Critical Thinking

*Reading and Writing in
a Diverse World*

Critical Thinking

Reading and Writing in a Diverse World

Second Edition

Joan Rasool   Caroline Banks   Mary-Jane McCarthy

WADSWORTH PUBLISHING COMPANY

I(T)P® An International Thomson Publishing Company

Belmont • Albany • Bonn • Boston • Cincinnati • Detroit • London • Madrid • Melbourne •
Mexico City • New York • Paris • San Francisco • Singapore • Tokyo • Toronto • Washington

ENGLISH EDITOR: Angela Gantner Wrahtz
EDITORIAL ASSISTANT: Royden Tonomura
PRODUCTION EDITOR: Deborah Cogan
DESIGNER: Kaelin Chappell and Ann Butler
PRINT BUYER: Barbara Britton
COPY EDITOR: Melissa Andrews
PERMISSIONS EDITOR: Robert Kauser
ILLUSTRATOR: Gary Palmatier
COVER DESIGNER: Cassandra Chu
COMPOSITOR: Thompson Type
PRINTER: Malloy Lithographing

*This book is printed on
acid-free recycled paper.*

For more information, contact:
Wadsworth Publishing Company
10 Davis Drive
Belmont, California 94002, USA

International Thomson Publishing Europe
Berkshire House 168-173
High Holborn
London, WC1V 7AA, England

Thomas Nelson Australia
102 Dodds Street
South Melbourne 3205
Victoria, Australia

Nelson Canada
1120 Birchmount Road
Scarborough, Ontario
Canada M1K 5G4

International Thomson Editores
Campos Eliseos 385, Piso 7
Col. Polanco
11560 México D.F. México

International Thomson Publishing GmbH
Königswinterer Strasse 418
53227 Bonn, Germany

International Thomson Publishing Asia
221 Henderson Road
#05-10 Henderson Building
Singapore 0315

International Thomson Publishing Japan
Hirakawacho Kyowa Building, 3F
2-2-1 Hirakawacho
Chiyoda-ku, Tokyo 102, Japan

Library of Congress Cataloging-in-Publication Data

Rasool, Joan.
    Critical thinking : reading and writing in a diverse world / Joan
Rasool, Caroline Banks, Mary-Jane McCarthy. — 2nd ed.
        p.   cm.
    Includes bibliographical references and indexes.
    ISBN 0-534-25692-9 (pbk.)
    1. English language—Rhetoric. 2. Critical thinking. 3. Academic
writing. 4. College readers. I. Banks, Caroline. II. McCarthy,
Mary-Jane. III. Title.
PE1408.R29   1996
808'.0427—dc20   95-23293

Dedicated to the Urban Education students
at Westfield State College

Brief Contents

Detailed Contents

PART II *Developing Reasoning Skills* **113**

CHAPTER 6   **Exploring the Unspoken: Finding Assumptions   187**

List of Readings by Chapter

CHAPTER 6   Exploring the Unspoken: Finding Assumptions

CHAPTER 7   Exploring Errors in Reasoning

PART III   *Extending Thinking Skills*

CHAPTER 8   Making Decisions and Solving Problems

CHAPTER 9   Reading Research Articles

CHAPTER 10 Evaluating Evidence

List of Readings by Theme

School Achievement and Success

Social/Cultural Understanding

Gender Issues

Empirical Inquiries

Social Controversies

Individual Perspectives

To the Instructor

Purpose of the Text

For several years we have been trying to develop a curriculum in critical thinking for our upper-level reading courses. We wanted to teach a critical thinking course that moved beyond teaching informal logic and reflected current understanding about the reading and writing process. While we wanted to teach our students how to analyze and debate, we also wanted to teach them how to collaborate. In addition, we wanted them to learn not only how to *challenge* each other's ideas, but also how to *listen* to each other's ideas.

We felt an obligation to our students to develop a text that would actively involve them and that would help them bridge the gap between their personal and social lives and the academic world. We wanted to make them more aware of their own thinking processes by having them read, write, and discuss a variety of topics at different levels of complexity. We hoped to expand their ability to elaborate on their own thinking and their ability to take in another's perspective. Finally, we wanted our text to provide students with analytical skills in reading, writing, and group participation that they could apply in their daily lives and in their other classes.

Critical Thinking: Reading and Writing in a Diverse World uses reading, writing, and discussion as vehicles for the development of students' critical thinking skills. This text can be used in any upper-level reading course. It is suitable as a critical reading text or as a critical thinking text at the college or college-preparatory level. English composition instructors who want to provide their students with structured comprehension and writing assignments and develop students' analytical skills will find this text useful. It is an appropriate supplemental text for use in first-year interdisciplinary courses being offered at several four-year colleges. It is also useful as a supplemental text in teacher preparation courses where instructors want to improve the critical thinking skills of their students. Several readings deal with issues of diversity and education that are relevant for prospective teachers.

Approach

First, the text encourages an *interactive dialogue* between reader and author. Activities and assignments are also designed to foster dialogue among class members. We believe that through spoken and written conversations we discover ourselves as thinkers.

Second, the *process of learning* is important. Students need to be aware of themselves as learners, aware of how they think and how they perceive their world. Our text emphasizes the process of students becoming aware of what they think. The Instructor's Manual describes the process of double-entry journal writing as a means of getting students to process information while they read. The text emphasizes discussion as a means of helping students clarify what they think. Finally, students bring their thoughts together through writing.

Because many students today are reluctant readers, particularly of expository texts, we have focused on reading as a social activity. Our experience has been that reluctant readers are more willing to read in order to discuss than to read simply to mark their texts. We want to create in our students the desire to communicate with us and with one another.

Third, the text provides students and instructors with *choice*. The process of selection helps build communication between student and instructor as well as commitment to learning. Each chapter begins with a checklist that presents an overview of the chapter. Students and instructors can preview the chapter and select those activities, readings, and writing assignments that are of interest. Of course, circumstances may make student choice inappropriate. In those cases the instructor should feel free to make the selections. Furthermore, instructors can choose to emphasize certain aspects of the text. For example, reading instructors may want to focus more on comprehension checks, while writing instructors may want to highlight writing assignments. Many of the discussion questions can be adapted to writing assignments.

Fourth, readings, writing assignments, and discussion questions reflect *different levels of difficulty*. We realize that instructors adapt textbooks to fit their needs. In our classes we have students at various skill levels and have found it valuable to be able to provide all students with challenging assignments. Moreover, we believe that all students will benefit from hearing and discussing answers to more complex questions than they may be ready to tackle on their own. Instructors may decide to assign specific assignments to certain students, or they may allow students the option of choosing. For example, students who always write from a personal perspective should be encouraged to select a more formal writing assignment. Some students may be asked to complete two writing assignments: one of their choice and one assigned by the instructor.

Coverage

Critical Thinking: Reading and Writing in a Diverse World is divided into three major sections: "Creating Common Ground," "Developing Reasoning Skills," and "Extending Thinking Skills." The three chapters in Part I, "Creating Common Ground," provide students with an orientation to the thinking tasks most often required in college. Students review the reading and learning process and its relationship to their success in studying. In Chapter 3 students are introduced to key concepts in critical thinking. They learn the difference between observations, interpretations, facts, and conclusions. They also learn the value of "investigating the obvious."

With this foundation students are ready for Part II, "Developing Reasoning Skills," in which they explore a variety of views and perspectives and learn several analytical skills. In Chapter 4 students investigate numerous factors that contribute to people's values and beliefs. In Chapter 5 they explore writers' perspectives in a variety of texts. Chapters 6 and 7 provide students with the analytical skills needed to evaluate ideas and conclusions.

Part III, "Extending Thinking Skills," moves beyond understanding and evaluating our own views and the opinions of others. Chapter 8 asks students to use their skills to make decisions and solve problems. Some instructors may choose to end their courses with Chapter 8; others may decide to include Chapters 9 and 10.

Instructors increasingly are expecting students to be able to read professional articles as well as evaluate statistical and research findings. Chapters 9 and 10 provide students with the background and expertise they will need to successfully complete upper-level course work.

Each chapter includes a set of chapter objectives that refer to the thinking skills emphasized in the chapter.

Special Features

■ The "To the Student" section that follows includes a list of reading terms and their definitions with which students should be familiar. Instructors can review this list and assign additional work to students who are weak in one of the areas.

■ The text does not assume that working well in groups or having good class discussions occurs naturally. The Introduction, "Circling the Square," presents students with strategies for working successfully in groups, and the section "How to Have a Good Discussion" in Chapter 1 offers additional information on how to prepare for class discussion.

■ Each chapter includes *Chapter Objectives* and a *Chapter Outline and Checklist*. This checklist can be used as a starting point for chapter study. Instructors and students can preview and select the activities and assignments they will complete. The *Introductory Chapter Activity* highlights a key concept in the chapter and is followed by text that explains the chapter information. A *Discussion Break* or *Activity Break* usually follows the instructional text in each chapter. The *Application* section of the chapter includes a series of readings, comprehension checks, discussion questions, and writing assignments.

■ The *Application* section contains several thematically linked readings from a variety of sources, including professional and student writings and college texts. In this way the students see how the same topic is discussed from several perspectives and levels of complexity.

■ Readings have been selected for their appeal to students, for their ability to generate productive thought and discussion, and for their capacity to build students' academic background knowledge.

■ The Application section ends with a "What Do You Think?" section. Open-ended discussion questions are presented; these are followed by several possible writing assignments.

■ Vocabulary study is flexible. Each of the readings has words listed in the margin. These words can form the core of students' vocabulary study. The Instructor's Manual includes several options for vocabulary instruction. Our emphasis is on understanding words in context.

■ This text is accompanied by an Instructor's Manual that provides teaching suggestions for each chapter. In addition to suggestions on vocabulary instruction, the Manual also includes possible answers to activities and comprehension checks. Suggestions for student evaluation at the end of each chapter are included.

Notes on the Second Edition

Changes made in the second edition of *Critical Thinking: Reading and Writing in a Diverse World* focus on the clarification and elaboration of key terms, the inclusion of additional articles and activity breaks for students, and the creation of a new section, "Extended Practice," to supplement students' work on analyzing arguments.

"You and Creative Thinking" has been added to Chapter One along with a relevant activity break and student essay on breaking old habits. Chapter Two introduces critical thinking and reading literature and includes a discussion of tone, figurative language, and diction. Chapter Three has been renamed and substantially reorganized and expanded. Terms such as *observations, interpretations, facts,* and *conclusions* are clarified and a new section on opinions has been added.

Chapters Five and Six now include "Extended Practice" sections; articles and guiding questions are provided to give students additional practice in working with argument analysis. There is an expanded section on inductive and deductive reasoning in Chapter Five as well as a more detailed explanation of how to use the argument outline. Chapter Six also includes an expanded optional essay format.

An additional activity break dealing with errors in reasoning has been added to Chapter Seven. Chapter Eight now includes a new section "Understanding Problems: Cause and Effect."

Eleven new readings have been added. Selections range from "La tierra es un satélite de la luna" by Leonel Rugama to the conflict between babyboomers and generation Xers, from questioning the benefit of lotteries to arguments made by corporate advertisers.

We continue to be indebted to our colleagues who have adopted this text and have offered many valuable suggestions to make it better. Any shortcomings that remain are our own.

Acknowledgments

We would like to thank the following colleagues for reviewing and commenting on our manuscript: Margaret Fieler, De Anza College; Pat Gent, Rogers State College; Patricia A. Janson, Suffolk County (New York) Community College; Teresa Kozek, Housatonic Community Technical College; Cathy J. Marsh, Pitt Community College; Victoria Sarkisian, Marist College.

Special thanks are due to Travis Tatum for contributing the introductory chapter, "Circling the Square"; to Bruce W. King for contributing Chapter 3, "Understanding Observations, Interpretations, Facts, and Conclusions"; and to Trudy Knowles for contributing the section on creative thinking in Chapter One. Mary Scanlon offered valuable examples of errors in reasoning.

Joan Rasool would like to acknowledge a longstanding gratitude to Nanci Salvidio for her role in this project. Without her valuable participation, this book would not have been possible. Baidah and Hala deserve recognition for their cooperation and understanding.

Finally, we appreciate the continued support of our editor, Angie Gantner Wrahtz.

To the Student

Welcome to *Critical Thinking: Reading and Writing in a Diverse World.* We believe that critical thinking is a powerful tool to use in your academic, personal, and professional lives.

Developing your critical thinking skills will help you better understand yourself and others. It can help you make decisions, solve problems, and work cooperatively with others. It can help you decide when to "think with your heart" and when to "think with your head."

Critical thinking skills also have particular importance in the academic world. Many college exams, essays, and research papers ask you to perform several kinds of thinking tasks. You might, for example, be asked to explain, summarize, or describe how the human immune system works. The thinking task here is to understand a certain body of information. Or you might be asked to explain the role and function of rites of passage in traditional African society. In this case you must interpret or infer certain information from what you have learned. Finally, you might be asked to evaluate the president's decision not to implement any new taxes. The thinking task here is to evaluate information and make a judgment.

The authors of this book believe that you can improve your reasoning skills by discussing, reading, and writing about a variety of social and academic topics. Your text has five major objectives:

- To develop your ability to read carefully and think critically about some of the topics that interest academics.

- To increase your awareness of multicultural issues in our diverse society and to increase your understanding of the role that culture plays in the formation of our opinions.

- To improve your expository writing skills. This is an essential skill used in writing research and essay papers and in answering essay questions on tests.

- To increase your academic knowledge. We recognize that you have already acquired lots of information, but our goal is to

increase your store of the kind of knowledge that schools —
especially colleges — reward.

■ To develop your capacity to become a more independent learner
as well as a contributor to the learning of other people. We want
you to become a more active reader, a more assertive
questioner, and a stronger group participant.

Format

We have adopted a conversational tone in our text because we believe
that through spoken and written conversations we discover ourselves as
thinkers. Each chapter begins with a list of objectives and a checklist.
You and your instructor can begin your chapter study by previewing the
topics and deciding what will be covered and when. You may also skim
over the reading selections and decide which reading and writing assignments you might want to complete. Each chapter is designed to
include choice in order to encourage more independent learning. The
Introductory Chapter Activity highlights a key concept in the chapter
and is followed by text that explains the chapter information. At times
you are asked to complete an activity or participate in a discussion.

The Application section contains several thematically linked readings from a variety of sources, including professional and student writings and college texts. You will have an opportunity to see how the same
topic is discussed from several perspectives and at different levels of
complexity. The Application sections also include discussion and comprehension questions and writing assignments.

Vocabulary and Terms

Each reading selection in the Application section has a number of words
listed in the margin. These words have been selected for vocabulary
instruction. Your instructor will explain how you should proceed.

Your text assumes that you are familiar with certain terms or phrases
used in discussing comprehension and writing skills. We have included

the following list of terms and a brief explanation for your reference. Some of these terms and phrases are discussed more fully in your text.

- *Previewing*. Previewing skills are the strategies you use to get an idea of what a reading selection is about before you read it thoroughly. The purpose of previewing is to prepare and focus your mind on the reading. Using these previewing skills will help you learn to read faster and to locate information and ideas more efficiently. Previewing skills include activating background knowledge, predicting, and skimming.

- *Activating background knowledge*. By reading the title, the introductory comments, and the source of a text or article, you can review in your mind what you already know about the subject or topic. If you possess a great deal of background knowledge about a topic, chances are the reading will be easy for you. If the text is about an unfamiliar topic, however, you may find it more difficult to comprehend.

- *Predicting*. Often with a careful reading of only a small portion of a text you can predict the outcome of a story or sequence of events. Trying to predict what will happen before you complete a thorough reading of a text engages your mind in the activity of reading. The result of actively "psyching out" the text is that you keep asking questions. This process can also aid your retention of the material for later recall.

- *Skimming*. Skimming involves a partial reading of a text. By reading introductory paragraphs and the first sentences of the other paragraphs, it is often possible to get the "gist," or the general idea, of the whole text. The purpose of skimming may be to quickly assess the whole text or to decide whether a more careful reading is needed.

- *Scanning*. Scanning is the process of moving your eyes through a text looking for specific information. Examples are looking up words in a dictionary, searching for a name in a phone directory, or consulting a map to find a specific location. The purpose of scanning is the efficient location of information. It is especially helpful when using reference materials.

- *Major ideas and supporting details.* The major ideas in a text are the general statements that give the overall idea of either a whole reading or individual paragraphs. The supporting details tell more about the major ideas.

- *Summarizing.* Summarizing is restating material briefly. You are "boiling down" the material to its essentials. You can summarize a text, ideas in your mind, or spoken material. Summarizing is a good test of comprehension.

- *Paraphrasing.* Paraphrasing is restating a word, an idea, or a whole text in your own words. Usually your restatement will simplify or clarify the original.

- *Outlining.* Outlining is a writing skill necessary for summarizing longer texts. It is also an organizing device for planning compositions, essays, speeches, and projects. In addition, it can be used for organizing information after it has been read. Preparing a written outline of the headings or key sentences of a text before a thorough reading can help you divide a long reading, such as a textbook chapter, into manageable chunks. This kind of outlining can be a planning aid.

- *Words in context.* Learning a word "in context" means trying to figure out its meaning by understanding the surrounding words. Read the following sentences:

The captain trimmed her ship's sails.
The barber trimmed his customer's mustache.

The meaning of "trimmed" is different in the two sentences. You might be sure of the second meaning, because it is more common. However, you may have to ask yourself some questions about the first usage: What meaning might make sense in this context? What clues to meaning can I find in the text surrounding this word? You may figure out that it means "to pull in tighter." Perhaps you will have to ask another person or look it up in a dictionary.

Recognizing Our Diversity

We live in a society that is becoming more diverse all the time. Our country includes large numbers of people from many different cultures and ethnic backgrounds. We participate in the dominant Anglo culture; however, we also may participate in other groups that include non-Anglo traditions. In Chapter 4 we discuss the influence culture can exert in determining a person's values as well as the positions they take on many controversial issues. Throughout this text we offer essays and articles that highlight some of the issues surrounding our becoming a more diverse nation. An expanded awareness of cultural perspectives is a valuable critical thinking tool in the academic world and in society at large.

Conclusion

We believe that you do your best when there are high expectations for your achievement and when you are shown how to succeed. We are committed to providing you with challenging information and exercises as well as instruction on how to be successful. We welcome hearing directly from students. If there are ways that we might make this text more useful and interesting to you, let us know!

Introduction: Circling the Square

We believe that many students experience schooling and education as an individual exercise. They are usually involved in some form of competition with other students over grades, over attention from the teacher, and even over the attention of other students in the class. This emphasis on competition can make it very difficult for them to work with one another. Since the idea of competition is so fundamental to their learning, it is not easy for them to share their ideas and thoughts with others. Competition assumes that in order for one person to win another has to lose. And obviously, no one wants to lose. For example, if Azanda's grades depend on how well or how poorly Tim does, she is not going to want to share information with him that might lower her grade.

We all spend a lot of time and energy trying to be independent and self-reliant. As a result, we may view those who seek or need help as being weak and less competent than those who can go it alone. This stigma presents problems for those who need assistance since they will be reluctant to seek it, and for those who want to give it since they may not know how to do so without offending the recipient. These are just a few of the problems that emerge when we work with others in a group.

What happens when we have to work with someone whose behavior and attitude make it difficult for us to be in the group, let alone to accomplish the task of the group? Members in the group become frustrated and angry, which makes the situation even worse. Many times the frustration can lead to angry outbursts and withdrawal from the group. More often people tend to withdraw quietly — the body may continue to be there, but the mind has wandered off. Sometimes members identify one individual as being responsible for the failure of the whole group. That person becomes the scapegoat even though the entire group is responsible for its success or failure. This kind of experience is not unusual; it happens in schools, in corporations, in government committees, and even in teachers' groups.

In spite of the difficulties, working with others is an extremely important part of the learning process. Indeed, being able to work with others is becoming a criterion for success in the working world. While we all have individual responsibilities and styles of doing things, we rarely can function in any organization without working closely with other people. However, the process of working successfully with others is not always intuitive and requires some awareness and knowledge of the social dynamics that emerge within a group. The more you know about how groups function, the better prepared you will be to work with others and the more effective you can be in accomplishing group tasks.

This Introduction will provide you with some ideas on how to work together in groups in meaningful and productive ways. Following our suggestions will improve your ability to learn from others and create a foundation for cooperative learning. Thinking critically does not simply mean arguing with others, it also means developing an ability to think and communicate with others. Not only will you be required to participate in groups for many activities and discussions in this book, you are liable to take part in groups throughout your life.

Getting Ready to Work in Groups

Working in groups can be an ideal opportunity to exercise some critical thinking skills, to learn more about how you interact with others, and to experience personal growth. In order for this process to be most beneficial, however, you need to pay attention to a number of important group development issues and to be aware of yourself as you experience this rather complex process. In this case, paying attention means being aware of your own feelings as you engage in the process — when you feel bored, excited, scared, or anxious. It also means trying to pay attention to the feelings of the other group members. As you can imagine, trying to maintain awareness of yourself and others while at the same time trying to accomplish some task can become very complicated.

Understanding the Role of Critical Thinking

Earlier, we mentioned the ability to think critically as one of a set of skills necessary to make a group function effectively. Critical thinking skills can be used to analyze and evaluate not only the tasks that the group has been asked to complete, but also the group process itself.

Most groups are formed to deal with some problem or issue that its members are interested in. Do you remember getting together with the other kids in your neighborhood to play a game or to answer the age-old question, What is there to do? In a sense, you got together to solve problems, and critical thinking skills were a necessity.

However, critical thinking in this situation is not competitive. The goal is not to "win" as is the case in formal debating; rather, critical thinking is cooperative and is used to share thoughts and examine ideas and solutions so that the group can accomplish its goals. As young children in the neighborhood, you did not get together to rationally debate whether you should do one thing or the other. Everyone simply presented suggestions, which were then discussed and acted upon.

Ideally, a group shares ideas, examines several possibilities, and then agrees on the single best option. A sense of humility in terms of learning and sharing is very useful at this point. When group members feel no need to dominate or to take charge, all members can contribute possible options. Sometimes the best ideas come from the most surprising source, perhaps from the person who speaks the least. If, on the other hand, the process becomes competitive, with different people vying for control, then individuals become critical of one another as persons. This immediately heightens the level of frustration in the group and reduces its chances of achieving its goals in a way that is beneficial to all members.

Heeding the Message, Not the Messenger

Within the group framework it is very important to distinguish between people and their ideas. The necessity for doing so is greater within a working group since the sharing of ideas is essential to enhancing the options available to the group and to increasing the probability of finding the best solution to the problem. You may have heard the story of the trucker who tried to drive his 12-foot 3-inch truck under a 12-foot-high overpass. The truck became stuck and traffic quickly backed up. Nobody knew what to do until a small boy suggested letting some air out of the tires. The boy's solution to the problem was simple and elegant. A lot of times adults do not listen to children because they assume children don't know or understand things. Similarly, when we work in groups there is the tendency to treat some group members as if they were children or as if their ideas did not count.

To avoid this kind of situation, members must feel free to express their ideas and thoughts. And the group must be eager to receive these ideas. This process is especially important during the brainstorming stages of problem solving. To compete for the best ideas and to criticize individuals or even ideas at this stage adversely affects the process. At this point members must have an opportunity not only to share ideas but to begin to define their roles in the group and to determine what the boundaries and norms of the group will be. A subtle process of establishing how people will act and behave is established by the members as they work with a given problem. By setting norms that assume a measure of cooperation and openness rather than competition, a group may provide a framework for resolving problems that benefits all its members.

Handling Disagreements

Having emphasized the need for cooperation and sharing, we must also acknowledge the need for disagreement within the group. This may sound like a contradiction, but to seek cooperation does not mean that the group must achieve conformity on the issues and problems it is dealing with. Indeed, the demand for conformity can be equally troublesome for the group. In business, conforming all the time is referred to as the "yes man" syndrome. In this situation people tend to agree with ideas because they think everyone else does so, especially if it is the boss's idea. So even if a group member secretly thinks the idea won't work, he or she feels pressure to "go along with the program" and not create any waves. As a consequence, a number of bad ideas are implemented because no one was willing to question them for fear of being perceived as a bad team member.

One of the measures of the effectiveness of any group is the degree to which the group is able to handle conflict and at the same time maintain its sense of cohesiveness while accomplishing its tasks. This particular process can be very difficult because most of us are not good at responding to those who disagree with us. We all tend to dislike those who do not share our opinions and beliefs. Consequently, we may take disagreements as personal attacks. In reality, however, you know you cannot determine the value or validity of an argument simply by looking at the person who presents it. Likewise, you should not dismiss an argument because the person who presented it was someone you don't like. In class discussion you need to separate disagreements over reasons presented from the people who make them.

Indeed, within the framework of a class discussion, some disagreement and diversity of opinions are essential in order to expand the knowledge base of the group as a whole. For example, in preparing for a debate, it is helpful to have someone on the team argue the opposing point of view. This person provides a framework for understanding how the opposing team might present its case and how the group may respond to a particular line of reasoning. If the team is made up of individuals who simply agree on the issues, then it becomes more difficult to anticipate problems and to find alternatives. Similarly, in just about any problem-solving situation, there are people who think up solutions and possibilities that others are not aware of. Thus those who offer alternative views should be sought after and appreciated for their contributions.

Expressing Appreciation

The act of expressing appreciation to group members for their efforts can help to strengthen the group so that it can successfully accomplish its task. This is a relatively simple procedure. At the end of a discussion, group members can simply say one thing about each member that they thought they did well or that was helpful to the group. Pay attention and develop an awareness for what people do right and you will start "seeing" it more often. Too often we spend time telling each other what we do wrong rather than what we do right. As a consequence, many people find it hard to accept compliments for their behavior and performance. In fact, strange as it may seem, we find it easier to believe the negative things said about us than the positive things.

Moreover, the process of expressing appreciation is not an easy one. Most of us have gone through life without receiving a lot of appreciation, and we in turn have often failed to appreciate others. For example, our parents raised us and provided us with food and shelter, and yet it is a rare child who has actually thanked them for their effort. We tend to take the work of others for granted, just as the things we do are taken for granted. By the same token, when we are ready to give someone credit for what they have accomplished or contributed, we sometimes are at a loss as to how to do it. And in the context of a group project, it may be particularly difficult.

The trick is to tell one another — without being insincere or manipulative — something positive about one another's behavior, participation, or performance. For example, it is always good to let someone know that you liked the ideas they brought to the group. This will encourage that person to continue making contributions. It is also important to thank people for whatever positive things they do — whether it's mediating between arguing group members, making all group members feel comfortable, or simply providing pencils and paper for each meeting. In order for this process to be successful, every member in the group must be included, not because it's wrong to exclude someone, but because each person *does* contribute to the group in her or his own way.

Providing Feedback

The process of expressing appreciation for one another's contributions is part of a larger process of providing feedback to group members and assessing what has happened in the group. A cooperative group should set aside some time to talk about itself. Members of the class should have the opportunity to talk about how they feel and about what is happening with the group.

Earlier, we mentioned that an effective group allows for differences and diversity of opinions. In order to prevent these differences or conflicts from becoming major issues in the group, members need to have space and time to talk about how they are experiencing the group and how they feel about what is happening. Any discussion about feelings and feedback or about people's behavior can be difficult. However, certain things can be done to make the process easier and to strengthen group cohesiveness.

The first part of the process has to be in the *establishment of group norms*. The members need to recognize that they can benefit from discussing not only their difficulties in being members of the group but also the problems they face in accomplishing the task. The group should set aside a small amount of time (ten or fifteen minutes) to talk about how it's doing as a whole and how each member feels about the way things are going. (Your instructor may facilitate the group's processing of its own experience by requesting that each student write a few paragraphs describing the group's process rather than the task.) Doing so at the end of a class will provide an opportunity for the discussion of group issues and for the expression of individual feelings and thoughts.

This format can be relatively simple. For example, group members could have exactly two minutes each to talk about their experiences and feelings about the group. While a person speaks, no one else is allowed to comment; indeed, no one should comment on what anyone else says. And no one should speak again until everyone has had an opportunity to speak for his or her two minutes. This means that all members will have a chance to express their reactions to the group. Those who are not talking should give the speaker their undivided attention. By doing this the group shows that it respects its own members and values what people have to say.

What might you talk about for two minutes? One of the things that might come up is how you feel about expressing your views. For many of us, thinking out loud produces a lot of anxiety and fear, not to mention confusion. Sometimes it is useful simply to tell other members that you are very anxious. The very act of verbalizing your anxiety can help to lessen it.

Another issue that often emerges is other members' behavior. Frequently, the behavior of group members is misunderstood. For example, a member may be late to class on several occasions or may not show up, but may not realize how this behavior is affecting the rest of you. During this feedback session members can *identify the behavior* and state how it makes them feel, but they *should not* interpret the behavior. The emphasis here is on feelings. For example, you can say, "When Joe is late for our class or when he does not show up for class, I feel that he does not care about what we are doing. And that upsets me." This is a simple statement that expresses how one person feels about Joe's behavior. You do not know why Joe is late or why he does not show up for the meetings. Joe may have very legitimate reasons for his behavior. But now Joe is aware of the impact of his behavior and he is free to respond to how you may feel about it. There is no accusation involved, nor are there any threats. There is only a statement on one person's feelings about the behavior. In this way, a dialogue is possible in which each person is free to respond to issues that affect the performance of the group. And every member is allowed to have direct input into the process and the work of the group. Such an approach should provide all of you with the opportunity to learn about the task and about yourself in a way that is not ordinarily available.

Conclusion

In this Introduction we have suggested that there are alternative ways to deal with tasks and problem solving in groups. (The box on page xliv highlights the suggestions we have made in this section.) We have argued that although our educational system and our society generally place a high value on competition, some problems can better be solved through cooperation and some forms of learning are enhanced through cooperation. Both competition and cooperation have a place in society and can serve a useful purpose. Consequently, it is necessary to be able to engage in both processes depending on the circumstances and one's goals.

In the academic environment grades are often perceived as the major criterion for the assessment of learning. We tend to assume that the higher one's grade point average, the more one has learned, thus creating greater competition for grades. This competition can be particularly intense in fields where the financial rewards are great and access is limited: law, engineering, medicine, and business.

However, the measure of one's learning is not limited to grades. It is possible to learn a great deal about a subject and receive a low grade or even no grade in the course. Moreover, there are some things for which grades cannot serve as an evaluation. No grade can be used to define what we learn about ourselves when we reflect on our life experiences. No one can give us a grade for the knowledge we gain from sharing what we know with others. And no one can give us a grade for how we feel about ourselves and about our relationships with others.

Techniques for Effective Group Discussions

1. Be aware of your own feelings in the group.

2. Pay attention to how other group members are feeling.

3. Set group norms of cooperation and openness. Avoid creating a competitive atmosphere.

4. Distinguish between people and their ideas.

5. Recognize the group's need for disagreement and diversity of opinions.

6. Take time at the end of class to express appreciation for the contributions of *all* group members.

7. Set aside time for the group to discuss itself. Discuss feelings of group members; give group members feedback.

✪ **DISCUSSION QUESTIONS**

Prepare for class discussion by writing down brief answers to the following questions.

1. Do you find it easy or difficult to express how you feel to another person? Have you been in a situation where someone told you how he or she feels about you? How did you respond?

2. Everybody behaves differently in different groups, but we all have a general pattern of behavior. Some people like to sit back and check things out; others like to take charge and get things done. What is your style of behavior in a small group? Why do you think you behave in that manner?

3. Why do you think "Circling the Square" was chosen as the subtitle for this Introduction?

Creating Common Ground

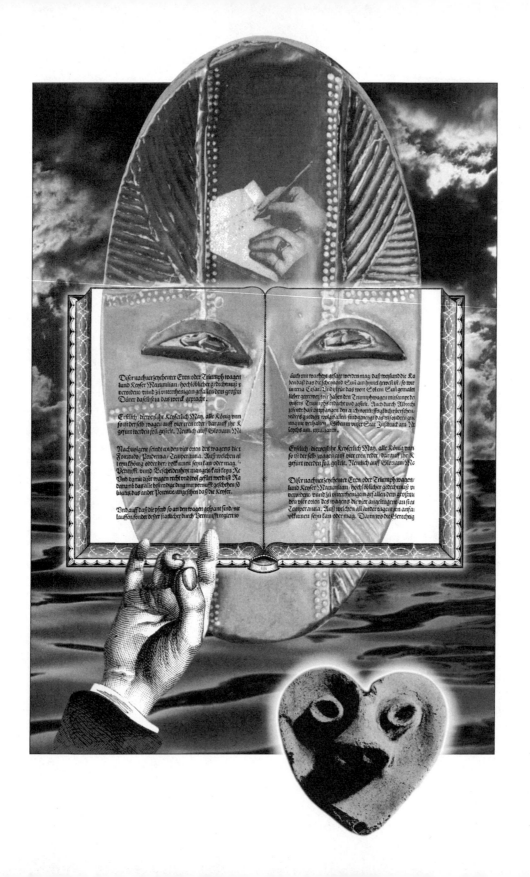

CHAPTER 1

Thinking Critically in College

After reading Chapter 1 you should be able to:

- define critical thinking
- recognize some of the assumptions that instructors make about students and critical thinking
- understand the difference between convergent and divergent thinking
- use brainstorming to generate solutions to problems
- participate in a focused class discussion
- describe how external factors influence academic performance

You may use the following checklist in planning your study of expectations in the academic world. Activities marked with a ✪ are to be completed in class. Some preclass preparation may be required.

CONTEXT FOR LEARNING

✪ _____ INTRODUCTORY CHAPTER ACTIVITY

_____ You and Critical Thinking

_____ You and Creative Thinking

✪ _____ ACTIVITY BREAK

_____ Underlying Assumptions in the Academic World

_____ How to Have a Good Discussion

✪ _____ DISCUSSION BREAK

APPLICATION: BUILDING SUPPORT

_____ APPLICATION ONE

_____ **"Peer Pressure and Academics"** by Martin Jones

_____ COMPREHENSION CHECK

_____ APPLICATION TWO

_____ **"Test Scores Don't Lie: Back to Basics"** by Diane Ravitch

_____ COMPREHENSION CHECK

_____ APPLICATION THREE

_____ **"Old Habits"** by Danielle Lewis

_____ COMPREHENSION CHECK

_____ APPLICATION FOUR

_____ **"Environmental Influences on Achievement"** by L. Steinberg

_____ COMPREHENSION CHECK

_____ What Do You Think?

✪ _____ DISCUSSION QUESTIONS

_____ WRITING ASSIGNMENTS

Take a moment and consider the last time you bought a major item; it might have been a car, a leather coat, a swimsuit for your two-year-old, or a new sound system. Write a short paragraph describing the decision-making process you went through as you made your choice. You might begin writing by asking yourself, "What made me decide to buy this particular item? What was I thinking?"

Share your answers in small groups of two or three students, and make a list of all the factors people considered as they made their purchasing decisions. Now, working together, revise your list to develop a set of purchasing guidelines for consumers. What factors should consumers consider before making a major purchasing decision? Discuss your guidelines with the whole class. Do the groups offer similar advice? Finally, discuss what kinds of thinking skills might be helpful in making decisions.

You and Critical Thinking

You are not a newcomer to critical thinking. Do you recall a time in your childhood when all you seemed to do was ask questions, enough questions to drive your parents crazy: Why does the water go down the drain? Why don't we celebrate Christmas? Why don't those people have a place to live? Why don't you trust me? Why don't you know why?

Questions and more questions. It was a frustrating time because often your parents did not know the answers to your questions, and even if they did they weren't sure you were old enough to understand the answers. In the best of worlds your parents kept their sanity, and enough of your questions were answered to keep your curiosity alive.

And then you were sent off to school. Perhaps school fostered your curiosity, bridging and supporting your experiences and background, and helped you expand your knowledge. Or maybe school overlooked or denied your background and experiences and did not tolerate questions of "Why?" Were you encouraged to ask "Why?" and to explore answers? Or were you simply expected to memorize? Were you rewarded for challenging the teachers, or punished for "having attitudes"? Some of you found school a good place to think openly; others became closet or secret thinkers.

Fortunately, your early childhood preoccupation with questions is a strength that you can bring to the present task of improving your critical thinking skills. Moreover, you are now at a stage of cognitive (reasoning) development where you can better analyze and evaluate the reasons you are given.

By improving your analytical skills you expand your options; you create more choices for yourself. Being able to follow the reasoning of others makes you an informed consumer of those ideas. Being able to explain your own views helps you convince others of the soundness of your ideas. Finally, you are in a position to better understand some of your preferences and feelings. You have the potential of basing some decisions on logic or feelings or on a combination of the two.

Critical thinking, then, entails asking questions, getting answers, and then asking still more questions about those answers. What is equally exciting is that you and your classmates are now in a position to turn the questioning spotlight on each other, allowing one another to investigate why you think and believe certain things.

Let's take a minute and consider our definition of critical thinking. Most of us regard thinking as an *activity* that goes on in the brain, and therefore we would probably agree that critical thinking involves some active mental process. But what is the nature of this activity? Perhaps in our life experiences we have met up with an overly critical parent, teacher, or friend who found fault with our every behavior, comment, or action, which has left us with a rather negative view of being "critical." One of our students wanted to know, "Does this mean we're going to learn how to insult each other?" We're used to *critical* meaning something negative — like the terms *dissing* and *dogging*. But our use of the word *critical* is not meant to be demeaning or insulting. Analyzing and evaluating are done for the purposes of interpretation and understanding, not to find fault and condemn.

Critical thinking means actively seeking to understand, analyze, and evaluate information. Readers think critically when they reflect on the ideas they have read; writers write critically when they reflect on the ideas they have written. Listeners listen critically when they focus on what is being said and not on what they want to say next.

A word of caution: Some students assume that critical thinking leads to endless debates and never-ending arguments. While we agree that debating is fun and helps sharpen our analytical skills, we will want to take the next step in critical thinking and talk about problem resolution and compromise in a world where simple solutions are hard to come by.

You and Creative Thinking

As a child you were not only a critical thinker, but also a creative one. You used boxes for boats and spaceships, and pieces of cloth for tents, bandanas, and sarongs. You explored the kitchen cupboards, the buttons on the VCR, and the lint between your toes with the inquisitiveness of the best scientists. You instinctively took risks and used your imagination to dream.

Creative thinking is an essential element to critical thinking. The process of creative and critical thinking can be seen as opposite sides of the same coin. Creative thinking uses divergent thinking. During the divergent thinking phase, the problem solver gathers information and generates a list of possible solutions. At this point in the process all possibilities remain open. Problem solvers believe that the more possibilities there are to consider, the greater the chance of finding the best solution (see Figure 1-1).

Critical thinking uses convergent thinking. This type of thinking involves analyzing and evaluating all the possibilities and coming to a specific conclusion or a solution to the problem (see Figure 1-2). Effective thinking requires both convergent and divergent thinking. It must first involve divergent or creative thinking. If we begin our convergent thinking too soon, we minimize the number of possible solutions. For example, Craig has a problem getting to his 8:30 a.m. classes. His first impulse is to drop the course. By not thinking divergently he closes off the opportunity to discover a solution that might work better for him and allow him to complete the course. If he followed the model for effective thinking shown in Figure 1-3, he would first generate a list of possible solutions: He could take the class at another time; he could go to bed earlier; he could take a nap in the afternoon; he could get a friend to tape the class for him; he could try to bribe the professor. The next step

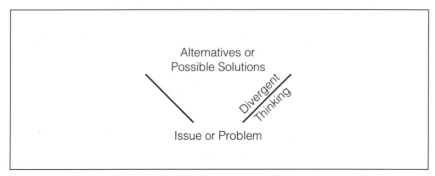

Figure 1-1 CREATIVE THINKING

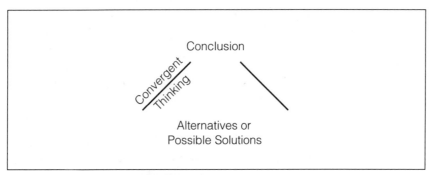

Figure 1-2 CRITICAL THINKING

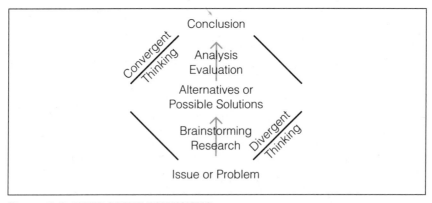

Figure 1-3 EFFECTIVE THINKING

would involve analyzing and evaluating each of the possible solutions. He might look to see if the same class is offered at a different time; he could check his schedule to see if he has time for a nap; and so on. After analyzing and evaluating each option, he makes his decision and arrives at a solution. Of course, the thinking process continues. As Craig implements his solution he may acquire new knowledge, gain added perspective, change his values, or have new experiences that make him reevaluate his original conclusion.

Changing thinking habits

Changing our way of thinking is like changing a bad habit, and habits don't die easily. Even bad habits are comfortable; they make us feel connected. When we try to break a habit we feel disassociated and uneasy. For example, lean back in your chair and clasp your hands together. Take a deep breath. You feel comfortable; you feel connected. Now clasp your hands together the opposite way. If your right index finger was on the top, shift your fingers downward so that your left is on top. How does that feel? If you are like most people, you will feel slightly uncomfortable and be very aware of your hands. You may want to shift your hands back to make things feel "right" again.

Thinking in new ways is similar to the preceding exercise. When we are asked to think in a new way, we resist and often want to return to our comfortable ways. Noncreative thinking is a habit you can break, but you need to take risks. Courses such as these can open you to new possibilities in thinking.

✪ **ACTIVITY BREAK**

1. This activity will help you think more creatively by encouraging you to think divergently. On a piece of paper write down twenty uses for a pencil other than its normal purpose. For example, a pencil can be used as a back scratcher. Then share your ideas with the class.

2. Brainstorming is a technique for coming up with possible solutions to a problem. When you brainstorm you need to follow two rules: (1) Generate as many possibilities as you can. Quantity is more important than quality. (2) Place no value judgment on any responses during brainstorming. In groups of two or three decide on a problem. You can brainstorm about anything — solutions to teenage pregnancies, ways to stop acid rain, what to do on your summer vacation, what to do with the 35 million extra copy machine lids that Xerox made, how to spend the $10,000 you won on the lottery. For ten minutes generate as many solutions to the problem as you can. Remember — do not judge or criticize people's ideas. The next step after brainstorming is to analyze all the solutions and see if they are possible, cost-effective, humane, reasonable, and so on. It is during this phase that judgment is necessary. In this exercise it isn't possible to fully analyze all solutions given the time frame; however, our goal is to highlight the process. (We discuss problem solving in Chapter 8.)

Underlying Assumptions in the Academic World

When we discuss the academic world, we are generally referring to the environment in which instructors teach and students study and learn. It is an environment where people recognize common goals, preferred forms of behavior and performance, and agreed-upon rewards. Some of these concepts are very well known to students. For example, students know that they must understand any information being presented and study it in order to do well in their schoolwork, and that if they do so, they will receive a degree as a reward. Other information or beliefs held by the academic world may remain hidden. For example, students sometimes wonder why they have to learn so much information that they won't have any use for in the future.

As with any group or organization you are a part of, it is always helpful to know the spoken and unspoken rules by which the members play. You certainly wouldn't start playing an unknown game, with your future at stake, without trying to learn the rules. You've been going to school since about age five, but you probably haven't been thinking about the tacit (unspoken) assumptions under which schools, particularly colleges, and academicians (that is, professors, instructors, and the like) operate when it comes to critical thinking.

Instructors' assumptions about critical thinking

Our first assumption about critical thinking in the academic world is that personal opinions need to be backed by logic and evidence in order to be accepted and/or respected. Statements such as "The rise in skin cancer is due to the thinning of the ozone layer" or "John Singleton's *Higher Learning* is a great movie" must be supported with reasons or evidence. Students are often offended when instructors challenge their opinions: "It's my opinion and I'm entitled to it. My opinion can't be wrong." You may be able to persuade your friends to accept this "love me, love my opinion" attitude, but the rules are different in the academic setting. You probably won't be asked to justify your taste in ice cream or your preference for leather jackets, but you will need to be able to explain how you perceive the world around you and how you think the world ought to be. For example, if you believe that a high school student's grades will drop if she has an after-school job, then you are expressing a view on *how* you see the world. If you believe that the federal government should prevent discrimination against AIDS victims, you are taking a position on how you think the world *should be*. Regardless of your views, you must be ready to defend your position, to explain your reasons, and to provide supporting evidence.

Our second assumption is the cornerstone to analyzing your views: Always ask "Why?" Nothing is taken for granted; everything is examined. We may like you and think you are the greatest; nevertheless, we are obligated to question all that you say and write. How do we know if what you say is true? If it is true, how do we know it supports your position? Even if we accept what you say, we must go one step further and ask how this information relates to what we already know: "What difference does this make in my life?" For example, if you have convinced us that the number of homeless people in this country is a problem, then we must extend our thinking to consider causes of and solutions to the problem. We should also consider the personal costs or benefits involved in solving or not solving a problem.

Our third assumption helps explain why academicians ask so many questions. They *like* ideas. They like to take an idea and turn it round and round in their minds, examining every aspect of it. For example, if someone told you that plants grow faster when you talk to them, you might begin to examine the idea by asking a series of questions: Can I believe this statement? If talking makes plants grow faster, does that mean they have feelings or the ability to reason? Are plants aware? Are they conscious? If they are, should we change our agricultural practices? Are there ethical and moral issues to consider?

Academicians enjoy tossing around ideas — even ones that may seem absurd — in much the same way that kids enjoy a pickup basketball game. When they play, they aren't thinking about whether the game will further their careers or is relevant to what they will be doing in five years; they play for the fun of it. They experiment with new angles for shots and new defense strategies. In the academic world the perspective is the same; ideas are tried out just for the fun of it and to see where they lead. Does this notion appeal to you? We hope so! By virtue of your continuing in school, you are "on the team," and we would like to increase the likelihood of your becoming one of the star players!

Although academicians enjoy playing with ideas, they do take their work seriously. They work toward understanding the world in which we live today, the world our ancestors lived in, and/or the world our children will inhabit. They are concerned about finding possible solutions to global problems. They take a great deal of pride in contributing to the education of those in their classes. And while they believe critical thinking is a powerful tool to academic success and to understanding our world, they are aware of its limitations. Learning how to think critically does not guarantee learning "The Truth." We will explore this idea more fully in Chapters 3 and 4.

Instructors' assumptions about students

Your instructors assume not only that you want to learn and are interested in their subject matter, but also that you want to be successful in their classes. One way for you to achieve academic success is to know what you think. Many students tell us that they either don't know what they think or don't know how to express it. How, then, do you discover what you think and why? You learn this by questioning yourself and by asking others to consider your views and express their own. Finally, we believe that by understanding and analyzing your own ideas, you will be in a powerful position to evaluate someone else's.

Instructors also assume that you would like to be respected by them and by your peers. We believe that being a student is an honorable position, worthy of respect. It is a privilege to watch students acquire knowledge and to guide them in their thinking. Instructors learn a great deal from their students, and in the ideal classroom student and teacher often exchange roles. Respect is something students bestow on the instructors who have earned it. It is reserved for instructors who know their subject matter, who show concern for students' learning, and who do not misuse their power.

How to Have a Good Discussion

We are all capable of thinking without speaking; in fact, research on small babies has shown how much thinking they are capable of prior to their acquiring language. However, we are strong believers that language facilitates the thinking process. Some people will tell you that the only way they know what they think is by hearing themselves say it! We want to encourage discussion throughout the text, but we want to be sure that these discussions are productive, that they help people clarify their views as well as understand the views of others. A good discussion is more than a conversational "free-for-all." Following are some suggestions on how to hold a good discussion.

Guidelines for Discussions

1. *Come to the discussion prepared.* If you know you will be discussing a certain topic because it is listed in the syllabus or your instructor has told you, take time to think about your views *prior* to the discussion. We cannot overemphasize our experience that good discussions don't just happen; they require planning and forethought.

2. *Be a good listener.* Rather than spending time mentally composing your next statement while another person is talking, listen carefully. Ask yourself if you understand what the speaker is saying. Be advised: This is difficult to do.

3. *Ask questions to clarify what someone has said.* Ask the speaker to explain certain points, or restate what the speaker has said in your own words and ask for feedback. Did you understand correctly?

4. *Keep the discussion on track.* Remember what you are discussing and stick to the topic. If you change focus be sure everyone is clear on the shift in direction.

5. *Appoint a discussion facilitator.* It is the facilitator's job to call on people to speak and to let the group know when group members are straying from the topic. The facilitator should also encourage participation from those who have not spoken by asking those students if they have any comments they would like to contribute. Finally, the facilitator can provide the group with feedback on its performance.

6. *Take risks.* Expressing your thoughts in public requires a fair amount of courage. Realize that each idea expressed is important. Your solution may not be the one people choose, but your comment may spark another, more workable idea. Ask the group to help you clarify your ideas.

7. *Don't take people's comments personally.* Remember to agree to disagree; just because group members disagree with you doesn't mean they don't like you. At the same time, remember to be critical of ideas, not people. Don't allow character assassinations!

Have we missed any? Some groups say they like to agree to confidentiality: Whatever is said during discussions is not repeated elsewhere.

A final comment: Many textbook publishers and college instructors shy away from topics that may create some tension among students in the class. As a result they rely on such topics as capital punishment, mercy killing, and drug abuse because they believe that students can argue these topics passionately but with some emotional distance. Topics and issues that relate to people's cultural experiences and perceptions, such as race relations, ethnic values, and sexism, can lead more easily to misunderstandings and confusion. However, given our increasingly pluralistic society, we feel that including discussions around these topics is essential if we wish to think critically. In the Introduction you read about how to work effectively in groups. Demonstrating mutual respect for class members and following the guidelines for discussions presented previously will give you a starting point for exchanging and clarifying your views in a group.

In the next section you are asked to discuss your answers to several questions. Keep these guidelines in mind as you proceed. Later evaluate your discussion according to the suggestions just listed.

✪ DISCUSSION BREAK

Prepare for class discussion by jotting down brief answers to the following questions.

1. How often are you asked to think in school? Has most of your learning involved only memorizing or have you had to think about what you have learned? Give some examples of the kinds of questions or assignments that make students think. What suggestions would you have for teaching people to think more or think more critically (that is, evaluate ideas and consider alternatives)?

2. Do you consider yourself to be a creative thinker? How has school encouraged or discouraged you from thinking creatively?

3. Some students tell us they aren't interested in becoming better thinkers. This statement always puzzles us; can you suggest some reasons why people resist becoming better thinkers?

4. Two of the sections in the chapter talk about assumptions instructors make about students and about critical thinking. Do you agree with these assumptions? Do they describe students or college work too simplistically? Explain your answers.

5. Why do people become teachers and professors?

Application: Building Support

APPLICATION ONE

Have you noticed that at times students don't show each other the same respect that they give to their instructors? Students who know too few answers are laughed at, while students who know too many answers are isolated. Pity the poor students who actually look as if they have done their homework! The greatest achievement seems to be getting high marks without appearing to work for them.

Preview the following essay by reading the title and the first and last paragraphs of the selection. What position do you predict Martin Jones will take regarding peer pressure and academic success?

Now read the entire essay to test your hypothesis.

Peer Pressure and Academics

BY MARTIN JONES

surpass

I was always a curious child. For as long as I can remember, it was my greatest desire to learn more. Learning gave me a feeling of power that far surpassed any of life's simple pleasures. I was not content to impress my peers with trivia. I felt a need to be prepared whenever a challenge or question arose. This preparation was my shield, my protection, my anchor. Knowledge made me feel strong.

I was very naive, however. Little did I realize that my strength— my ability to focus my thoughts, concentrate and reason—brought others some pain. My peers felt threatened. Small in stature and meek in heart, my desire to learn shone through me like sun rays through the holes of an old barn roof. At first I was totally oblivious to those peers who noticed "my weakness." However, they did not hesitate to spotlight my "strange" ideas that differed from the group. I would often analyze their behavior to the point of justifying the criticism that I tolerated.

oblivious

I was often alone and kept outside distractions at a minimum. I liked it that way. Alone I tackled intellectual challenges one by one like a row of dominoes. But unlike the crowds of Paris that awaited Lindbergh after his great success, there was no such cheering for mine. Because of what I saw defined as success around me, I saw my actual successes as failures. Popularity was verification of success and in my solitude there was none. My "success" remained a fantasy.

verification

I began to do research on those who were considered popular and who had what I badly wanted and needed. Many were athletes. Others were physically beautiful. The rest were simply good at stirring up trouble and attracting attention to themselves. Their humor was based on degradation. Their discussions were equally short on inspiration. Yet, they enjoyed all of the trappings of success.

Enter my logic. I attempted to imitate them. I failed. Why? I was not being myself. I did not give the greatest performance either, and it showed. They ridiculed my acting, making it difficult to continue. Thus, I gave up my futile quest for popularity. Once again I withdrew and much of my past motivation dissipated. Frustration came and depression followed. These two imps dogged me for the years to come.

dissipate

Looking back I realize that I have spent more time concentrating on negative attitudes towards me than I have on appreciating the positive ones. There were many good people who liked my behavior. Although most of them were older than me, the support was still there. Among the younger supporters, there were others like myself, but because I had wanted to please everyone, I continued to dwell on "lost votes."

Today I feel as though I have overcome this personal conflict. I now take pride in whatever topics interest me and pursue them with zest and without shame. There are times when I blame myself for so many years of self-oppression. I wonder where I would be if I had not felt such a barrier to my success. I will never know, but I do know that the experience has brought me to where I am and I do not intend to stop.

COMPREHENSION CHECK

Write brief answers to the following questions.

1. What topic does Martin write about in his essay? What does he say about this topic? (In other words, paraphrase the main idea of this reading.)

2. What strategies did Martin use to overcome "this personal conflict"?

3. How did Martin's peers define "success"?

4. What did Martin mean in the following sentences? Refer to the context of the essay.

    a. "I would often analyze their behavior to the point of justifying the criticism that I tolerated."

    b. "These two imps dogged me for the years to come."

    c. ". . . there were others like myself, but because I had wanted to please everyone, I continued to dwell on 'lost votes.'"

5. How did Martin's perspective change over time?

APPLICATION TWO

The next reading selection, written by a historian of education at Columbia University, comes from a popular magazine, *The New Republic*. It addresses the same topic of peer pressure and academic achievement, but discusses the issue within a broader social context. Preview this article by reading the first sentence of each paragraph in the selection. Taking time to preview an article will help you to increase your comprehension. What topic is the article discussing? What overall view do you predict the author will express?

Test Scores Don't Lie: Back to Basics

BY DIANE RAVITCH

When I was in public high school in Texas in the 1950s, one of the last things a girl wanted was a reputation as a good student. Girls who got good grades were "brains," and brains were socially handicapped. Most girls strived to cultivate the June Allyson image: a follower, not a leader; cute and not too smart, or at least not so smart that the guys felt threatened.

Apparently — despite the women's movement and the presence of significant numbers of successful women as role models — it is still considered inappropriate in most schools and colleges for girls to seem "smart." As a female student at Hunter High School in New York City recently explained, "I make straight A's, but I never talk about it. . . . It's cool to do really badly. If you are interested in school and you show it, you're a nerd." In elite institutions, where students are chosen for their academic ability, girls are more willing to challenge the boys academically than they are in non-selective schools and colleges. But with the demise of most single-sex girls' schools and colleges, there are now even fewer institutions where girls can be leaders and achievers without feeling like freaks. The popular culture — through television, movies, magazines, and videos — incessantly drums in the message to young women that it is better to be popular, sexy, and "cool" than to be intelligent, accomplished, and outspoken: Madonna has replaced June Allyson.

demise

In 1986 researchers Signithia Fordham and John U. Ogbu found a similar anti-academic ethos among both male and female students at an all-black high school in Washington, D.C. They noted that able students faced strong peer pressure not to succeed in school. If they did well in their studies, they might be accused of "acting white." Fordham and Ogbu observed that "peer group pressures against academic striving take many forms, including labeling (e.g., 'brainiac' for students who receive good grades in their courses), exclusion from peer activities or ostracism, and physical assault."

ostracism

These attitudes, whether expressed by boys or girls, blacks or whites, discourage academic achievement. If boys or girls who study are derided as "goobs" and "dweebs" — two of the many pejorative terms for good students catalogued in a recent *New York Times* survey of teenage slang — then most boys and girls are going to avoid studying. Permissive parents and permissive educators don't help the situation by leaving adolescents adrift in a culture shaped largely by the mass media. A national mathematics assessment released in 1988 revealed that American teenagers know the basics taught in elementary school, but their academic performance trails off as they get older and peer pressures begin to take effect. Only half of all 17-year-olds "reached a level of proficiency asso-

pejorative

ciated with material taught in junior high school mathematics."

Unfortunately, outside the cultural bubble inhabited by Madonnas and dweebs lies a real world, and in that world poor academic achievement is not without consequences. Last March a comparison of students in 17 nations reported that our fifth-graders ranked eighth out of the 17; our ninth-graders ranked 16th out of the 17 (beating out Hong Kong only); and our 12th-graders ranked last in biology, third from last in chemistry, and fourth from last in physics. Just a few weeks ago another international test of mathematics and science was released by the Educational Testing Service, with the same dismal results. Compared to 13-year-old students in Ireland, South Korea, Spain, the United Kingdom, and four provinces in Canada, our students scored last in mathematics and well below the mean in science.

There is a growing real world correspondence between our declining test results and our declining economic prowess. Those countries that promote hard work and self-discipline in school have surged ahead, eroding the technological edge that we once enjoyed. According to the *New York Times*, Japan's annual share of American patents grew over the past 15 years from four percent to 19 percent, while our own share dropped from 73 percent to 54 percent. Experts point to the lack of a well-educated labor force as one of the prime causes of our diminishing economic position. Government policy is partially responsible, as are inadequate levels of savings and investment. But we have wounded ourselves, socially and economically, by failing to nurture scientists, engineers, inventors, and, in fact, a general citizenry who can read, write, compute, and adeptly use technology. In the 17-nation science study, the bottom quarter in the ninth grade of U.S. schools is described as "scientifically illiterate."

So what are we doing about it? Among the nations that regularly lead the world in international competitions, like Korea and Japan, there is a strong core curriculum that begins in elementary school. U.S. educators should be demanding that all future *liberal* teachers get a solid liberal education, one that includes math, science, history, literature, and foreign language; and some educators are. Educators and concerned citizens should also be insisting that all children learn science and mathematics and history and literature and a foreign language in every grade from elementary school onward; but few educators are, because they either don't believe in doing so or know there aren't enough qualified teachers to offer *curriculum* such a rich curriculum.

What we shouldn't be doing is denying that a problem exists, or jettisoning objective measures that reveal our educational shortcomings. Yet that has been one effect of the anti-testing movement, which just won a federal court order in New York banning the use of Scholastic Aptitude Tests as the *sole criterion* for awarding state scholarships, on the grounds that the SAT (the nation's most widely used college admission test) discriminates against girls. Judge John M. Walker, noting that boys get higher scores than girls, ruled that this use of the test to distribute scholarships violates the equal protection clause of the Constitution.

Down this path lies a great deal of foolishness. Racial and gender *disparity* disparities crop up on most objective measures of academic performance. On the science tests that were given to students in 17 nations, boys outscored girls in every country, and the gap increased with each age level; only among the most advanced seniors in Hong Kong and Sweden — and only on the biology exam — did girls outscore boys. In the history assessment, boys usually outscored girls, and sometimes the differences were startling. For example, in a national history assessment in 1987, boys were more likely than girls to locate the Rocky Mountains on a map, to know that Columbus discovered the New World before 1750, and to know that the Great Depression occurred between 1900 and 1950. Are these gender-biased questions? It doesn't seem so.

Some of the differences between the genders and the races on tests of subject matter can be accounted for by different course-taking patterns. For example, white males tend to take more advanced courses in science than do females and members of minority groups. Something else is amiss, however, because even when girls and blacks and Hispanics take physics, the white males still outperform them by a considerable margin. Since I don't believe that white males have a genetic edge, I have to conclude that deeply ingrained self-deprecation and ever present peer pressures combine to depress the aspirations and achievements of girls and minority students.

deprecation

Thus, if the SAT were abolished, there would still be gender disparities and racial disparities on other tests. But since I happen to think that the SAT has outlived its usefulness as a college admission test, I am not going to raise a hue-and-cry about its potential demise. Far better in determining whether a student deserves admission to a selective institution would be a test that measures what he or she has actually studied — or should have studied — in science, history, literature, mathematics, and foreign language. Because the SAT is content-free (except in its mathematical questions), high schools can afford to ignore content. If the SAT were replaced by achievement tests, high schools would be likelier to teach the subjects that matter, and students would be likelier to take them. Both developments would narrow the achievement gap that places us at a disadvantage in international comparisons.

But no matter what kind of test is used, we will continue to have serious cultural problems undermining educational achievement: the negative attitudes of students who jeer at those who do well in school; the negative attitude of parents who urge their sons to strive and achieve but not their daughters; and the negative attitude of educators who accept the destructive peer culture, not acknowledging their responsibility to establish a climate in which academic achievement, hard work, and brainpower are honored.

We could tackle the achievement gap by following the lead of Judge Walker in New York and rejecting the validity of all tests in which white males consistently outperform females and members of minority groups. Maybe we could even stop participating in international assessments that tell us how badly we are doing compared with other countries.

Or we could take a hard look at the social and cultural attitudes among teenagers and adults that discourage girls, blacks, and Hispanics from seeing themselves as future engineers, doctors, and scientists; and then we could think hard about ways to change the peer pressures that put down academic achievement. We will continue to lose ground and squander our educational resources until teenagers and their parents come to recognize that academic achievement requires the same motivation and active involvement as achievement in sports or music.

COMPREHENSION CHECK

Write brief answers to the following questions.

1. How well did you predict Ravitch's view? What is her position?

2. What does Ravitch mean by "anti-academic ethos" (paragraph 3)? Try to figure out the meaning from the context before consulting a dictionary.

3. What groups does Ravitch cite as examples of where this ethos can be found? Do you believe her examples are correct? Are there other groups that should be included? If so, name some.

4. Whom does Ravitch blame for these negative attitudes toward studying (paragraph 4)? What evidence does she provide to support her belief? Do you agree with her? Explain.

5. What relationship does Ravitch believe exists between poor academic performance and economic strength? On what does she base this claim (paragraph 6)?

6. Ravitch offers an educational solution based on what other international competitors do (paragraph 7). What assumption (unstated belief) is she making about schools in the United States and in countries such as Korea and Japan?

7. Ravitch continues her discussion of possible solutions by telling her readers what they shouldn't be doing (paragraph 8). One thing she advises against is eliminating standardized tests. How does she explain the "racial and gender disparities [that] crop up on most objective measures of academic performance" (paragraph 9)? Explain why you agree or disagree with her.

8. What do you think Ravitch means by "serious cultural problems" (paragraph 12)?

9. What solutions does Ravitch offer (paragraph 13)? What would she like to see happen?

APPLICATION THREE

Habits are hard to break — especially ones your parents developed in you over the years. In this essay Lewis talks about how old habits have influenced her now that she is in college. As you read the passage be aware of both the gratitude and the frustration Lewis feels toward her past. How do you think habits are related to creative thinking?

Old Habits

BY DANIELLE LEWIS

It is so hard to break old habits! Ever since I can remember, I was trained to do certain things at certain times. Like most others, the important thing I learned was always to obey my parents even if I really didn't want to.

My parents have always been there to guide my way. They had set enough rules so that no matter which way I stepped, I was still out of place. I worked so hard to live by all their rules and regulations. I perfect strived to perfect everything I did so I could hear their praises instead of a "How To Do" lecture. But they would not let me fall, even as off-balanced as I was at times, because they were right there to catch me. If I was too wobbly though, they would straighten me up rather quickly. For the most part, I was an obedient child, and I am grateful to my parents and society for molding me into the person I am. I'm proud of myself for putting up with so much and not rebelling by using drugs or alcohol, or by developing a bad attitude.

Now I'm an eighteen-year-old in college with more freedom than I have ever had before, until I go home, and then I'm their little angel. You know, the child they know they can count on to be honest. Well, one of the rules my parents taught me was that all that was said in the family was kept to the family and was not to leave the house. Since I have been here, the rules have changed a bit. All that is said or done here is left here when I go home. Sometimes it is so hard not to discuss school, friends, and certain incidents with them.

This is when I resent the person I have become. I am not very creative because I've always been judged on preciseness and not crea- *preciseness* tivity. I went through most of high school wearing a mask, until I was alone or with a friend, and then I could be myself. There were even times when I had to take a close look in the mirror to find out if I was really in there somewhere. Once I found myself, I felt secure until the mask fell on my face again. Then that little insecure girl and all her fears were wound up in a knot again.

I came to college so that I could escape my home life, spread my wings, and discover who I am and what it is I really want in life — not what to do and how to do it. I want to solve my own problems. I no longer want to live in fear of hurting my self-image. I want to be treated as an adult, but most of all, I want to be friends with my parents. I want them to actually sit down and listen to what I have to say without criticizing.

These are the goals I had hoped to fulfill my first year of college. Well, most of the rules and regulations my parents had set for me are still in effect. I feel as if I am betraying them if I choose a different method of living. How do I break the habits they have instilled in me after all these years without a feeling of betrayal? A compromise is in order, but it's hard to straighten a warped record.   *warp*

COMPREHENSION CHECK

Write brief answers to the following questions.

1. What blocks to creative thinking did Lewis encounter as she was growing up? How has this affected her?

2. In what ways has being in college changed Lewis?

3. What are Lewis's goals for herself?

4. Lewis ends her essay with the statement "A compromise is in order, but it's hard to straighten a warped record." What does this statement mean? Who is the compromise between, and who is the warped record?

APPLICATION FOUR

The fourth reading selection comes from a college psychology textbook. In this selection the author presents four key environmental factors that influence academic performance. The writing follows a consistent pattern: Each environmental factor is presented and explained, findings from relevant research are cited, and examples are given. The Comprehension Check for this reading provides you with an organizational structure for summarizing the information contained in the text. Preview the selection by reading the first and last paragraphs. Then read the whole passage carefully, filling in the chart as you go.

Environmental Influences on Achievement

BY L. STEINBERG

situational factors

Ability and effort may play a large role in influencing individual performance, but opportunity and situational factors also have a great deal to do with achievement (Featherman, 1980). Many of the differences in academic or occupational achievement observed among adolescents are due not to differences in adolescents' abilities, motives, or beliefs, but to differences in the environments in which these abilities and motives are expressed.

School environments differ markedly—in physical facilities, in opportunities for pursuing academically enriched programs, and in classroom atmosphere, for example. Many school districts, plagued with shrinking tax bases, are characterized by decaying school buildings, outdated equipment, and textbook shortages. In some schools, problems of crime and discipline have grown so overwhelming that attention to these matters has taken precedence over

plague
characterize

learning and instruction. Many young people who genuinely want to succeed are impeded not by a lack of talent or motivation but by a school environment that makes academic success virtually impossible.

impede

The school, of course, is not the only environment that makes a difference in adolescent achievement, and few would argue that schools should accept full responsibility for adolescents who do not succeed at a level consonant with their ability. If anything, the evidence suggests that important aspects of the *home* environment are better predictors of adolescents' academic achievement than important aspects of the school environment (Coleman et al., 1966).

Researchers have focused on three ways in which the adolescent's home may influence his or her level of achievement. First, studies have shown that authoritative parenting is linked to school success during adolescence. In one recent study, sociologist Sanford Dornbusch and his colleagues (Dornbusch et al., 1987) demonstrated that adolescents whose parents were authoritative consistently performed better in school than their peers whose parents were permissive or autocratic. Interestingly, the poorest school performance was observed among adolescents whose parents were inconsistent in their child rearing. That is, even though adolescents whose parents were autocratic received lower grades than students

autocratic

whose parents were authoritative, adolescents whose parents used a mixture of autocratic and permissive techniques performed even worse. In general, these findings are in line with a good deal of research suggesting that consistent, authoritative parenting is associated with a wide array of benefits to the adolescent, including higher achievement motivation, greater self-esteem, and enhanced competence (Maccoby and Martin, 1983).

A second way in which the family influences adolescent achievement is through parents' encouragement. Studies have shown that adolescents' achievement is directly related to the level of achievement their parents expect them to attain. Adolescents whose parents expect them to go on to college are more likely to do so than adolescents of equal ability whose parents expect less of them (Featherman, 1980).

Finally, studies have also shown that the quality of an adolescent's home environment — as measured simply in terms of the presence of such items as a television set, dictionary, encyclopedia, newspaper, vacuum cleaner, and other indicators of family income — is more strongly correlated with youngsters' levels of academic achievement than is the quality of the physical facility of the school they attend, the background and training of their teachers, or the level of teacher salaries paid by the school district (Armor, 1972).

correlate

With this in mind, it is important to point out that a disheartening number of young people in this country—a disproportionate number of them from minority groups—live in overcrowded, inadequate housing and come from families that are under severe economic and social stress. Their neighborhoods may be dangerous centers of crime and violence. And their diets may be sorely deficient in protein and other nutrients necessary for intellectual development. These obstacles to success disproportionately afflict youngsters from minority backgrounds. Put succinctly, many American youngsters do not grow up in an atmosphere that is conducive to academic achievement.

There is also evidence that friends influence adolescent achievement as well. But contrary to the notion that the influence of the peer group on adolescent achievement is always negative, recent studies suggest that the impact of friends on adolescents' school performance depends on the academic orientation of the peer group. Having friends who earn high grades and aspire to further education appears to enhance adolescent achievement, whereas having friends who earn low grades or disparage school success may interfere with it. For example, according to one extensive study of friends in school (Epstein, 1983a), students' grades changed over time in relation to the grades of their friends. Students with best friends who achieved high grades in school were more likely to show improvements in their own grades than students who began at similar levels of achievement but had friends who were not high achievers. Peers also exerted a small but significant influence on each other's college plans. Among low-achieving adolescents, for example, those with high-achieving friends were more likely to plan to continue their education than those with low-achieving friends.

The potential negative impact of friends on achievement is vividly seen in a recent study of black male peer groups in an inner-city school (Fordham and Ogbu, 1986). These researchers found that bright black students in this school had to live down the "burden of acting white" and face criticism from their peers, who referred to them as "brainiacs." When a small group of these students were placed in an environment in which all their peers were high achievers, the derision and negative labeling did not occur, however.

Situational factors affect occupational as well as educational attainment. In the opinion of many social critics, strong institutional barriers impede the occupational attainment of women and members of ethnic minorities (Ogbu, 1978). These barriers may be especially strong during adolescence, when young people are steered away from some educational and occupational pursuits and toward others—not on the basis of abil-

disproportionate

conducive

institutional

ity or interest but because of gender, socioeconomic background, or race. Anthropologist John Ogbu (1974) has argued that many minority youth do not believe that the labor market will be open to them and, consequently, do not believe that there is sufficient payoff for investing a great deal of time in schoolwork. Studies by sociologist James Rosenbaum (1976, 1978) indicate that the ways in which schools determine which students are exposed to which curricula restrict the opportunities of those students who are placed in the slower tracks and perpetuate these students' academic disadvantages. The courses they encounter are likely to be less stimulating and less intellectually enriching than those taken by their peers. And students placed in the slower tracks tend to come disproportionately from minority groups and the economically disadvantaged — partly because their academic test scores warrant remedial placement, but partly as a consequence of their social background (Featherman, 1980).

warrant

Even after adolescence, a variety of social obstacles may lead to differences in occupational attainment among various ethnic groups and between men and women. Sociologist Margaret Marini (1980) finds, for example, that although men and women enter the labor force at similar levels of occupational status, men have much greater occupational mobility — primarily because their movement is not constrained, as is women's,

by marital and childbearing commitments. The single most powerful influence on sex differences in the years of schooling completed, for example, is not that men and women have different abilities and motives, but that women marry younger (Marini, 1978). Because women tend to marry younger than men, they tend to leave school earlier.

Thus although psychological factors play an important role in determining occupational and scholastic success, it is impossible to examine achievement during adolescence thoroughly without taking into account the broader environment in which individuals pursue their educational and occupational careers. Moreover, distinguishing between motivational and environmental factors is hard: They typically go hand in hand. Living in an environment that offers few opportunities for success induces feelings of learned helplessness, which in turn leads individuals to feel that exerting any effort to succeed is futile. Attending school in an environment where achievement is not encouraged engenders attitudes and beliefs inconsistent with striving for achievement. Rather than viewing achievement during adolescence as determined by one single factor, such as ability, it is more accurate to say that patterns of achievement are the result of a cumulative process that includes a long history of experience and socialization in school, in the family, at work, and in the peer group.

cumulative

Complete the chart on page 31 to check your understanding of the information contained in the textbook reading.

What Do You Think?

This section is divided into two parts: "Discussion Questions" and "Writing Assignments." The division is somewhat arbitrary in that all the questions and assignments could be discussed either orally or in writing; however, discussion questions tend to be more open-ended in order to promote greater thinking. Some of the ideas generated in class discussions may be useful in your writing assignments. You and your instructor may choose to respond to only some of the discussion questions or complete only one of the writing assignments.

We view writing as a process. What you write should go through several stages of writing and revision. Peer-editing — having fellow students read and comment on your writing — can be a valuable tool in the revising process. We also believe that writers write best when they truly want to convey something to the reader. In the Writing Assignment section of each chapter, we try to balance your choosing a writing topic with our providing topics or questions that reflect writing expectations in college.

✪ DISCUSSION QUESTIONS

Prepare for class discussion by jotting down brief answers to the following questions.

1. Are Martin's experiences in Application One, "Peer Pressure and Academics," similar to any you have had? How do peer groups play a major role in students' study habits? How can peer groups make the difference between a student graduating and dropping out?

"Environmental Influences on Achievement"

Introduction _____

_____

Environmental Influences	*Examples*	*Research*
1. _____	_____	_____
	_____	
2. _____		
a. _____	_____	_____
	_____	
b. _____	_____	
	_____	_____
c. _____	_____	
	_____	_____
3. _____	_____	_____
	_____	
4. _____	_____	_____
	_____	

Factors after adolescence _____

_____

Conclusion _____

_____

2. Have you experienced similar attitudes from your peers? What advice would you offer to someone who is having problems similar to Martin's?

3. Do you agree with Ravitch's argument in Application Two, "Test Scores Don't Lie"? Take a moment to consider your own views. Even if you agree with her view of how things are, do you think this is necessarily a problem? What experiences have you had that support her ideas?

4. Ravitch suggests that "we could think hard about ways to change the peer pressures that put down academic achievement." Is she being naive in suggesting this as a solution? What concrete steps do you think could be taken to help? Be ready to elaborate on your answers.

5. In Application Three, Lewis talks about how difficult it is to break habits. What habits of thinking or behavior do you have that you would like to break? What attitudes would you like to change? What habits have you been able to break? What suggestions or strategies could you offer others?

6. In Application Four, "Environmental Influences on Achievement," Steinberg reports the findings mentioned in the Ravitch article (that is, the negative impact of friends on achievement), but focuses more on the "opportunity and situational factors" contributing to academic success. How would you rank these factors? Which factors do you think are more influential? Explain your answers.

7. What knowledge or experience do you have regarding classes in the "slower track"? Under what conditions might these "remedial" courses be a self-fulfilling prophecy for academic failure?

8. How do you respond to the following statement: "Authoritative parenting is associated with a wide array of benefits to the adolescent, including higher achievement motivation, greater self-esteem, and enhanced competence"?

WRITING ASSIGNMENTS

Select one of the following topics and in a few paragraphs develop a thoughtful written response.

1. Prior to writing his essay, Martin generated a list of ideas related to his topic. Using one or more of the following ideas as a starting point, write a few paragraphs in which you agree or disagree with Martin. Be sure to add your own ideas, examples, and experiences.

    a. Terms such as *bookworm, nerd,* and *dweeb* are frequently used as derogatory statements toward academically motivated students.

    b. The most popular students in school tend to be athletes.

    c. Among male students, studying is often viewed as an effeminate activity.

    d. Among Black students, studying is often viewed as a Caucasian activity.

    e. Many Black male students often receive both the effeminate and the Caucasian label if they study.

    f. Students who are victimized by peer pressure may suffer from low academic achievement.

    g. Parents and counselors are sometimes unable to provide the necessary support for these students to deal effectively with academic peer pressure.

2. Putting yourself in "another's shoes" is an excellent way to develop your critical thinking skills. Write a sympathetic description of someone who exerts peer pressure on others. Be creative; you may decide to write a short narrative piece to get your point across.

3. Complete the chart on page 35 for the article "Test Scores Don't Lie." Now write a brief summary of the major points. Finally, write a paragraph explaining your reaction to Ravitch's ideas. Be sure to explain your ideas and include examples.

4. With a friend develop a creative writing piece. You might first brainstorm the kind of piece (that is, poem, play, story) you intend to write, then brainstorm the topic or vice versa. Use your imagination and take some writing risks. For example, if you have never written a poem, try to now; if you have never used description in your writing, be sure to include some.

5. Using the information you supplied to complete the chart on page 31, write a summary of the reading selection "Environmental Influences on Achievement."

6. Each of the readings discusses how external factors influence academic performance. Having read the four selections, compare the writing styles used by the different authors. Consider the focus of the readings, the amount of information presented, and the way it is organized. Finally, discuss which one was easiest to understand, most interesting, and/or most informative. Be sure to explain your answers.

"Test Scores Don't Lie"

The Problem

1. What it is _____

2. The causes

    a. _____

    b. _____

3. The consequences

    a. _____

    b. _____

    c. _____

The Solutions

1. Alternatives

    a. _____

    b. _____

    c. _____

2. Best choice and why _____

    _____

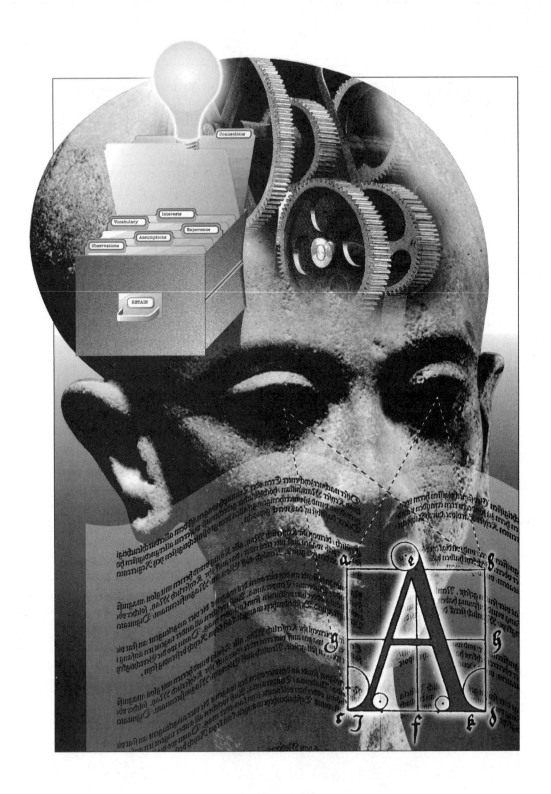

CHAPTER 2

Reading for Meaning

After reading Chapter 2 you should be able to:

- list several factors that make comprehension easier
- implement a set of study and reading strategies that promote high academic performance
- recognize the dangers in stereotyping the academic achievements of any particular group of people

You may use the following checklist in planning your study of factors affecting comprehension and academic performance. Activities marked with a ✪ are to be completed in class. Some preclass preparation may be required.

CONTEXT FOR LEARNING

✪ _____ **INTRODUCTORY CHAPTER ACTIVITY**

_____ Factors That Influence Comprehension

✪ _____ **ACTIVITY BREAK**

_____ Distinguishing Between Studying and Understanding

_____ Misconceptions About Reading

_____ Reading Literature

_____ Guaranteeing Academic Success

✪ _____ **DISCUSSION BREAK**

APPLICATION: BUILDING CONNECTIONS

_____ **APPLICATION ONE**

_____ **"Literally Handicapped"** by Vicki Anderson

_____ **COMPREHENSION CHECK**

_____ **APPLICATION TWO**

_____ **"Berkeley Mathematician Strives 'to Help People Get Moving'"** by B. T. Watkins

_____ **COMPREHENSION CHECK**

_____ **APPLICATION THREE**

_____ **"Asian-American Students: The Myth of a Model Minority"** by Frank H. Shih

_____ **COMPREHENSION CHECK**

_____ **APPLICATION FOUR**

_____ **"The New Americans"** by R. J. Wilson

_____ **COMPREHENSION CHECK**

✪ **INTRODUCTORY CHAPTER ACTIVITY**

For this activity select a passage that you do *not* understand and bring it to class. You may choose, for example, an excerpt from a textbook, an article in the Constitution, a paragraph from an essay, or something from *Sports Illustrated*. The only criterion is that you do not understand the majority of the text. On a separate piece of paper list several factors that might explain why this selection is difficult for you to understand. Now share your reading selection with two or three classmates. Do you understand some of their passages? Compare your list of reasons for not understanding. Are they similar? As you read Chapter 2, keep your list of reasons in mind to see if they match up with those described here.

Factors That Influence Comprehension

The following series of examples will help you think about how people understand or comprehend written materials. What factors make it easier for us to understand and remember? How exactly do we make sense of what we read?

Knowing more about *how* you learn ultimately will help you understand more from your textbook reading. Also, it will help you study and learn more from your lecture notes. Finally, it will help you become more aware of the way you think.

Example One   Read the following two lines to yourself:

A B C D E F G H
11 12 13 14 15 16 17 18

Did you "read" the first line as a set of letters? Did you "read" the second line as a set of numbers? Look closely now at the number 13 and the letter B. The actual marks on the paper are the same. What accounts for the fact that most people "read" letters in the first line and numbers in the second?

If you say it has something to do with the information surrounding the written symbols, you are correct. What words or sentences mean has a lot to do with what goes before or after them. We often think that meaning comes from the marks on the page, but meaning also has a lot to do with what is in our heads. We "see" what we expect to see.

Our brains really are quite remarkable organs. Our eyes register the world as upside down and backward, and vibrating slightly. It takes our brains to sort out and make sense of all the incoming information.

Example Two   Read the following sentence:

The notes were sour because the seams split.

Do you understand each of the *words* in the sentence? Can you define each of them? Assuming that you can, does the sentence make sense? Probably not. Some people think that understanding is a matter of adding up all the definitions of a group of words in order to achieve meaning; that is, definition + definition + definition + . . . = meaning. In our sample sentence we can see that this does not hold true. If you are now told that you are in Scotland listening to a group of bagpipe players, does it begin to make more sense? Again, the meaning comes from more than just the words. What implications does this have for your understanding your lecture notes or your textbook? Simply that you need to look for meaning in more than just the individual words or sentences.

Example Three   Read the following passage. When you have finished write one or two sentences summarizing it.

> Rocky slowly got up from the mat, planning his escape. He hesitated a moment and thought. Things were not going well.

What bothered him most was being held, especially since the charge against him had been weak. He considered his present situation. The lock that held him was strong but he thought he could break it. He knew, however, that his timing would have to be perfect. Rocky was aware that it was because of his early roughness that he had been penalized so severely — much too severely from his point of view. The situation was becoming frustrating; the pressure had been grinding on him for too long. He was being ridden unmercifully. Rocky was getting angry now. He felt he was ready to make his move. He knew that his success or failure would depend on what he did in the next few seconds.

What did you write down — something about a wrestler trying to break out of a hold or a prisoner trying to escape from custody? Some students have even said the paragraph is about a dog! Who is right? The passage is ambiguous (that is, it could have several possible meanings). Researchers used this passage in a study to find out how important a person's background was to comprehension. Students who were college physical education majors more often reported the wrestling interpretation, while members of the general college student population chose the prisoner scenario.

What does this mean in terms of understanding? It shows that readers come to a reading task with expectations that influence their comprehension. When their expectations match the writers' intentions, comprehension comes easily. When there is a mismatch of background knowledge, however, confusion and misunderstanding often result.

So much of what we understand depends on what we already know. Understanding, then, is much more individualized than most people realize. Of course, as a student you strive to understand your textbook, but clearly the more knowledge you have in common with the writer, the easier your comprehension task will be.

Example Four   In what area do you consider yourself to be an expert: Sports? Politics? Soap operas? Music? Choose an area and call yourself the expert. Now imagine a friend of yours who knows very little about this area and call him or her the amateur. For the sake of our example we will say that you know 5,000 facts related to your field while your friend knows only 100. You both are sitting in a classroom when in walks a professor who, it turns out, knows all the facts that you both know and who also comes up with fifty new facts that neither of you knows. You are told that you have twenty minutes in which to learn the new information. Who will have the easier time? Will you, the expert whose head is filled with information on the topic? Or will your friend, whose brain is relatively clutter-free on this topic? If you chose yourself, you are correct. Why? For several reasons. First, you are obviously more interested in the area and thus will find the learning more interesting. Second, you will be able to relate and connect the new information to facts you have already stored in your brain. One of the cognitive truths of life is that the more you know, the more you can learn. You may be familiar with the saying "Money makes money"; in this case, knowledge makes more knowledge possible.

How does this relate to studying? Imagine you and a friend are enrolled in the same course, and even though you seem to be studying all the time, your friend manages to get better grades than you with a third less effort. "My friend must be smarter," you say, or even, "I must be stupid." Well, chances are your friend already knows more about the subject or knows more about how to study than you do. Perhaps she studied harder than you last year or had more demanding teachers. New information "fits" into her "knowledge bank" more easily than into yours and gets learned faster. "Not fair," you say. Maybe not, but because your situation is due to lack of knowledge and not lack of brainpower, you can do something about it.

Example Five   In a study done by researchers on reading, two groups of students were given a passage to read. One passage dealt with shopping at a grocery store; the other dealt with dining at a restaurant. Each passage contained the same number of foods bought or eaten, and both passages were the same length and reading difficulty. After reading one of the passages, each student was asked to recall the foods in the order presented in the passage.

One group did significantly better at remembering the items. Which group would you pick? In fact, the restaurant passage readers remembered more; the interesting question is "Why?" According to some research studies, over time the brain develops mental structures, described as "schemata," to organize information about common events and circumstances. We might have schemata for such things as doing the laundry, getting to school in the morning, or partying Friday night. We might not all share the same schemata for the same activities, but we could assume that the more similar our experiences, the more similar our schemata might be.

In this example the restaurant passage readers would call upon their "restaurant schemata" to help take in and remember the incoming information while the grocery passage readers would use their "grocery shopping schemata." But what would allow the restaurant readers to remember more of the items in order? Because dining in a restaurant is usually more structured than shopping in a grocery store, the "regular" schemata for eating in restaurants offers our restaurant passage readers fewer surprises. Incoming data fit easily into the appropriate "slots," and thus the restaurant passage readers have an easier time remembering the foods. For example, we eat our soup before our steak and our steak before our dessert, but when we go shopping we might just as easily put a dessert into our cart before a T-bone steak.

When it comes to remembering information, the structure or the organization of the information helps. What relationship does this have to learning? In part it means that acquiring information also means learning how the information is organized. How information is connected is probably as important as the information itself.

How can this be true? Let's take a personal example. Consider your birth date and today's date as two points on an imaginary time line. One point indicates that you were born, the other that you are still alive. In truth, neither of these facts is particularly interesting in and of itself. What makes your life interesting is what *connects* these two facts — all the dots or events on the line that link these two dates. The same analogy can be made for information. Two facts in isolation are not very interesting or informative. It is *how* the facts are connected that is significant.

It may seem impossible, but the more you already have stored in your brain, the easier it is to store more. This is true because you are able to make appropriate connections between what you know and what you want to know.

Example Six   Imagine that your psychology professor has asked you to participate in a psychology experiment. You arrive on time and are escorted into a dark room containing a blank screen. You are told that this is an experiment to discover how much information people can see and recall when it is presented to them for only a split second. You focus your attention on the screen, and the following information flashes before your eyes:

x t r h q a t l o b g k c m j w

You immediately write down all the letters you can remember in the order in which they were presented. The rest of the experiment continues in the same manner, with the following information being presented to you one line at a time:

th st ch tr ph sh pr qu cr br

walk   case   quick   window   tap

What television show are you watching?

After the experiment is completed the researcher goes over the answers with you and says your answers are similar to those of most other subjects. In line 1 you were able to recall between 5 and 7 individual letters, and for each subsequent line you were able to recall additional letters until the final line where you were able to recall all 32 letters and the question mark. The researcher asks, "How do you account for this? You could 'see' only 6 letters in line 1 but all 32 letters in line 4." You respond, "Well, the last line makes sense and the first line doesn't."

We agree. In addition, we think your performance says something about the way in which you can make learning and remembering easier for yourself and your brain. When you try to learn material that is not connected or is not related to anything already stored in your brain, you can learn some of it, but not very much. When you ask your brain to remember information that is connected and makes sense, it can do a much better job. This may sound like basic common sense, yet all too often students try to store information that the brain only perceives as a string of unrelated letters. Once again, *connection* is the key word here. Add to this the concept of organization and you increase the chances of remembering a thousandfold.

✪ ACTIVITY BREAK

For each of the following statements, write down the example or examples that illustrate the comprehension concept mentioned. The statements represent a summary of the points presented as they relate to understanding, learning, and remembering.

_____   1.   In many ways understanding is unique to a person. Meaning is *constructed* by the reader or listener.

_____   2.   Meaning is more than the summation of the definitions of the words in a passage.

_____   3.   Comprehension of a written text or lecture depends, in part, on the *context* in which it is found as well as the *expectations* of the reader.

_____   4.   Information you *understand* is remembered more easily than information that makes little or no sense.

_____   5.   Knowing how information is *connected* and *organized* facilitates remembering that information.

_____   6   *Relating* new information to information already known aids in comprehension.

_____   7.   The more you understand, the more you *can* understand. The more you understand, the more you *can* remember. The more you remember, the more you *can* remember.

Distinguishing Between Studying and Understanding

"I know I know the answer; I just can't say it."

"I know right where it is in the book; I just can't remember it."

"I know I knew it last night."

— The voices of desperate students

Let's take a minute to distinguish between studying and understanding. We are excluding here rote types of learning where the task is to memorize without regard for comprehension. *Understanding* means having information make sense. When you understand something you can imagine the brain receiving the information and nodding in agreement. "No problem here," says the brain. Understanding is the first step to effective studying. Studying is made easier when material is first understood.

Students often spend hours preparing for their first exams only to flunk miserably. "Why bother," they say, "it makes no difference. When I don't study I flunk, and when I do study I flunk." What students often fail to realize is that they have only really studied to the point of having a literal (basic) understanding of the information. They need to study to gain a deeper level of understanding. For example, they can ask themselves a series of questions: What makes this information significant? How does it relate to what I already know? Do I agree with these ideas? What are the implications or applications of this information? By answering these questions students interpret and evaluate the information.

Most studying involves reading lecture notes and assigned chapters in the text. Students who don't like to read tend to be passive readers, content to let their eyes float over the print. Moreover, they are often misinformed about what good reading involves.

Misconceptions About Reading

Unfortunately, several misconceptions about reading prevent many readers from assuming greater control over their reading and thereby affect how efficiently they read and how well they learn. Which of the following misconceptions might be "getting in your way"?

Misconception 1: Done correctly, reading is easy and/or fun

Belief in this misconception may be due to students' early reading experiences with teachers who, eager for them to be successful readers, steered them away from materials they couldn't read aloud without 90 percent accuracy. Thus, for instance, if Trevia stumbled over too many words, it was assumed she needed an "easier" book. As a consequence, she developed a very low reading frustration level. Now when Trevia struggles to read difficult material, she quickly gives up.

Of course we would like you to find reading easy and fun, but when it is not, it does not necessarily mean that you aren't reading "correctly." Some reading material is just difficult, either because the topic is unfamiliar, the material is complex, or the selection is badly written. Some reading material is not inherently entertaining, but the information within it is important. When the reading seems difficult you need to stop and assess the situation: Why are you reading this — what is your purpose? What is causing the difficulty? How can you minimize frustration and maximize comprehension?

Misconception 2: Readers should understand everything they read

Here is a situation where you must take more responsibility for the reading. How much you should comprehend from a reading depends on your purpose: Are you looking for an answer to a particular question? Do you just want to know the author's position? Will you be required to take a test on the material? As a reader you need to decide what your purpose is before reading and let that guide you in how much you need to comprehend. If you are assigned material to read in a course and the instructor hasn't set forth any purpose, you should ask about it.

Misconception 3: Good readers should read quickly

Speed should not be confused with flexibility. Good readers are flexible readers and vary their reading rate depending on their purpose. Some students bemoan the time it takes to read ten pages in their history texts, but the unhappy truth is that some material does take considerable time to read well. It may, indeed, take you an hour to read and remember the important ideas in ten pages of history. If you need to acquire only a general understanding of the author's viewpoint, then you can go more quickly. Your reading rate also depends upon the writer's style, the complexity of the material, and your background knowledge. Does this sound familiar? It should; reading is an interaction between the reader and the writer. When the reader and the writer use the same language (vocabulary and style) and share similar interests, knowledge, and experiences, then comprehension will come more easily and the reading will go more quickly. When any of the variables clash, then comprehension will take you more time.

Misconception 4: Reading is done with the eyes

At this point misconception 4 should not come as any shock to you. Reading is only incidentally visual; in fact, were you to lose your eyesight you could learn to read with your fingertips. Although your eyes receive the print stimuli, it is your brain that processes and understands the data. Reading is a cognitive or mental process. It is the reconstruction of the writer's meaning. Thus you can understand why speed reading courses that rely on eye movement exercises may not be very effective. Simply learning how to move your eyes more quickly will not guarantee that you understand what passes before them. (Sometimes these courses offer additional exercises that do increase your flexibility as a reader or help you develop more reading concentration; however, eye movement exercises alone will have little impact on your comprehension.)

Reading Literature

So far in this chapter we have discussed several factors within readers and within texts that influence how well a reader understands what has been written. We have also made a distinction between studying and understanding and cautioned students to see them as different tasks. Finally, we have looked at several misconceptions that students often make about the reading process and how this can affect their approach to reading assignments.

Our comments have assumed that most of your reading assignments are information based where the text is there to inform, teach, or persuade. *What* is being said takes precedence over *how* it is being said. And in all likelihood these are the kinds of texts that will form the core of your general education requirements and maybe your major. However, we shouldn't overlook another "type" of reading that transports the reader into a world created by the writer. We are speaking of literature — plays, poetry, short stories, and novels where *how* authors tell their stories is equally as important as *what* they say.

When students read, they need to be aware of some of the differences between fiction and nonfiction. Nonfiction writing is focused on conveying ideas, and the writer strives for clarity; points are explained by example or elaboration. Writers organize their thoughts carefully to make it easier for readers to follow. You may have noticed all the headings and outlines that textbooks — including our own — have to help the reader follow the sequence of ideas. Writers try to use words that are unambiguous (have only one meaning) and use sentence structures that allow the reader to follow their logic. This does not mean that nonfiction writers don't write eloquently or inspire their readers; they can and do. However, literary writers — perhaps unconsciously — use a variety of literary techniques to convey meaning; students in literature courses often spend time studying different literary terms and a writer's effectiveness in using them in order to better understand a piece of literature. The following excerpt from *The Life of Samuel Johnson* by James Boswell highlights some of the key differences between expository and literary writing.

> He [Mr. Johnson] received me very courteously; but, it must be confessed that his apartment, and furniture, and morning dress, were sufficiently uncouth. His brown suit of clothes looked very rusty; he had on a little old shrivelled unpowdered wig, which was too small for his head; his shirt-neck and knees of his breeches were loose; his black worsted stockings ill drawn up; and he had a pair of unbuckled shoes by way of slippers. But all of these slovenly particularities were forgotten the moment that he began to talk.

If our goal in describing Samuel Johnson were merely to inform the reader of the "facts," our excerpt might read as follows:

> Mr. Johnson was courteous when we met, but I have to admit his apartment, furniture, and clothes were in poor taste. His brown suit was old; he was wearing a powdered wig that was too small; his shirt collar and short trousers were loose; his

black stockings were falling down; and he wore a pair of un-
buckled shoes for slippers. But I forgot all about his sloppy
dress when he began to talk.

What's missing in the "translation"? Take a moment and share your
thoughts with a class member. Did you point to certain words like *rusty*
or *shrivelled*? These are words that enhance the reader's understanding
of the description. A writer's choice of words, or *diction*, is important to
the effectiveness of the piece. What do such phrases as "his black
worsted stockings ill drawn up" or "all these slovenly particularities"
add to your understanding?

Read the following passage in which Boswell transcribes some of
Johnson's conversations. As you read you may want to "translate" the text
into a more expository form as we did above. Doing this may help you
uncover other aspects of the author's literary style.

Madness frequently discovers itself merely by unnecessary
deviation from the usual modes of the world. My poor friend
Smart showed the disturbance of his mind, by falling upon his
knees, and saying his prayers in the street, or in any other
unusual place. Now although, rationally speaking, it is greater
madness not to pray at all, than to pray as Smart did, I am
afraid there are so many who do not pray, that their understanding is not called in question.

Boswell also includes a conversation between Johnson and Dr. Burney regarding the fate of "this unfortunate poet, Christopher Smart."

Burney: How does poor Smart do, Sir; is he likely to recover?

Johnson: It seems as if his mind had ceased to struggle with the
disease; for he grows fat upon it.

Burney: Perhaps, Sir, that may be from want of exercise.

Johnson: No, Sir; he has partly as much exercise as he used to
have, for he digs in the garden. Indeed, before his confinement,
he used for exercise to walk to the alehouse; but he was *carried*
back again. I did not think he ought to be shut up. His infirmi-
ties were not noxious to society. He insisted on people praying

with him; and I'd as lief [likely] pray with Kit Smart as anyone else. Another charge was, that he did not love clean linen; and I have no passion for it.

Figurative language is a literary term that describes the many ways in which language is used nonliterally to create an image or comparison. Literal language uses words according to their exact definitions, while figurative language expands on exact word-for-word translations. The term *figurative language* has several specific categories; however, we need only bear in mind the more general definition. Figurative language is the result of all the pictures and images created by the words. For example, the passage above presents the image of Smart being preyed on for praying! Smart's illness is like an extended metaphor comparing physical, mental, and social diseases. Madness is treated like a human being and "discovers itself," while Smart's mental illness has an appetite and grows fat. Mr. "Smart" is judged "dull" by society and locked away. Finally, there is something ludicrous about a man being confined in a madhouse for not "loving" clean linen.

The last literary term we will discuss is *tone*. Tone refers to the emotional meaning authors bring to their writing. It is an important part of understanding written text. For example, read the following sentence in as many different ways as possible.

I am meeting my brother today.

You may be nervous ("Oh boy! I'm finally meeting my brother after all these years"); you may be excited ("Hurray! I'm meeting my little baby brother today"); you may be discouraged ("Well, I knew I would finally have to face him"). It is clear that how a reader interprets an author's tone will make a big difference in how something is understood. Reread Boswell's excerpts. What tone does he bring to his writing? Do you think he likes Johnson or thinks he's a fool? How do you know? Given that Boswell wrote in the late 1700s, it may be more difficult for present-day readers to be sure of his tone. Being familiar with the meanings of words and literary techniques and reading carefully can make interpreting tone easier.

Analyzing literature uses critical thinking skills in a different context. Understanding literature is more than understanding the facts in a story or knowing the main points and the events that lead up to them. Studying literature means understanding the author's use of language. It also means interpreting a piece of literature for ourselves because literature is often ambiguous and open to several interpretations. Finally, keep in mind that the goal of reading literature is not to whiz through the pages, reaching the last line on the last page as quickly as possible, but to soak up the linguistic sights as you move along.

Guaranteeing Academic Success

Guaranteed academic success or your money back! If only it were as simple as commercial advertisers would have us believe about any number of products.

In order to succeed in college you need to use your brain, but you don't have to be brilliant. In fact, in our combined sixty-two years of teaching we have rarely met anyone who did not have the basic intelligence to complete an undergraduate degree. You need to know such things as how cells divide, what three branches make up our government, and what 23 percent of sixty is. For those students who come to college knowing lots of history, biology, and math, learning will be easier. In the first section of this chapter we tried to explain why this is true and what makes learning more difficult for those who lack this academic knowledge. Even if you are one of these latter types, don't despair. There are materials, strategies, and courses like this one that can help you "fill in the gaps."

Learning new study strategies can help you achieve academic success, but students sometimes make the mistake of thinking that such strategies work magic. They don't. In fact, we have seen students use all the right strategies and still not learn anything! Ultimately, *you* decide how, what, and if you will study. This leads us to two critical factors that can determine college success: the ability to think about what you are learning and the personal power that you bring to the task.

What do we mean by "personal power"? Imagine being able to promise your friends that you could make them study for six hours, work out in the gym for two more hours, and eat nothing but healthy, nonfattening foods every day! Imagine promising yourself that you would never skip another class, turn in another paper late, or leave anything until the last minute and know that you really meant it! What would make it possible? Personal power.

Our experience has shown that motivation and self-discipline are two key components of personal power; and of the two, self-discipline is the more important. Motivation alone does not guarantee success. Students complain that while they are truly interested in the material as it is being presented in class, once they return to their dorms they are incapable of sitting down and doing the reading and reviewing necessary to do well. "I just can't seem to make myself" is the familiar refrain. If a student is in the unfortunate predicament of lacking both motivation and discipline, we usually hear "It's all *so boring*." We suggest that you set some goals, establish a study schedule, work with some friends, and set up a system of rewards for work completed. You may want to adopt the study group approach described in Watkins's article in Application Two in this chapter.

Our single most valuable piece of advice, however, is this: *Go to all your classes.* Go when you are half asleep; go even if you aren't understanding the lectures; go even if you are already failing. If you can't structure your time, let someone else provide the external control. Good luck!

✪ DISCUSSION BREAK

Prepare for class discussion by jotting down brief answers to the following questions.

1. How would you define "personal power"? Do you agree that discipline and motivation are the keys to academic success? Consider your own history of self-discipline and motivation. In what areas do you have the most discipline? What factors or experiences contributed to developing that discipline and motivation? What steps can you take to transfer these strengths to other areas? Be as specific as possible.

2. Consider this situation: You are a faithful watcher of the well-known soap opera "As the Universe Expands." You have two friends, one who watches the program once in a while and another who has never seen the program. On two separate occasions each one pays you a visit while you are watching the show. Both ask you the same question: "What's happening?" How will you answer? Is your answer influenced by your questioner's knowledge of the program? If so, what can be said about the relationship between background knowledge and comprehension?

3. Take a poll to find out areas in which your classmates consider themselves either experts or amateurs. Do the same thing with regard to academic subjects. How should you change or modify your studying to take into account your status as an amateur or an expert? Be as specific as possible.

4. The six examples discussed in the section "Factors That Affect Comprehension" were designed to provide you with some insights into how your brain functions. Given what you now understand about how the brain "learns," of what use is cramming? Be prepared to explain your answer.

5. Which misconceptions about reading have you always believed? Should we add a fifth misconception: Students believe reading is unnecessary? Recall the circumstances that helped form your beliefs. How have these misconceptions affected your interest and motivation in reading? How will this information change the way you approach difficult texts in the future?

6. What kinds of material do you read for enjoyment? Do you read more fiction or nonfiction? What are your favorite kinds of literature? In what ways are you aware of *how* the writer conveys meaning? What literary techniques do you use in your creative writing? Explain your answers.

Application: Building Connections

APPLICATION ONE

Do you take being able to read for granted? Do you know an adult who cannot read? What kind of coping skills has he or she developed? The reading selection "Literally Handicapped" describes with great sensitivity the writer's relationship with her godfather, who is functionally illiterate. Preview the essay by reading the title and the last paragraph. What do you think the author means by "literally handicapped"?

Literally Handicapped

BY VICKI ANDERSON

It was two weeks before my high school graduation. Equipped with forty glossy copies of my senior picture, and a list of friends and relatives, I sat down and began a most difficult task: saying farewell forty times to forty different people in forty different ways. After all, aren't all high school seniors expected to leave outstanding farewell speeches on the back of their graduation pictures before they depart into the "real world"? However, my problems came to a temporary end as I came to a particularly special loved one on my list. His picture was by far the easiest to sign. "I love you," was all I said. It's not that I couldn't think of yet another witty phrase. The reason is quite simple. Because he was forced to drop out of school to help support his brothers and sisters, this friend of the family never received a formal education. Although he planned to return to school one day, the opportunity never arose. At the age of seventy, my godfather is functionally illiterate. Had I decided to write my godfather a long detailed letter on the back of the picture, he probably would have politely put it away until he had a chance to read it in privacy at his own pace. However, my godfather is not alone. According to Joseph Berger in his article "Price of Illiteracy Translates into Poverty and Humiliation," more than twenty-three million people in this country share his problem (*The New York Times*, September 6, 1988, A1). Because of the

functionally
illiterate

many social, personal, and economic problems that illiterate adults must face, it is obvious that efforts to reduce this problem are crucially needed. Perhaps the first necessary step towards reducing this problem is to focus on the severe handicaps endured by illiterates. It is impossible to hide from the destructive impact of illiteracy on one's life.

My godfather is a proud man. He has learned how to disguise his illiteracy perfectly through the years. One would never guess that he must rely on others for such basic things as balancing his checkbook, interpreting legal documents, and writing formal letters. But the fact is that this charming man who spent his life gaining a reputation as one of the best automobile mechanics in the state has suffered from a very severe problem all his life. In his article "Daughter of a Slave Seeks Freedom from Illiteracy" (*The New York Times*, September 9, 1988, A12) George James states that adult illiteracy can contribute to strong feelings of inadequacy and poor self esteem which often result in the individual feeling handicapped. James refers to Helen Elmore, a functional illiterate, who claims that illiteracy is "like a handicap, because you have to depend on others to do certain things for you and then sometimes it makes you feel you're not like a completely whole person." Joseph Berger supports this view (A12, B8). Berger states that "illiterate people's lives are crippled by their inability to read and write. . . ." Berger implies that the inability to perform such functions as vote in a presidential election, complete a job application or read labels on potentially dangerous bottles of medicine only contributes to the handicaps illiterate adults must face in their everyday lives.

imply

It's hard not to wonder what my godfather does in his spare time besides enjoying the company of his many friends and relatives. I have never visited my godfather when the radio or television was not on. There are probably many households that have a television on as much as he does, but for my godfather his situation is a result of his illiteracy. Although he can read simple magazine articles and books, I know that he relies on the radio and television to keep himself informed of everyday things that happen around him. My godfather has the intelligence to read and write; he just never had the time or the opportunity to perfect such an essential skill.

perfect

However, Berger claims that perhaps the most "disheartening" handicap illiterates must face is their inability to help their children to read or write. Not being able to do such things as read a bedtime story to your child or help him/her with reading or writing assignments can cause any parent to experience feelings of inadequacy, humiliation and embarrassment. I can not remember a time when my godfather read me a bedtime story or helped me with a school assignment but I can remember all the exciting, interesting, and educational stories he told me about his childhood and life experiences, and I must say, they were better than any story from a book. And although he may not have helped me with any schoolwork, he has taught me many things that I will value all my life.

In conclusion, it seems obvious that the plight of illiterate adults is an issue that deserves special attention. Although there are a significant number of programs designed to help illiterate adults in learning how to read and write, there is not enough attention given towards the emotional, social, and economic handicaps they must face. An increase in programs that not only teach reading and writing skills but also confront the many problems that go hand-in-hand with illiteracy would be of great benefit for illiterate adults. Many illiterate adults are capable of improving their status, if they only had the chance.

COMPREHENSION CHECK

Write brief answers to the following questions.

1. What problems are nonreaders in this society likely to face?

2. How does Helen Elmore describe illiteracy? Would you agree?

3. What factual information or sources does Anderson include in her essay? What function does this information serve?

4. How does Anderson respond to Berger's claim regarding "the most 'disheartening' handicap illiterates must face"?

5. What feelings are expressed in this essay?

6. What purpose(s) did Anderson have in writing this essay?

APPLICATION TWO

The following excerpt from an article that originally appeared in *The Chronicle of Higher Education* describes one study technique that seems to be very effective. Read the excerpt to determine why the author thinks this technique is so successful. Keep the following questions in mind as you read: Would this approach work for you? What are the advantages and disadvantages to collaborative work (that is, to working with someone else)? If you think this approach would be ineffective, what alternatives can you suggest?

Berkeley Mathematician Strives "to Help People Get Moving"

BY B. T. WATKINS

For the last decade, Philip Uri Treisman has been a mathematician with a mission.

In 1978, while he was a graduate student at the University of California at Berkeley, Mr. Treisman began to experiment with a collaborative workshop. . . .

The research that led to Berkeley's workshop program began in 1975 when Mr. Treisman, who was working with teaching assistants in the mathematics department, learned that 60 per cent of black students but only 12 per cent of Chinese students failed freshman calculus. His search for an explanation for that dra-

matic difference provided the data for his doctoral dissertation, as well as the teaching technique for the workshop.

"I did something on the edge"

Mr. Treisman began his research in the traditional manner. He developed a set of hypotheses, interviewed students about their study habits, and conducted a faculty survey.

When he got nowhere with that approach, Mr. Treisman says, "I did something on the edge."

He persuaded 20 black and 20 Chinese students to let him videotape them while they were working on their mathematics assignments. For 18 months, he trailed the students.

"I moved in with the students and set up cots in their rooms. I wanted to see first hand how they went about learning calculus in the university. I wanted to know who they actually spoke with when, and what they did when they got stuck."

Because the students were unable to study normally with Mr. Treisman peering over their shoulders, the visits did not go quite as planned.

"I was in their bedrooms. It was 2 a.m. I had a videotape, and they would get stuck," he says. "They would turn around and say, 'How do you do this?'

"I love mathematics, so I would turn off the equipment, roll up my sleeves, and we'd spend a few hours doing mathematics."

In the course of those discussions on their own turf, Mr. Treisman says, the students were willing to talk about the reasons for their success or failure in mathematics and the effect that coming to a large, predominantly white university had had on their morale and sense of self-esteem.

"I learned a tremendous amount," he says.

All of a sudden, says Mr. Treisman, the traditional hypotheses proposed to explain the academic failure of black students — weak academic preparation, lack of motivation, little family support, low income — "just fell apart."

The key to the difference in academic performance between the black and the Chinese students emerged from "the ways these students interacted with each other in the university," says Mr. Treisman.

"Eighteen of the 20 black students never studied with other students. The two who studied together dropped out of school and married each other at the end of their freshman year. They were the only example of black students studying together in calculus," says Mr. Treisman.

"These students maintained a rigid separation on campus between their intellectual lives and their social lives," he says. "Many of them said that if they had mixed their social lives and their study, they would never have gotten to the university. Now, the separation made it impossible for them to figure out exactly what was going on."

In contrast, says Mr. Treisman, the Chinese students worked together in informal groups. "By the first midterm, 13 of the 20 Chinese students had found study mates, and they organized what they called in Cantonese 'study gangs.'

"These students would study for four hours alone on the average and do a lot of independent work. They would come together as the penultimate stage of their study. They organized their lives around common classes and common academic goals."

penultimate

Mr. Treisman says: "The students would ask each other questions. How many hours did you stay up last night? What do you think is going to be on the test? How do you feel about this particular financial-aid person?"

Everything a surprise for blacks

"One of the common questions, whose meaning I only learned two years later, was, How are you dealing with the food? This was the local idiom in Cantonese for How are you dealing with the white folks? Or, actually, how were they dealing with me."

As a result of such collaboration, Mr. Treisman says, the Chinese freshmen knew exactly what was going on in their courses. For the black students, everything was a surprise.

"The black students became extraordinarily demoralized," he says.

In the 1977 fall term, Mr. Treisman organized a workshop similar to a study gang for three black freshmen who were about to fail calculus. For six hours each week, the students labored together on tough problems carefully constructed by Mr. Treisman to use basic formulas without seeming to be remedial.

By the spring term, he says, the students were solving difficult problems from old examinations and textbooks used in honors courses.

Along with calculus problems, Mr. Treisman says, he dispensed advice on academic and personal matters, hints for dealing with the financial-aid and housing offices, and anything else that seemed necessary.

Of the original workshop students, Mr. Treisman reports, the first completed a bachelor-of-science degree with honors and a master's in civil engineering at Berkeley, while the second completed a bachelor's in electrical engineering with a high grade-point average. The third married the second and "stopped out" in good standing to have a child.

In fall 1978, encouraged by his initial success, Mr. Treisman persuaded 42 students to participate in what soon became the mathematics workshop program.

COMPREHENSION CHECK

Write brief answers to the following questions.

1. What was the purpose of Treisman's research?

2. How did Treisman go about collecting data? What did he find was the most effective way to obtain the information he wanted?

3. What were Treisman's findings?

4. What is meant by the following statement: "Treisman's workshops did more than teach mathematics"?

5. How does Treisman account for the success of his workshops?

APPLICATION THREE

In Application Two, "Berkeley Mathematician Strives 'to Help People Get Moving,'" Treisman describes the academic success of Chinese students and their use of study groups. Many articles written recently recount numerous other academic achievements of Asian-American students and often refer to them as the "model minority." Under these circumstances it would be easy to conclude that Asian-American students face few, if any, academic problems. The next selection, "Asian-American Students: The Myth of a Model Minority," addresses that misperception. Preview the article by reading the information about the author (under the picture), noting the two article subheadings, and reading the pull quotes (that is, the excerpts set in italic).

Asian-American Students: The Myth of a Model Minority

BY FRANK H. SHIH

The extraordinary success some Asian Americans are enjoying in a few areas has created the misconception of an exemplary minority and has detracted from a need to accurately assess the costs and sacrifices involved for those who manage to reach such high levels of achievement.

The educational achievements of Asian Americans have recently generated much publicity. News articles have repeatedly directed our attention to the outstanding academic successes of this group. For example, we read of the disproportionately large number of Asian Americans reaching the finals of the prestigious Westinghouse Science Talent Search and of others who, despite having to catch up in

English, become high school or college valedictorians. It has also been reported that Asians as a group have the highest score on the math section of the Scholastic Aptitude Test while taking it at a rate greater than any other group. The capstone on these accomplishments, however, is the growing rate of Asian enrollment at top universities: 14 percent at Harvard, 20 percent at MIT, and 25 percent at Berkeley, percentages so dramatic that many are afraid schools have placed limits on Asian admissions.

These "new whiz kids," as *Time* magazine recently called them, have been touted as a modern success story in the old American tradition. We are told that their penchant for hard work and their drive for excellence have enabled them to overcome great obstacles in a country many have only recently called their own. The successes in education appear to have paid off. According to the U.S. Census Bureau, Asian/Pacific Islander households have the highest average and median incomes of all ethnic categories, including whites.

generalization

These achievements have led to the perception of Asian Americans as the model minority. This generalization, implying that all are high achievers, has not been dampened by indications that recent immigrants are from better-educated classes and thus tend to hold high educational aspirations for their children. Neither has it been emphasized that the notion of success

is narrowly defined, focusing almost exclusively on the group's performance in specific areas, such as science and technical fields, and on test scores and percentage of enrollment in certain schools. Household income may also be a poor indicator if one accounts for the number of wage earners in each family or the total hours worked — both probably high for Asians.

There is also an assumption that life is going extremely well for Asian Americans on college campuses, and a new racial stereotype has emerged of the dedicated, disciplined, and very bright Asian student who has neither extracurricular interests nor social needs. Moreover, they are perceived to be content with academic accomplishments and with college life.

These images, as positive as they may seem, impact negatively on this group. It is unfortunate that the extraordinary successes some are enjoying in a few areas have brushed aside any discussion of their unique problems and have detracted from a need to accurately assess the costs and sacrifices involved for those who manage to reach such high levels of achievement.

At the State University of New York at Stony Brook, for instance, Asians in this year's freshman class received the highest math scores on the SAT's but had the lowest in the verbal section compared to other ethnic groups. A study at UCLA of Chinese students has documented that those with low verbal scores compensate for the deficiency in English by carefully avoiding classes that appear to require a high degree of language skills. Besides limiting access to the full range of courses that the university offers, researchers also found that the failure to develop English skills forces these students to spend longer hours on their homework.

There are important social ramifications as well. This deficiency contributes, for instance, to the tendency of Asian Americans to isolate themselves by socializing only with those who speak their own languages. It also increases the reluctance to take advantage of student services and participate in social activities. And, finally, the lack of adequate communication skills will be a tremendous handicap when they enter the job market.

It is clear that not all Asian-American college students are underprepared in English. But for those who are, limited proficiency in English exacerbates the alienation and cultural margination that many Asian Americans feel to a degree. The college campus, after all, is a cultural environment that is vastly different from that of an average Asian-American home. Adjusting to campus life — from norms regarding male/female relationships to the food served in the cafeteria — is thus more difficult for them than for the traditional white

exacerbate

student. The dissimilarity between the two cultures, however, is more subtle than can be deduced from behavioral patterns.

The principles governing social conduct in Asian societies is fundamentally different from those of Americans. For Asians, social interaction must always be congenial, and behavior is carefully crafted towards maintaining group harmony. This so-called "situation centeredness" contrasts with American emphasis on individualism. For example, while Asian mannerisms and speech express self-deprecation and deference to others, these traits are seen as weaknesses in a culture that emphasizes looking out for number one and the importance of asserting one's opinions. The differences are such that even with fluency in English, social interaction for many Asian Americans may involve a certain amount of anxiety.

Family pressures add another dimension. This is felt in two ways. In Asian societies, a person's social identity is closely associated with the kin group, an identification that is fostered by a strong sense of shame and guilt. Asian children are taught that they bear the responsibility for the honor or shame of each member of their family. Because success or failure is shared with one's family, the consequences of one's actions are greatly magnified, making success more imperative and the fear of failure more intense. A second form of

situation centeredness

© Pamela Gentile 1992

family pressure can be seen as a corollary of the first. Though the tight-knit family structure deserves much credit for the group's achievements, it should also be mentioned that parents' expectations are high. Moreover, career goals are usually determined by parents. Thus, realizing these expectations — sometimes an awesome task in itself — is made more difficult by having to do so in a field that is not of the student's choosing.

How do Asian-American students under these circumstances cope with the emotional, social, and academic stresses? Are there psychological consequences? The evidence we have indicates that,

like the larger population of Asian Americans, these students are experiencing greater levels of emotional and social adjustment difficulties and have a higher rate of unreported mental health problems than do Caucasians. Not surprisingly, assimilation has some effect: those who are recent immigrants tend to have a greater degree of unhappiness and anxiety. However, research has shown that Asian values are retained even among those relatively assimilated and that all Asian students may at one time or another experience similar forms of distress.

Racial visibility is another factor that compounds the problem. Shedding the foreigner image and

assimilation

gaining acceptance by the majority is difficult for Asian Americans because of it. The extent to which this creates cultural identity problems for those who have been Americanized remains to be fully explored.

Some suggestions

There are a number of ways professors and other college professionals can respond to the needs of Asian-American students. Because a large number of these students major in the sciences and mathematics, it would seem appropriate for educators in these fields to take the lead and use their influence in the role of advisors on personal as well as academic issues. The following suggestions can be helpful:

- Question the student's choice of course electives. For example, those with limited conversational English could be reminded to take English as a Second Language courses. In classes that are attended in large numbers by Asian Americans who are non-native speakers of English, professors could emphasize that proficiency in writing and reading are necessary not only in course work but also especially when one begins to look for employment and later pursues promotions.

proficiency

- Encourage participation in social activities, as a way of improving one's conversational English and meeting new friends.

- Refer students to the campus counseling or psychological center when signs of emotional strain are apparent. In many instances, merely suggesting that the person seek help will not be enough, as students feel intimidated by the prospect of having to articulate personal problems to someone outside the family. The feeling of being stigmatized and, in particular, of bringing disgrace to one's family will also be a problem. In addition, for therapy to be successful, the counselor will have to be sensitive to cultural issues as well as Asian perceptions of the therapeutic experience.

articulate

stigmatize

Because in Asian cultures the body is a legitimate vehicle for articulating psychological problems, emotional suffering is often concealed. Asian students who complain of physical ailments should be asked directly if there are emotional problems.

- Address the issue of academic pace. When a course load appears to be too demanding, ask the student to consider reducing the amount of credits. The value of education in

Asian societies is such that these students feel compelled to maximize semester credits and not "waste" the opportunity.

- Inquire about the student's physical well-being and take an interest in his or her study/exercise/eating routine. Under extreme pressure to do well, students may sacrifice good health habits. In addition, Asian Americans, especially those who are recent immigrants, have a hard time adapting to non-Asian meals.

Professors should also inform those who provide campus services of the particular needs of Asian Americans and the way such needs are met. The campus infirmary, for example, must understand that traditional Asian attitudes concerning medicine influence the way psychological problems are expressed. Because in Asian cultures the body is a legitimate vehicle for articulating psychological problems, emotional suffering is often concealed. Asian students who complain of physical ailments that are not supported by a physical examination should be asked directly if there are emotional problems.

Research also shows that Asians perceived counselors in their own racial group to be more credible. There should be a concerted effort by administration and faculty to hire Asian student and professional staff proportional to the student population.

Conclusion

Asian-American students are a heterogeneous group. The diverse cultural and linguistic representation and differing degrees of adaptation to American life complicate efforts to assess their needs. Some of the problems many of them face are unique, while others, though common to all college students, are made more acute by their distinct cultural heritage. Those who are recent immigrants, especially on campuses where Asian students are relatively few, are most vulnerable to socio-emotional distress. It is with this group that college and university administrators should be most concerned.

heterogeneous

assess

Racial stereotypes, even those meant to be complimentary, tend to dehumanize individuals.

Racial stereotypes, even those that are meant to be complimentary, tend to dehumanize individuals. In the effort to meet the needs of Asian Americans, faculty as well as administrators should be aware that the current misconception of Asians as a model minority obscures some of the needs of this group while allowing other problems to be overlooked. This image of success may in fact be altogether false when all the facts are known. Nevertheless, we do know that high grade point averages do not translate into high salaries — not to mention successful careers, when one is unable to communicate effectively. Academic achievements, even in more than one area, will not guarantee happiness when the individual is uncomfortable with the cultural environment.

For Asian Americans, a college campus remains an excellent place to learn the skills to prepare for a rewarding career. For recent immigrants, it is ideal for acquiring language skills and for broadening their understanding of their adopted culture. A college education, then, should prepare the students to participate fully in all aspects of American life. This will assure all of the benefits that come from the rich blend of two distinct cultures — Asian and American.

[NOTE: References for this article have been deleted.]

Frank Shih is the Associate Director at the Center for Academic Advising at State University of New York at Stony Brook, Stony Brook, NY 11794-3375.

COMPREHENSION CHECK

Write brief answers to the following questions.

1. What topic is Shih discussing? What overall point or idea does he want his reader to understand from reading his article?

2. What misconception do many people hold regarding Asian-American students?

3. On what evidence is this misconception based?

4. What assumptions do people make about Asian Americans?

5. What negative consequences result from these assumptions?

6. What suggestions does Shih have for college professors and other professionals who work with Asian Americans? How might college students make use of these suggestions?

7. What does Shih mean by this statement: "Racial stereotypes, even those meant to be complimentary, tend to dehumanize individuals"?

APPLICATION FOUR

Has society always regarded Asian Americans as a "model minority"? History tells us emphatically not. The following excerpt, taken from a history text, explains how immigrants from the 1840s to the 1920s were received. Glance quickly at the passage. What makes this selection difficult to preview?

To facilitate your understanding, the Comprehension Check for this selection includes an outline format that, when completed, will list the major points covered in the passage. Keep the outline headings in mind as you read the excerpt.

The New Americans

BY R. J. WILSON

In 1790, when the United States took its first census under the new Constitution, nine out of ten Americans (except for the black slaves in the South) had English or Scottish ancestors. This pattern changed somewhat with the immigration of the 1840s and 1850s — the "old" immigration — when large numbers of German, Scandinavian, and Irish immigrants began to arrive. Although their languages might be strange to American ears, most of the Germans and Scandinavians were at least Protestants. And although many native-born Americans resented the Catholicism of the Irish, these immigrants at least spoke English. In 1865 the United States had only about 200,000 inhabitants who had been born in southern or eastern Europe. They were easily absorbed in a total population of about 40 million.

inhabitants

By 1914 this picture had changed dramatically. A "new" immigration—mainly from Italy, Russia, and Austria-Hungary—flooded into the United States. Poverty drove many of these people from their home countries. Some men left to avoid the military draft, which discriminated against the poor. Jews wanted to escape the official anti-Semitism of Russia and Poland. Armenians fled from persecutions carried out by the Turkish government. The new immigrants were drawn to the United States by advertisements of cheap steamship transportation, by rumors of free land and golden opportunity, and by a massive propaganda campaign conducted by railroads anxious for workers and for customers to buy up their lands.

anti-Semitic

. . . The new immigrants were not only different in culture, language, and religion, they behaved in ways different from those who had preceded them. They moved into a society that was no longer predominantly agricultural and rural, but urban. So they did not fan out onto farms as many of the old immigrants had done. Instead, they followed the lead of millions of other Americans and settled into cities. Two thirds of foreign-born residents in the United States lived in towns and cities by 1900.

precede

Bewildered and often victimized in America, new immigrants clustered together in their own city neighborhoods, or "ghettos." People from a particular province or even a particular village would move into buildings on the same block, re-creating much of the culture of their Old World homes. As the new immigration swelled, so did antiforeign sentiment. Ghetto dwellers earned a reputation among "native" Americans for being clannish, dirty, superstitious, and generally undesirable. They were considered strange, chattering in their old languages, and somehow suited only for city life. Actually, of course, they were no more "natural" city dwellers than were the English who had come to Virginia and Massachusetts in the seventeenth century. They were simply caught in a phase of the industrial revolution—the creation of an urban society.

sentiment

Immigrants from Asia—almost all from China and Japan—were among the most ghetto-bound of the newcomers, rigidly segregated in their "Chinatown" communities. And for generations, neither the Asian Americans nor native-born whites believed that they ever could or should become integrated into American life. Most of the Asian immigrants believed that Western civilization was a form of barbarism, something to be resisted in every possible way. Few American officials paid any attention to whether Asian-American children attended public schools. No one thought it necessary for them to learn English. They were

harassment

culinary

the victims of harassment, cruel jokes, and vicious cartoons. The state of California had special taxes for "foreign miners." Murderous riots against the Chinese took place in every major Western city during the 1870s and 1880s. The Asians' subtle and sophisticated way of cooking attracted some favorable attention, but even their food came into the American diet and language as "chop suey," an unkind culinary joke.

In California, especially, the Chinese immigrants were the objects of a double discrimination. Almost every American of European ancestry believed Asians were racially inferior. But white workers also resented competition in the labor market, especially during times of economic depression and high unemployment. In the 1870s the California Workingman's Party began to agitate for a law forbidding any person from China to hold a job. The effort succeeded. In 1879 a clause was added to the state constitution of California that forbade any employer to hire Chinese workers. But no state had a constitutional right to forbid immigration. That was up to the national government. In 1882 an act of Congress put a ten-year prohibition on Chinese workers entering the United States as immigrants.

And so the new society that grew out of the industrial revolution was an intensely segregated society. As a result of the railroads and the rush of pioneers to the West, Native Americans were confined to their shrinking reservations. Blacks, Asians, and European immigrants in the towns and cities were just as confined to their ghettos. The very meaning of the word *American*, as it was normally used, reflected these racial and ethnic segregations. Being an American meant, to most people, *not* being "colored," *not* being Catholic or Jewish, *not* having Slavic or Greek or Polish ways and words. The two most intensely debated questions of the day among "native" Americans—that is, Protestant white people whose ancestry was British or northwest European—were: What could be done to slow down or stop the "foreigners" from coming? Who among them (if any) had a chance to become "Americans"?

Fill in the blanks in the outline based on your reading of "The New Americans."

The New Americans

   I. Description of the United States population prior to 1914:

   _____

   _____

   _____

  II. New immigrants after 1914:

   _____

   _____

 III. Differences between "new" and "old" immigrants:

   _____

   _____

   _____

   _____

 IV. Treatment of Asian immigrants:

   _____

   _____

   _____

   _____

  V. Description of new society during industrial revolution:

   _____

   _____

APPLICATION FIVE

Our final reading is a poem written in Spanish and translated into English. Poetry often uses figurative language and creates images to convey its meanings. If you are bilingual you will also be able to read and understand the poem in language contexts. Is the poem's message altered in the translation? Read the poem carefully.

La tierra es un satélite de la luna

BY LEONEL RUGAMA

El Apolo 2 costó más que el Apolo 1
el Apolo 1 costó bastante.

El Apolo 3 costó más que el Apolo 2
el Apolo 2 costó más que el Apolo 1
el Apolo 1 costó bastante.

El Apolo 4 costó más que el Apolo 3
el Apolo 3 costó más que el Apolo 2
el Apolo 2 costó más que el Apolo 1
el Apolo 1 costó bastante.

El Apolo 8 costó un montón, pero no se sintió
porque los astronautas eran protestantes
y desde la luna leyeron la Biblia,
maravillando y alegrando a todos los cristianos
y a la venida el papa Paulo VI les dio la bendición.

El Apolo 9 costó más que todos juntos
junto con el Apolo 1 que costó bastante.

Los bisabuelos de la gente de Acahualinca tenían menos
        hambre que los abuelos.
Los bisabuelos se murieron de hambre.
Los abuelos de la gente de Acahualinca tenían menos
        hambre que los padres.
Los abuelos murieron de hambre.
Los padres de la gente de Acahualinca tenían menos
        hambre que los hijos de la gente de allí.
Los padres se murieron de hambre.

La gente de Acahualinca tiene menos hambre que los hijos
    de la gente de allí.
Los hijos de la gente de Acahualinca no nacen por hambre,
    y tienen hambre de nacer, para morirse de hambre.
Bienaventurados los pobres porque de ellos será la luna.

The Earth Is a Satellite of the Moon

Apollo 2 cost more than Apollo 1
Apollo 1 cost plenty.

Apollo 3 cost more than Apollo 2
Apollo 2 cost more than Apollo 1
Apollo 1 cost plenty.

Apollo 4 cost more than Apollo 3
Apollo 3 cost more than Apollo 2
Apollo 2 cost more than Apollo 1
Apollo 1 cost plenty.

Apollo 8 cost a fortune, but no one minded
because the astronauts were Protestant
they read the Bible from the moon
astounding and delighting every Christian
and on their return Pope Paul VI gave them his blessing.

Apollo 9 cost more than all these put together
including Apollo 1 which cost plenty.

The great-grandparents of the people of Acahaulinca were less
    hungry than the grandparents.
The great-grandparents died of hunger.
The grandparents of the people of Acahaulinca were less
    hungry than the parents.
The grandparents died of hunger.
The parents of the people of Acahaulinca were less
    hungry than the children of the people there.
The parents died of hunger.
The people of Acahaulinca are less hungry than the children
    of the people there.
The children of the people of Acahaulinca, because of hunger,
    are not born
they hunger to be born, only to die of hunger.
Blessed are the poor for they shall inherit the moon.

translated by Sara Miles, Richard Schaaf, and Nancy Weisberg

Write brief answers to the following questions.

1. What images does the poem convey? How does the poet's use of language help convey those ideas?

2. What do you think the poem is trying to say? Explain your answer.

3. Leonel Rugama was born in Nicaragua. He was a member of the Sandinista National Liberation Front and died in 1970 while fighting against his country's ruling dictator. How might this information add to your understanding of the poem?

4. Rugama refers to the people of Acahaulinca. Is knowing who these people are necessary to understand the poem?

5. If you are able to read both the Spanish and English versions, explain any differences between the two poems.

What Do You Think?

Prepare for class discussion by jotting down brief answers to the following questions.

1. What is the relationship between intelligence and being able to read? How do we perceive nonreaders?

2. Why is literacy so important in our society? Has it always been as important as it is today? Have our needs for certain kinds of literacy changed over time? As we move into the twenty-first century, will knowing how to read become more or less important? Explain your answers.

3. In Application Three, "Asian-American Students," Shih writes: "we do know that high grade point averages do not translate into high salaries — not to mention successful careers, when one is unable to communicate effectively." What are the basic forms of communication we use in this society? How does culture affect communication?

4. What are your communication strengths? What options are available for students on your campus who would like to improve their skills?

5. Consider your own personal experiences dealing with issues of stereotyping, family expectations, cultural differences, and ways of dealing with stress. Are any of your experiences similar to those described for Asian-American students?

6. Why do you think there has been such a dramatic change in people's stereotypic perceptions of Asian Americans between 1900 and 1992?

7. In Application Four, "The New Americans," Wilson states that in the early 1900s "the very meaning of the word *American,* as it was normally used, reflected these racial and ethnic segregations." What is your definition of an American?

8. Some sociologists use the metaphor of a "melting pot" to describe how our diverse society joins together to form one common culture, while others claim that we can be more accurately described as a "vegetable stew" or "tossed salad." How would you explain these metaphors? Which one do you think is more accurate? Explain your reasoning.

9. What new information have you gained from the chapter readings? Will it have any effect on the way you think or behave? Explain your answers.

10. What might Rugama have said if he had decided to write a political essay rather than his poem "La tierra es un satélite de la luna"?

Select one or two of the following topics and in a few paragraphs develop a thoughtful written response.

1. Describe yourself as a reader. What are your strengths? Your weaknesses? Consider the information you have learned about factors of comprehension. Have you had experiences in school that supported or hindered your interest and ability in reading? What kinds of reading do you enjoy most and/or do most often?

2. Defend or refute the following position: Society places too much emphasis on schooling. A person spends twelve to sixteen years in school and then uses only a tenth of the knowledge learned there on the job. The only reason we have all this schooling is to keep people out of the job market and unemployment down.

3. If a student graduates from high school and can read only at the third-grade level, does he or she have the right to sue the school?

4. Describe a place, person, or thing. Try to let your words convey what you want to say (that is, let the reader understand through the words you choose, the images you present, and the tone you set).

Understanding Observations, Interpretations, Facts, and Conclusions

After reading Chapter 3 you should be able to:

- differentiate among facts, observations, interpretations, and conclusions
- distinguish between facts and interpretations in written material
- combine facts with interpretations to arrive at reasonable conclusions

You may use the following checklist in planning your study of observations, interpretations, facts, and conclusions. Activities marked with a ✪ are to be completed in class. Some preclass preparation may be required.

CONTEXT FOR LEARNING

✪ _____ INTRODUCTORY CHAPTER ACTIVITY

_____ Clarifying Terms

✪ _____ ACTIVITY BREAK

_____ Facts

_____ Questioning the Obvious

✪ _____ ACTIVITY BREAK

_____ Counterintuitive Facts

_____ Generating Conclusions from Facts

✪ _____ ACTIVITY BREAK

_____ Differences Between Conclusions and Interpretations

_____ Opinions

_____ GUIDED READING ACTIVITY: FACTS AND INTERPRETATIONS

_____ **"A Tale of Arsenic and Old Zach"** from *Newsweek*

APPLICATION: SEEING AND BELIEVING

_____ APPLICATION ONE

_____ **"Open Letter to Salman Rushdie"** by Florence Miller

_____ COMPREHENSION CHECK

_____ APPLICATION TWO

_____ **"In Saudi and US Women, Common Feeling Is Pity"** by Colin Nickerson

_____ COMPREHENSION CHECK

——— **APPLICATION THREE**

——— **"Infinite Sets"** by William P. Berlinghoff and
Kerry E. Grant

——— **COMPREHENSION CHECK**

——— What Do You Think?

✪ ——— **DISCUSSION QUESTIONS**

——— **WRITING ASSIGNMENTS**

✪ **INTRODUCTORY CHAPTER ACTIVITY**

As members of a foreign civilization you find yourself stranded on the
planet Earth at Your College, USA. You know little about this primitive
life form, and although you fear for your safety, you think some attempt
must be made to investigate. You have been ordered to collect information. Specifically, you have been told to make observations, verify facts,
make some interpretations, come to some conclusions, and offer some
opinions.

1. Break into groups of two or three. Have one person in each group
   divide a piece of paper into five blocks. Label each block with one
   of the following headings: Observations, Facts, Interpretations,
   Conclusions, and Opinions.

2. Now complete the chart with appropriate information. Take note of
   any disagreements you may have over where to place information
   properly.

3. Discuss your charts with other groups. How would you define an
   observation, a fact, an interpretation, a conclusion, and an
   opinion?

Clarifying Terms

A good starting point for developing critical thinking skills is being able to decipher what observations, facts, interpretations, conclusions, and opinions are, but agreeing on definitions for these terms can be complicated. In part this is due to narrow definitions that are used in academic disciplines and broader definitions that are used in everyday conversation. For example, the definition of *opinion* in the dictionary is much broader than the one found in a logic textbook. (We will discuss this later in the chapter.) Another complicating factor among the terms is that their definitions aren't distinct; sometimes they overlap. A fact or interpretation may at some point become a conclusion. Looking carefully at each of the terms may help resolve some potential confusion. We then examine how the terms "fit together."

Observations

An *observation* involves having direct contact or experience with an object or event. This contact can occur through any of your senses. For example, a list of observations could include seeing a basketball player make a three-point shot; hearing someone say, "Boris Yeltsin is a great leader"; feeling a person's pulse; and investigating the flavor of tofu. Stop for a moment and make note of three observations. Compare your observations with others in the class. Do you all agree on what an observation is?

Interpretations

Your observations must be objective; that is, they should report the information but not your *interpretation* of the information. An interpretation is your explanation or understanding of events. One way of learning to differentiate observations from interpretations is to first make an observation and then develop as many interpretations as possible.

Differentiating between observations and interpretations

Distinguishing observations from interpretations requires vigilance because the two processes can happen almost simultaneously. We observe something and quickly decide (interpret) what it means. This technique is practiced by most mothers almost automatically. Frequently, a mother's observation such as "My baby is crying" is followed immediately by an interpretation: "He wants me to rock him." If the baby continues crying after she rocks him, she rejects her first interpretation and tries another one: "He's hungry." If he rejects food and continues crying, she may move on to any of the following interpretations:

1. He needs changing.

2. He is sick.

3. He has gas pains.

4. He hurt himself on the crib.

5. He has diaper rash.

A mother who is able to generate a wide repertoire of interpretations of her child's crying is far more likely to successfully meet her baby's needs than a mother who can only come up with one or two interpretations. Likewise, you will be a far more effective thinker if you are able to consider many possible interpretations beyond your immediate reaction.

✪ **ACTIVITY BREAK**

Working in groups of two or three, make a list of three or more possible interpretations for each of the following observations. Do not be judgmental about the quality of your interpretations; simply try to generate as many as possible.

1. Enrollments at historically Black colleges are on the rise.

2. The bomb explosion resulted in many deaths and injuries.

3. The United States landed the first man on the moon.

4. There are more female elementary school teachers than male elementary school teachers.

5. He applied for a union job but was turned down.

6. She was having dinner with her best friend's boyfriend.

7. The jury found the policeman guilty of excessive force.

Notice that an *accurate* observation becomes a fact. An observation that is influenced by your perspective, your values, or your preferences, however, is an interpretation. The interpretation may be correct, but we should reserve judgment if we have no proof. As we have already seen, interpretations that seem true can turn out to be wrong. If you are quick to accept interpretations because they are your own or because someone offers you an impressive-sounding argument, you may be erroneously perceiving interpretations as facts.

Recognizing interpretations in reading

Reading is a process of reconstructing the writer's meaning and being able to separate a writer's facts from his or her interpretations. What you read is not necessarily factual. If *Time* magazine reported that "the president was furious over Congress's proposed federal budget," can you be absolutely certain that the president *was* furious? His fury is the *Time* reporter's interpretation, not an observation. (What might have been the reporter's observation?) Perhaps the president only wanted to *appear* furious to pressure Congress or to win public support. Your observation should not be "the president was furious," but rather "according to *Time* magazine, the president was furious."

Here is an intriguing point: You can turn any of your personal interpretations into observations by prefacing each one with "It is my opinion that . . ." Assuming you are being truthful, it is a *fact* that the statement is your opinion. The catch is that this type of observation is one about your own personal feelings, and not about something you have witnessed going on externally.

Facts

Is an observation a fact? Is an interpretation a fact? We all agree that it is important to "get the facts straight," but we need to agree on what constitutes a fact. Part of the reason we spend so much time investigating "facts" is to help you develop a mindset for investigating the obvious. We all think we know facts when we see them, but what assumptions are we making, and when does a fact and a subtle interpretation (explanation/translation) begin? Being able to distinguish between reasons that are facts and reasons that are interpretations is a valuable skill in analyzing and evaluating writers' views (which we will discuss in Chapter 5). Here we consider several definitions of the word *fact*.

Definition 1: A "fact" is something most of us agree is true

According to this definition, the following are facts:

1. We need food to survive.

2. Jews celebrate Passover.

3. Most leaves are green.

4. Drug abuse can be dangerous.

Most people would say these statements are true. Therefore, according to our definition, these statements are facts.

Or are they? If most people agree on something, does that make it true?

Look at statement 3 again. It isn't true; most leaves are really brown. When leaves die, they turn brown and fall to the ground. In temperate forests, most leaves do not decompose the first year. One can find intact leaves in the forest that are three or more years old. Green leaves represent only one year's growth; there is at least a two years' supply on the ground in most forests. In truth, there are more brown leaves than green leaves even though most people believe the opposite. But according to our definition, it is a fact that most leaves are green, *even though it is not true.*

Let's consider another example. At one time, most people believed that the earth was flat. Was it a fact? If you accept definition 1, then it *was* a fact — and yet it was not true! Since definition 1 allows falsehoods to masquerade as facts, we propose rejecting this definition.

Definition 2: A "fact" is something that is true

With this definition in mind, let's look at some other statements and try to decide which are facts. From the following list of statements, indicate which one you think is most likely to be a fact by placing a 1 in the blank to the left, followed by a 2 for your second choice, and so on down to 6.

_____   1.   Abraham Lincoln was a president of the United States.

_____   2.   11 + 1 = 12.

_____   3.   Christianity is the only true religion.

_____   4.   God exists.

_____   5.   The earth is roughly spherical.

_____   6.   Columbus discovered America.

Now place an asterisk next to the statements that you believe are definitely true. According to our new definition, those statements are our facts. But this raises an important question: How do you *know* that they are true? What is it that makes you sure?

If you are a critical thinker, chances are your first statements are ones that can be proven true beyond a reasonable doubt. If you are able to find irrefutable evidence that something is true, then you are likely to accept it as a fact. Statement 2, for example, could be proven by placing eleven pennies on a table and then placing one more penny on the table; counting them all will show that the total is 12. Indisputable evidence appears to be a more useful definition of *fact*.

Definition 3: A "fact" is something that can be proven beyond a reasonable doubt

How do you know when you have proven something beyond a reasonable doubt? Statements 3 and 4 about religion are difficult to prove. Evidence can be given supporting these statements, but we would suggest that no definite proof exists. Indeed, an important part of most religions is *faith*, which implies believing something without absolute proof.

The statement about Columbus discovering America can be supported by what is written in many history texts and reference books. For example, *The Standard American Encyclopedia* has the following entry:

> Columbus, Christopher (in Spanish, Cristoval Colon; in Italian, Cristoforo Colombo, his real name), the discoverer of America; born in Genoa between Aug. 26 and Oct. 31, 1451.

However, additional historical evidence suggests that this encyclopedia is wrong. A Norse explorer, Leif Eriksson, landed in North America around 1000 A.D., almost 500 years before Columbus. Some sources suggest that a group of Danes, urged by an explorer named Naddod, arrived in America even earlier. Furthermore, Native American Indians were already there to greet each group of European explorers, and had been living in America for thousands of years. Shouldn't they be credited with the discovery of America?

It appears that statement 6 is *not* a fact. However, if we rephrased this statement to read "some sources give Columbus credit for discovering America," we now have a fact, according to our current definition.

History texts also support statement 1: "Abraham Lincoln was a president of the United States." Since we found that many reference and history books are not accurate about Columbus, should we trust them to be truthful about Lincoln? Why should we accept historical statements about Lincoln's presidency but not historical statements about Columbus's discovery of America? Can we be sure Lincoln was once president? There are currently no eyewitnesses that Lincoln even existed. We have no evidence other than historical documents.

One important difference is that no historical document disputes that Lincoln was president, while some dispute that Columbus discovered America. *Assuming* that historians are trying to tell the truth, and *assuming* that their unanimous agreement is sufficient evidence that Lincoln's presidency did occur, we propose that statement 1 be accepted as fact. It is a fact because the statement has been shown to be true beyond a reasonable doubt.

Questioning the Obvious

The key word in declaring Lincoln's presidency a fact is *assuming*. The assumptions we make about historians and historical documents are essential to our declaration. We suggest that *nothing* can be proven to be a fact unless we make at least some assumptions. Even the most obvious fact is open to some doubt.

The statement "$11 + 1 = 12$" is a fact, *assuming* that we are using the decimal number system. There are other number systems for which $11 + 1$ does not equal 12. For example, in the binary number system, $1 + 11 = 100$! Without getting into the mathematics of this statement, our point is that every fact is based on certain assumptions. If we *assume* that photographs of the Earth taken by space satellites are not falsified or distorted, and there have been no major changes in the Earth's shape since the photographs were taken, then statement 5 ("the Earth is roughly spherical") becomes a fact.

Often, assumptions form the basis of questioning the obvious. Children believe that Santa Claus's existence is a fact based on the assumption that their parents are always honest with them. Once this assumption is challenged, what seemed like an obvious truth to children becomes a myth.

It may seem obvious to you that humans are the most advanced form of life on Earth. Even critical thinkers who agree with this statement will examine it carefully and consider how it might be challenged. The statement makes many assumptions. It may assume that we know about every life form there is on Earth; but any biologist will tell you that new species are discovered every year. Or it may assume that, if there were a life form superior to ours, we would know about it; but perhaps a superior life form would not *want* to reveal itself to us. Also, what is meant by "most advanced"? Does it mean that we are the most intelligent life form? The strongest? The most persistent? Consider this: Scientists tell us that the family of humans (Hominidae) has been in existence for about 4 million years. An insect called the silverfish (often considered a pest because it eats and damages human belongings) has been around for about 400 million years. It has survived several mass extinctions. Some 360 million years ago, many species of plants and animals died out, possibly because of a mass cooling of the Earth. The silverfish survived. Sixty million years ago, the mighty dinosaurs became extinct; still the silverfish persisted. If silverfish have a point of view, they would regard humans merely as newcomers to Earth, and as a convenient source of food. "For them we are a young, trial species with the ability to alter its environment modestly, thus allowing our kind to increase to ridiculous numbers for the express purpose of creating habitat and food for a few species of *their* kind. Good but probably not dependable providers. Will very likely disappear in the next mass extinction. Better not get accustomed to them" (Sue Hubbell, *Broadsides from the Other Orders: A Book of Bugs.* New York: Random House, 1993).

⊛ **ACTIVITY BREAK**

1. Return to the chart you made in the Introductory Chapter Activity. Check the items you placed under Observations, Facts, and Interpretations. Is their placement still correct? Use the definitions presented above to explain your examples to other members of the class.

2. Questioning the obvious is a good link to both critical and creative thought. Here is a list of statements that many people would say are obviously true. Think about them. What issues can you raise that might lead people to question the truth of these statements?

   a. Water boils at 100 degrees Celsius.

   b. In basketball, the best team always wins.

   c. Men are physically stronger than women.

   d. There are twenty-four hours in a day.

   e. Winter begins in December.

As you can see, it is often difficult to be certain about what constitutes a fact. We believe that at least some doubt is associated with any fact, and this doubt often lies in whether the assumptions associated with the fact are accepted. (In Chapters 5 and 6, we talk more about the role assumptions play in developing an argument and in writing persuasively.)

Based on what you have read and discussed so far, we suggest adopting the following definition of *fact: something that can be proven to be true beyond a reasonable doubt, based upon certain assumptions.*

Counterintuitive Facts

Did you know that the matter in your body came from exploding stars? Or that when you see the sun, you are looking 8.3 minutes into the past? These statements may sound false — that is, may seem counterintuitive — yet science and mathematics have proven them true, based upon certain assumptions. Your intuition will tell you many facts are false, yet they have been proven to be true.

Usually, these facts do not seem true because they appear to contradict our everyday experiences or are outside our experiences. This helps explain why so many people once refused to believe that the Earth is sphere-shaped. Just look around you: Your eyes clearly tell you that the Earth is basically flat.

Do not reject statements too quickly simply because they seem impossible. Find out what the underlying assumptions are. Find out how the statements came to be accepted as facts. At that point, you will be in a much better position to make a critical, intelligent judgment about the truth of a statement.

Generating Conclusions from Facts

Facts are used to generate conclusions. Some of the ways we use them to arrive at conclusions are to (1) interpret them, (2) combine them with other facts, and (3) include them with interpretations.

Interpreting facts to arrive at conclusions

Let us imagine that Michael telephones his girlfriend, Rachael, and the *fact* is that all he hears is the phone ringing at the other end of the line (this is fact 1). He *interprets* that to mean she is not home. Is his interpretation a fact? Probably, but he cannot be certain. Maybe he dialed the wrong number. Maybe she was asleep or in the garage, or didn't feel like answering the phone. Maybe she was with another man! While Michael may feel confident that his first interpretation is correct, he really needs more facts to be certain.

His next move is to drive over to her house. He knocks on the door, but there is no answer. That no one answers (fact 2) is another fact that supports his interpretation. He lets himself in with the key she has given him and finds her on the couch reading the newspaper with her Walkman turned up full blast (fact 3). She tells him that she has been home listening to music and didn't hear the phone ring. (What is fact 4?) He interprets this fact to be the truth, and is finally ready to make his final interpretation: She did not answer his call because she did not hear the phone ring. His final interpretation is his conclusion. A *conclusion* is a finalized opinion or judgment based on an exhaustive review of available data, including facts, assumptions, and interpretations.

Because certain facts were not immediately available, Michael was tempted to let his first interpretation become his conclusion. As he gathered more facts, however, he found out that his interpretation was wrong. He needed to avoid drawing a conclusion until he had gathered as many facts and interpretations as possible.

Not all conclusions are valid. Conclusions vary greatly in degree of truth, depending on the strength of the supporting factual evidence. Some evidence may be missing. Is it possible, for example, that Rachael heard Michael drive up, let her other boyfriend out the back door, put on her earphones, and turned up the volume in order to deceive Michael?

Combining facts with facts to arrive at conclusions

Look at the following list of some of the facts about a certain piece of chalk:

1. It is 6 centimeters long.

2. It has a diameter of 1 centimeter.

3. It weighs 14 grams.

4. It costs 5 cents.

5. It is yellow.

6. It tastes unpleasant to me.

7. It is used to express human thoughts and feelings through forming pictures, words, and diagrams.

8. It is made primarily of calcium, carbon, and oxygen.

9. It was once part of a living creature many thousands of years ago.

10. There are tiny particles in the chalk that are traveling over 5 trillion miles per hour.

11. If you were to try to count the atoms that make up the piece of chalk, it would take you thousands of years.

12. Someday the chalk's matter will be vaporized by the explosion of another star — our sun.

13. This list represents a very tiny portion of the facts about the piece of chalk.

Combining these facts in various ways can lead to many conclusions. A mathematician would use facts 1 and 2 to conclude that the volume of the chalk is 1.5 cm^3 (cubic centimeters). A physicist would use facts 1, 2, and 3 to determine that the chalk has a density of 14 g/cm^3. A critical thinker might conclude that some facts about chalk — facts 9–13 — are not obvious to everyone. An educator who believes in an interdisciplinary curriculum would draw the conclusion that a piece of chalk has characteristics that draw several academic disciplines together, including mathematics (facts 1–4), economics (fact 4), philosophy (fact 7), and the sciences (facts 8–13). In each case, only facts are used to generate conclusions.

If we limit ourselves to facts, we are likely to feel very confident that our conclusions are correct. However, limiting ourselves to facts can also limit the number of conclusions we can generate.

Combining facts with interpretations to draw conclusions

Examine the photograph on page 94. Some of the facts about the photograph are:

1. It is a picture of two men without shirts.

2. One of the men is Black and the other is white.

3. They have their arms around each other.

These facts lead to some very different interpretations. Fact 3 taken alone might suggest that the photograph's theme is human compassion. Combining facts 2 and 3 implies that the photograph's message is interracial harmony and brotherhood. Combining facts 1 and 3 suggests homosexuality. Without additional information, any of these interpretations could be argued as reasonable. Indeed, any combination of these interpretations seems valid: Perhaps the photograph is about human compassion, interracial brotherhood, *and* homosexuality.

Embrace, 1982 Copyright © 1982 The Estate of Robert Mapplethorpe

✪ **ACTIVITY BREAK**

Let's add a fourth fact to our list: The photographer was considered to have been a great artist. Develop a list of interpretations that might be reached by combining fact 4 with any one or more of the first three facts. Now, assuming no other facts are available, generate a conclusion.

_____

_____

Differences Between Conclusions and Interpretations

Perhaps you are wondering, What is the difference between a conclusion and an interpretation? This is a good question. In many cases, the distinction is not clear-cut. Generally, an interpretation is an incomplete list of facts and one's reactions to those facts. For example, imagine that you are an imprisoned felon reading a newspaper account of police brutality. What is your interpretation likely to be? Now imagine that you are a law enforcement officer reading the same article. How is your interpretation likely to differ? The facts are the same, but the officer and the felon probably have very different interpretations.

Recall that a conclusion is the final interpretation of an exhaustive examination of all available data. In the case of the police brutality incident, it is up to a court of law to gather all the facts, listen to all the opinions, combine these facts and opinions in every possible way, and arrive at a final interpretation of the incident. It is hard to guarantee that a conclusion is valid or true. (In Chapter 6 you will learn how to analyze and evaluate arguments.)

New facts may later emerge to show that a conclusion is wrong. Conclusions are not necessarily facts; they are our best judgment, given what we have to work with. If later evidence demonstrates that a conclusion is wrong, we need to acknowledge it and admit that we made a mistake in our final judgment. It is not always easy to do this because it can hurt our pride and be embarrassing. But if we are wrong, it is better to let go of our old conclusion and seek a valid one. This step is often what separates the critical thinker from the less astute.

Finally, arriving at a valid conclusion is not necessarily the end of the process. Conclusions, together with values, facts, interpretations, beliefs, feelings, and other qualities, come together to form a person's view of the world. We look at this process in detail in Chapter 4.

Opinions

"In my opinion college students don't drink too much."

"In my opinion abortion is murder.

"As I see it, it's not my fault I'm flunking this course."

Our everyday conversations are full of opinions. There isn't a topic for which someone doesn't have an opinion. Opinions are as plentiful as the pennies in our pockets. They tend to be based more on feeling than on fact. When someone says, "I am entitled to my opinion," she is saying that she does not have to support her position. People often use the term *opinion* to refer to an argument they are making in which they hope to persuade you; however, technically an opinion is a claim without support.

According to Hurley in *A Concise Introduction to Logic*, opinions are "expressions of what someone happens to believe or think at a certain time. . . . Because there is no claim that this belief is supported by evidence or, in turn, that it supports some further conclusion, there is no argument." In a course on critical thinking, opinions, by themselves, don't carry much weight even if they are presented by experts in the field. The value of opinions is that they offer us a starting point in our thinking. Once we know our opinion we can begin to examine how we arrived at this position, and based on our investigation, we may change our opinions.

GUIDED READING ACTIVITY *Facts and interpretations*

To this point, we have limited our work with facts and interpretations to two isolated examples. Now we would like to extend these skills to an actual reading. Readers need to be able to recognize those statements in a passage that are facts and those that are the author's interpretations. To complete this activity, do the following:

1. Read the following excerpt from an account of the exhumation of Zachary Taylor's body and the subsequent investigation for signs of foul play. Look for the facts and interpretations reported by the author.

2. Divide a piece of paper in half with a vertical line. Label the left column "Facts" and the right column "Interpretations." Now reread the article, listing major facts in the first column and possible interpretation(s) in the second column. Make a note of the source of each interpretation. (For example, is it the author's interpretation or your own?)

3. Look at the results produced by your authors when they completed this exercise.

A Tale of Arsenic and Old Zach

FROM *NEWSWEEK*

Coming, as it did, during a relatively peaceful and sultry week in late spring, the exhumation of the 12th president fascinated Americans out of all proportion to its possible historical significance. If the experts in forensic anthropology find lethal levels of arsenic in Taylor's hair and bones, Lincoln will lose the distinction of being the first president assassinated. . . .

First with the urge to pry off Taylor's coffin was a silver-haired Southern woman named Clara Rising. A former humanities professor at the University of Florida at Gainesville and the author of a historical novel, "In the Season of the Wild Rose," Rising traces her intense interest in Taylor to a gathering of Civil War enthusiasts she attended in January 1990. Chatting there with Betty Gist, the owner of the Kentucky farm where Taylor lived as a young man, Rising began to realize how much the president's political foes had gained by his death. "They were dancing on his grave," she said last week, her voice ringing with contempt. Rising's strong feelings led her to the library and eventually to a Gainesville-based forensic pathologist, Dr. William Maples. She showed him contemporary accounts of Taylor's five-day death agony, which had been ascribed to cholera morbus, a catch-all phrase then used to describe a variety of intestinal illnesses. Maples said it sounded more like "a classic case of arsenic poisoning. . . ."

The test results should come back this week, but whether we will know the absolute truth about Taylor's final days seems less than certain. Arsenic, like other heavy-metal poisons, is a relatively easy substance to find in hair and bones, even many centuries after death. The fact that the president was not embalmed, at the request of his wife, Margaret, will also facilitate matters: 19th-century undertakers often relied on arsenic-laden potions. But some experts believe that Taylor's alleged enemies would need to have been terribly patient murderers, bent on killing the president at a slow but steady rate, for any evidence to have survived. "If it's an acute poisoning, one that happened all at once, there will be no way to tell," says Paul Sledzik, curator of anatomical collections at the National Museum of Health and Medicine, in Washington. The arsenic, he says, wouldn't have time to penetrate the bone. . . .

The following list shows the results we obtained when we did the exercise. Keep in mind that this is *one* set of answers, not the *only* set.

Facts

1. Experts will look for lethal levels of arsenic in Taylor's remains.

2. Political foes of Taylor felt they had much to gain by his death.

3. Clara Rising showed Dr. William Maples descriptions of Taylor's death.

4. Arsenic is easy to find in a person's hair and bones.

Interpretations

1. Presence of lethal levels of arsenic will mean he was assassinated. (article's author)

2. Taylor's foes considered assassinating him. (Clara Rising)

3. It sounded like arsenic poisoning. (Maples)

4. If Taylor died from arsenic poisoning, it will be detected. (reader)

5. The president was not embalmed. (Embalmers often used arsenic.)

5. Any arsenic detected will not be from embalming, but from another source. (reader)

6. Some experts believe that only a gradual poisoning will show up. (A massive single dose, says Sledzick, would not have time to penetrate the bone.)

6. Negative test results will not rule out death by a single large poisoning. (Sledzick)

During our second reading, we concentrated on finding the major facts (those relating to the causes of Taylor's death) and listing them in column 1. Interpretations for these facts are often mentioned in the article; these are listed in column 2. In some cases, no interpretation is stated, leaving it entirely up to the reader.

Notice that interpretations 4 and 6 conflict. This is because interpretation 4 was made before we had written down fact 6.

The anticipated conclusion of this article — whether Zachary Taylor was assassinated — was not provided, since the necessary tests had not been performed when the article was written. In the next issue of *Newsweek*, however, the following conclusion appeared: "Tests on [Taylor's] recently exhumed remains revealed that he died of natural causes and not, as rumored, from a lethal dose of arsenic." What facts might have led to this conclusion? Is there anything in the original article that raises a question concerning the validity of this conclusion?

Application: Seeing and Believing

APPLICATION ONE

In "Open Letter to Salman Rushdie," Florence Miller gives her account of a summer job orientation day held recently in an elementary school in East Harlem, New York. Ms. Miller worked for thirty-five years as a teacher and counselor in New York City's schools. Her letter appeared in *The Nation*. As you read it, try to separate fact from interpretation.

Open Letter to Salman Rushdie

BY FLORENCE MILLER

parochial

A few years ago, I worked as part-time guidance counselor in a small parochial elementary school in East Harlem, New York. The school got a windfall — money to run a summer day camp with jobs for ten neighborhood teenagers. More than sixty applied for the jobs, putting the staff in an awkward bind. All the applicants had attended the school at one time or another. The teachers remembered them as uniformed fifth and sixth graders, but what to make of these enormous, sexy, noisy, extravagant 15- and 16-year-olds? Which ten to choose? Who were the most worthy?

Graduate school graduates all, the teachers drew up a checklist — sensitivity, respect for others, motivation, leadership quality, need — looked it over and burst out laughing. Neediness was a given. All the applicants were needy. As for the rest, finding a dependable way to identify those fine characteristics would take more time than anyone had to give, and even then, so what? Checklists, like despair, don't offer much latitude.

So, being sensible women, they tossed the list and made a new plan. The teachers and the teenagers would spend a Saturday together getting reacquainted. It would have a name — Summer Job Orientation Day — and would include socializing, traditional group exercises, discussions, questions and answers. The teachers would lead some groups, drop in on others, keep their eyes open and next day, at breakfast in the convent, they'd decide on the kids they thought needed the jobs most and who appeared likely to work responsibly. Perfect.

That was in December. The famous Saturday was scheduled for March, and it was a March Saturday all right. Gray, rainy, dark. A day for reading, stretched out on the living room couch and peacefully falling asleep during the Met Opera broadcast. I could hardly wait.

ciao

Disaster one. Sister Madeleine broke her ankle late Friday afternoon in the gym. Could I please fill in for her? Ciao, *Tosca*!

Disaster two. What with all that sensitivity and attention to relevant criteria, no one remembered to tell the custodian to keep the heat up for Saturday, so the school, always a little moist, was inhospitably cold and dank.

Disaster three. Eighty kids, not sixty, showed up. The word had spread and then, as now, decent summer jobs were pure gold in East Harlem. "Never mind you don't have an application," parents must have insisted. "You just be there. The sisters won't throw you out." Having solved the problem of shall there be six groups of ten or ten groups of six, there was all that math to do over and worse, not enough chairs. The kindergarten was, of course, the only classroom we could get into, and the mood soured as we realized we would be either sitting knees to chin all day long in those miserable little chairs or dealing with "I don't sit in no baby chair. No way!" We could have predicted. . . .

Disaster four. Heriberto! He had attended the school briefly but memorably in fourth grade. He was now about 17, living with a friend in the neighborhood because his family had thrown him out. He was thin, drawn tight, radioactive. Theresa opened the first large group session at 9:30. At five to 10, Heriberto came in, carrying an economy-size bag of potato chips. He greeted his friends one by one, eyed and dismissed Theresa without interest, elaborately embraced a couple of the girls and came to rest on the back of a kindergarten chair, teetering not quite all the way back to the wall. Yo, Heriberto!

The morning went according to plan, more or less. Some groups were lively, others dull. Heriberto and his potato chips were a royal pain wherever they were but that was to be expected. Everyone perked up when the pizzas were delivered at noon. Hot and cheesy, they tasted wonderful in that icy building, and lunchtime was a cheerful mess of greasy napkins, laughter and screeching remember-whens. The afternoon wasn't too bad and I considered forgiving Madeleine for breaking her ankle. My last small group was to do the "bomb shelter" exercise, and then we would all go home.

The bomb shelter exercise runs as follows: War has been declared. The city will be bombed. A nearby shelter offers safety. Ten people rush to the shelter but there is room inside for only five. Who will live and who will die? The ten are: a doctor, female; a pregnant woman;

a retired general, male; a farmer, male; an artist, female; a construc-tion worker, male; a schoolboy, male; a housewife; a historian, fe-male; a priest. The group has half an hour to discuss the problem, agree unanimously on who survives, then select a representative to present and defend the decision when all the small groups reassemble for a final meeting.

I had led the exercise many times before and knew that the doctor and the general would be first into the shelter. They always were. Proponents of the pregnant woman would be challenged by "She could lose the baby and die, right?" There would be a miniseries romance between the shy, handsome construction worker and the beautiful, abandoned housewife. (Don't ask me. It never fails.) "He can build them a house after." "But what if, ya know, one of them can't make babies." "He'll do it with the doctor but he'll always love her the best." The priest and the farmer would be last pick, the odds favoring the farmer. The artist, the historian and the schoolboy would be left to the bombs. They always were.

engross The discussion was engrossing. The meaning of survival was everyday reality to these young people. They knew more than neces-sary about life and death, violent death, random death, unfair death, youthful death. Even Heriberto's sauntering late entrance didn't in-terrupt the flow of passionate opinion and advocacy. I called time for the first vote. Ten votes each for the doctor and the general; odds and ends for the construction worker, the housewife, the pregnant wom-an, the farmer and the priest. One vote for the historian.

Heriberto! Some in the group laughed. Others, including me, were annoyed. Come on, Heriberto. It's been a long day. Grow up. But Heriberto wasn't playing. He seemed genuinely astonished that his was the only vote for the historian. His reasons? "Because." Nidia, a formidable young woman, took the floor to tell him that she had no time for nonsense (she didn't use the word "nonsense"), that the vote had to be unanimous, that the next vote would be the last vote and that he'd better vote the right way. Another poll and again, one vote for the historian.

We could hear other groups breaking up and going toward the lunchroom for the last meeting of the day. One of the girls — I don't remember her name — was tearful. She had to be at her supermarket job by 5, and she wanted her fair chance at this summer job. She looked my way for backup but, fortunately, I kept my mouth shut as Heriberto began to explain his choice. The historian has to survive, he said. Someone must keep a record of what happens in the world. Someone has to write it all down so that people will know what happened before them. If it isn't written down, it will be forgotten and that would be terrible and wrong. People's lives must never be forgotten.

That isn't exactly what he said, but it's close. He had no golden tongue; he stumbled, mumbled, cleared his throat and repeated himself. It took a while to disconnect Heriberto of the potato chips from this earnest young man trying to persuade us that remembrance is an obligation and slowly, slowly, we understood. At a quarter to 4, just a little behind schedule, the historian got into the shelter.

> earnest

This is a true story, so it doesn't end with Heriberto's triumphant address to the final assembly and greater glory to come. It was Nidia who represented the group and she was terrific, relishing the moment and gracefully crediting Heriberto with the substance of the case for the historian. Sometime during the crush of goodbyes, Heriberto told Sheila, the principal, that he hadn't come for the job, only to hang out with his friends, and that he wouldn't be around that summer. He drifted away and I don't know what happened to him. I do, however, remember him clearly and so, following his instruction, I wrote it all down so that you can remember him too.

> relish

COMPREHENSION CHECK

Write brief answers to the following questions.

1. What statements do you believe are facts in Miller's "letter"?

2. What statements are interpretations?

3. Are some statements presented as if they were facts when they might really be interpretations or exaggerations? Which statements would fit into this category?

4. How does Miller feel toward Heriberto? How does she interpret the events of the Summer Job Orientation Day? What statements in her account lead you to your opinion?

5. How might the essay have differed if Heriberto had written the account? How might it have been the same? If there are statements that would have been the same, would they most likely have been facts, interpretations, or conclusions?

6. How might Nidia have recounted the story? What statements do you think might match those of Heriberto and Miller?

7. Miller plays the role of a historian. What do historians do? Do they simply record the facts? Explain your answer.

APPLICATION TWO

The following newspaper article relates how women from two different cultures view each other. Read it critically; that is, read it with the intent of distinguishing facts from interpretations.

In Saudi and US Women, Common Feeling Is Pity

BY COLIN NICKERSON

DHAHRAN, Saudi Arabia — The American servicewomen arriving by the thousands to this desert kingdom, where men may still take four wives, look sadly on their Saudi sisters cloaked head-to-toe in black abaay, eyes invisible behind the veils prescribed by Islamic custom.

cloak

"Even when you see them, they seem invisible. I simply cannot imagine their lives," said Navy corpswoman Kim Kanode, 31. "You feel lucky to be from America, where women may have a way to go but have still come a long way. These women are centuries behind. I just pity their lives."

Saudi women, meanwhile, admit to being amazed — stunned, really — by the spectacle of US troop carriers rumbling through their streets carrying rifle-bearing women in combat helmets. But even the most progressive among them feel no envy.

progressive

"I feel pity for these American girls with their guns," said a female engineer in her 30s. "Saudi women so often have looked to the West for inspiration. But how can we believe training women to kill and destroy is progress?"

Saudi Arabia, birthplace of the Prophet Mohammed and most conservative of Islamic nations, denies women rights that are taken for granted in other Moslem lands. Women cannot drive cars, must adhere to an ultramodest dress code enforced by religious police, and are barred from public places, including most restaurants and all swimming pools.

ultra

It is a country of sexual paradox, where over the past two decades women have been encouraged to pursue advanced degrees and enter professions ranging from medicine to economics. Yet it is also a country where a female surgeon, say, or a full university professor requires written permission from a male "custodian," husband, father, brother, even teenage son, before she can travel abroad.

paradox

Dating is unknown. Premarital sex, if discovered, would bring public censure and shame not only to the woman involved but to her extended family. Adultery may be, and occasionally is, punished by death.

censure

A female doctor in Jeddah recalled the humiliation of having her pay docked for two weeks when religious police discovered her making medical rounds in a long dress that police charged revealed too much ankle.

dock

"The long beards harass housewives and doctors alike. It is very democratic," said she, alluding to the whiskered imams, the religious teachers who oversee enforcement of Saudi morals.

Yet the doctor, who requested anonymity like most of the Saudi women interviewed, said she would never want to see her country become "liberalized" in the same way as the United States, where she lived for several years and earned her undergraduate degree.

"Saudi may be one extreme, and much change is needed here, especially for women," she said. "But America is another extreme, and it also is in need of change. An American woman can drive and has many freedoms. But she cannot walk the city streets in safety. If she has children she must always worry about drugs and molesters. Are sex movies and homeless people on the street a sign of liberty?

"Americans confuse permissiveness with freedom. There should be a balance," she said. "Saudi Arabia, at least, is not a kingdom of crime and fear. I may be required to wear a certain clothing, but in my country I walk in serenity and peace."

permissiveness

She cited the strong bond of the family as one of the Saudi culture's great strengths. "Everywhere I go in my country there is some cousin or uncle or friend who will take me in, feed me, and let me feel I am at home. Saudis care for one another in a way I do not believe Westerners do."

Write brief answers to the following questions.

1. What facts about American women are contained in the article?

2. What facts about Saudi women are reported?

3. According to the Saudi woman's interpretation, how is she better off than American women?

4. According to the American woman, how is she better off than Saudi women?

5. What similar conclusion does each woman draw about the other?

6. What observations can you make about the article? What are your interpretations of these observations? What are your conclusions?

APPLICATION THREE

The discipline of mathematics provides a perfect vehicle for demonstrating what we have been saying about the relationship between assumptions and facts. Much of the study of mathematics depends on establishing facts, called theorems. These facts are based on some beginning assumptions known as postulates or definitions.

The next reading is from a mathematics textbook. In it the authors explore the facts about infinity. It is not easy reading: It will require that you read very slowly at times. You may need to reread some passages several times before the meaning becomes clear. As you read, be aware of how the authors define *equivalent*. This definition becomes a key assumption in their argument about infinity.

Also read to discover the seemingly counterintuitive conclusion the authors come to about the size(s) of infinity. If we accept their definition, we will come to the same startling conclusion: There is more than one size of infinity. This is because no one-to-one correspondence between decimals and natural numbers exists. The set of decimals is *larger* than the set of natural numbers, even though the set of natural numbers is infinite!

Infinite Sets

BY WILLIAM P. BERLINGHOFF AND KERRY E. GRANT

literal

In its most literal sense, infinite means "unbounded, endless, without limits of any kind"; but these definitions are not much more informative than the word itself. *compound* The confusion is compounded by the fact that nothing in the world around us seems to possess this property, with the possible exceptions of space and time, which appear to be limitless, but certainly are finite as far as the experience of any individual is concerned. Even a quantity as vast as the total number of electrons and protons in the universe can be calculated, at least approximately, and is thereby bounded by some large but finite number. (In 1938, A. S. Eddington proposed a number for this: 10^{79}.)

The first outright encounter with infinity usually comes from a consideration of numbers themselves. Very early in their mathematical experience, children discover that there is no largest number because 1 can be added to any number to get a larger one. The natural numbers are thus envisioned as an endless chain stretching out "to infinity," a place just beyond the farthest cloud and off limits to sane, stable people. This pathway to infinity has a definite starting point and is composed of *discrete* discrete numerical steps, but it op-erates like a treadmill; you can walk as far as you like, but your goal will be as far away when you stop as it was when you began.

Contrasted with this discrete, step-by-step idea of infinity is the predominantly geometric idea of continuous infinity. Although a straight line can be shown to be infinite because one can "step off" intervals in either direction as far as one likes, there is no need to "step" at all. Because there are no gaps in the line, it is possible to proceed as far as is desired without singling out specific points along the way.

"But," you say, "this is really the same kind of process. One simply glides from one point to the next, thus taking very small but definite steps."

The Greeks considered a line (and time) to be composed of a succession of adjacent points (or *succession* moments) until Zeno showed how that assumption led to absurd results. . . . There is no "next" point to any given point and there are no gaps anywhere, so the set of points that make up a line appears to constitute a kind of infinity that is somehow different from that of the natural numbers. One might even speculate that these two infinite *speculate* sets are of different "sizes," so to speak.

If, just for the sake of argument, we suppose that there are indeed at least two different sizes of infinity, are there more? What about the set **I** of integers or the set **Q** of rational numbers? **I** contains no smallest number, so the infinity appears two-sided, in some sense. Between any two rational numbers there are infinitely many others. Does that mean **I** and/or **Q** somehow represent larger sizes of infinity than **N**? If infinity is truly limitless, can there be "larger" or "smaller" infinite sets, or different sizes in any sense? To answer these questions (and others that probably are starting to occur to you) we need to define precisely what we mean by an "infinite set," and we must define "same size."

For instance, consider the sets

$$A = \{ a, b, c, d \}$$

and

$$B = \{ \square, \triangle, \bigcirc, \square \}$$

Are these two sets the same size? Before this question can be answered reasonably, we must specify what we mean by "same size." Clearly, if we are talking about the area of the page each occupies, the answer is *No*. However, the size question as it concerns us in this chapter is more accurately translated by asking if A and B have the same number of elements, and in this case the answer is *Yes*. But what does "same number" mean, especially in the case of infinite sets? Must we have particular

numbers of elements before we can decide whether or not two sets are the same size in this sense? We certainly can use numbers to count the elements of A and B; but saying that A and B are the same size just means we ended up with the same number in each case. Now, counting is nothing more than matching things up with part of a known set (the natural numbers 1, 2, 3, . . .). If we are going to match up sets, there is no need to use numbers at all; we can directly match the sets we want to compare. Thus, we can pair off the elements of A and B as in Figure 6.1 and conclude that A and B are the same size.

$$A = \{ a, \quad b, \quad c, \quad d \ \}$$
$$\updownarrow \quad \updownarrow \quad \updownarrow \quad \updownarrow$$
$$B = \{ \square, \ \triangle, \ \bigcirc, \ \square \ \}$$

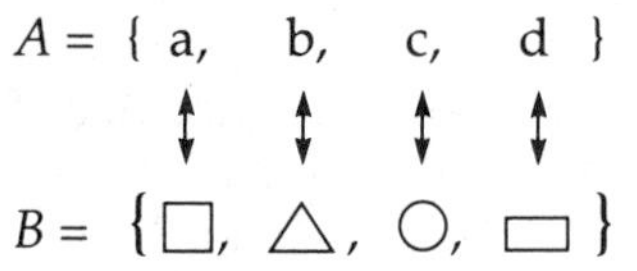

Figure 6.1 Corresponding elements in sets A and B.

As we prepare to investigate infinite sets, where counting all the elements is a hopeless task, it is useful to have a formal definition of this simpler comparison process.

Definition

A **one-to-one** (or **1-1**) **correspondence** between two sets A and B is any rule or process by which each element of A is associated with exactly one element of B and each element of B is associated with exactly one element of A.

Definition

Two sets A and B are **equivalent** if there exists a one-to-one correspondence between them. We shall write this as $A \leftrightarrow B$.

When we say that two sets *have the same size*, we mean that they are equivalent.

Example 6.1 There are many different 1-1 correspondences between the sets

$$A = \{a, b, c, d\}$$

and

$$B = \{w, x, y, z\}$$

Two of them are

$$A = \{ \; a, \quad b, \quad c, \quad d \; \}$$
$$\updownarrow \quad \updownarrow \quad \updownarrow \quad \updownarrow$$
$$B = \{ \; w, \quad x, \quad y, \quad z \; \}$$

and

$$A = \{ \; a, \quad b, \quad c, \quad d \; \}$$
$$B = \{ \; w, \quad x, \quad y, \quad z \; \}$$

Example 6.2 The matching

$$A = \{ \; a, \quad b, \quad c, \quad d \; \}$$
$$\updownarrow \quad \searrow \; \updownarrow \quad \updownarrow$$
$$B = \{ \; w, \quad x, \quad y, \quad z \; \}$$

is not a 1-1 correspondence (even though the two sets are equivalent). Although each element of A corresponds to exactly one element of B, the element x in B is not matched with anything in A, and y is matched with two elements of A.

Example 6.3 There is no way to put the sets $\{a, b, c, d\}$ and $\{x, y, z\}$ in 1-1 correspondence. Therefore, these two sets are not equivalent.

Example 6.4 A 1-1 correspondence between the set of all natural numbers and the set of all negative integers is given by

$$\{ \; 1, \quad 2, \quad 3, \quad 4, \quad \ldots, \quad n, \quad \ldots \; \}$$
$$\updownarrow \quad \updownarrow \quad \updownarrow \quad \updownarrow \quad \quad \updownarrow$$
$$\{ -1, \quad -2, \quad -3, \quad -4, \quad \ldots, \; -n, \quad \ldots \; \}$$

We cannot list every pairing in the correspondence, but the pattern given allows us to determine specifically how each element in either set is matched with an element of the other. For instance:

> The natural number 37 is matched with the negative integer -37; the negative integer -45 is matched with 45; etc.

Definition

A set A is **finite** if it is empty or if there is a natural number n such that A is equivalent to $\{1, 2, 3, \ldots, n\}$. A set is **infinite** if it is not finite.

This definition says that a set is infinite if its elements cannot be counted completely, no matter how fast we count or how much time we take. It fits well with the intuitive sense of infinity described at the beginning of this section and at the same time it makes good mathematical sense. So, let us move on to the first major question we face:

Are all infinite sets equivalent?

In other words, can two infinite sets *always* be put in 1-1 correspondence? If so, then all infinite sets are the same size (in this sense). If not, then there are actually different sizes of infinity! Intuitive reactions ("gut feelings") about that question vary widely. Since we human beings have never encountered actually infinite collections of things in our material experience, all of our attempts to deal with them must involve projecting our finite experience into an area in which its applicability is unknown. Therefore, we must rely on logical reasoning to guarantee the validity of any statements we make about infinity. In particular, we must apply the formal definitions carefully, and then be prepared to accept the consequences of our reasoning, regardless of whether or not they conform to our intuitive feelings.

intuitive

applicability

COMPREHENSION CHECK

Write brief answers to the following questions.

1. Why do Berlinghoff and Grant think that the concept of infinity is so hard for us to grasp?

2. What are the two different ways that a line can be used to demonstrate infinity?

3. **I** represents the set of integers. What are integers?

4. **Q** is the set of rational numbers. What are rational numbers?

5. **N** is the set of natural numbers. What are natural numbers?

6. What is Berlinghoff and Grant's definition of *counting*?

7. What are equivalent sets?

8. Berlinghoff and Grant's definition of a *finite set* may seem difficult to understand. How can you explain (or reword) it to make it clearer?

9. What are two ways of checking to see if finite sets are equivalent? Which of these ways can be used to see if infinite sets are equivalent?

10. What does the last sentence in the reading mean? Why do you think Berlinghoff and Grant included it?

What Do You Think?

✪ **DISCUSSION QUESTIONS**

Prepare for class discussion by jotting down answers to the following questions.

1. The Earth's spheroid shape is a counterintuitive fact. Somehow, though, you have been convinced that the world is *not* flat, in spite of what your eyes tell you. What did it take to make you accept this fact?

2. It is a fact that if you look at our second closest star, you are seeing the star the way it was over four years ago, not the way it is today. Based on your previous discussion, what would it take to convince you that this is a fact?

3. Consider the theme of the Saudi–American women article, only from a gender point of view. What are the advantages of being a member of your sex? What advantages do members of the opposite sex have? First discuss this with someone of your own gender; then pair up with a member of the opposite sex to compare your findings. Which of the findings are facts? Which are interpretations?

4. Speculate about time.

   a. Did it have a beginning? Will it have an end? What do your answers suggest about time?

   b. Do your answers to question 4a imply time is most like the set of integers, the set of natural numbers, or the set of natural numbers from 1 to 100?

   c. If time had no beginning, how is it possible that we ever arrived at the present year? If it did have a beginning, how is it possible that there was no time *before* its beginning? (Here we have a conflict of intuitive thoughts. Discuss this conflict of intuitions.)

WRITING ASSIGNMENTS

Select one of the following topics and in a brief essay develop a thoughtful written response.

1. Think about a snowstorm. In terms of facts and interpretations, how might each of the following people be likely to describe the snowstorm: a poet, a ski lift operator, a student, a mathematician, a historian, an artist, a scientist, and a farmer?

2. Consider the following scenario: A student enrolls in a one-credit class. After the professor says he will not fail anyone, the student stops attending and eventually gets an F. The professor did not expect a student to interpret his statement to mean that no one had to participate. The student is not on the graduation list because she is one unit of credit short. A part-time teacher believes the professor has been unfair and so turns in a fake grade for her so that she can graduate. The registrar accepts it, but is skeptical. The professor is furious. The student, furious at the professor at first, is relieved when she is allowed to graduate.

    Given this set of facts, take the role of the student, the professor, the part-time teacher, and the registrar. Write the story as interpreted by each of these people. Based on the facts and the interpretations you have made, what is your conclusion? Did the characters act morally? Defend your answer.

3. In a small group, select a current political issue. Develop a list of characters who are directly involved in this issue. Have each member of your group select one of the characters and, assuming the role of that person, write a first-person essay. In the first paragraph describe the background of your character. Continue the essay by describing the character's position on the issue, supporting it with facts and his or her interpretations of the facts. Then read each other's essays. What are your conclusions? How do they compare with the conclusions of other members of your group?

Developing Reasoning Skills

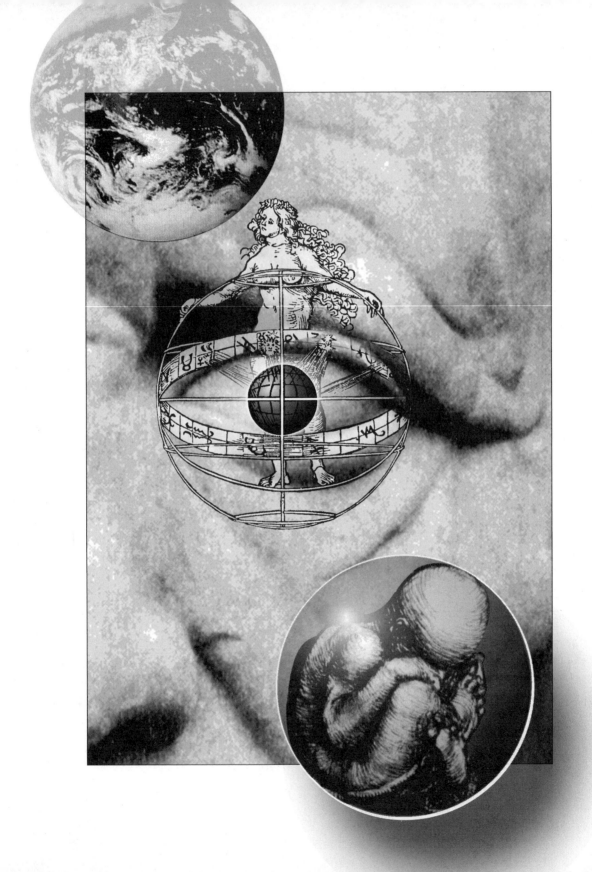

Exploring Perspectives in a Diverse World

After reading Chapter 4 you should be able to:

- list a number of factors that influence your worldview
- describe how values influence your views
- assume different roles and present different viewpoints
- define reasoned opinion

You may use the following checklist in planning your study of different perspectives. Activities marked with a ✪ are to be completed in class. Some preclass preparation may be required.

CONTEXT FOR LEARNING

✪ _____ INTRODUCTORY CHAPTER ACTIVITY

_____ Different Perspectives

_____ The Role of Values in Developing Worldviews

✪ _____ ACTIVITY BREAK

_____ Reasoned Conclusions

✪ _____ DISCUSSION BREAK

APPLICATION: BUILDING CONNECTIONS

_____ APPLICATION ONE

_____ **"Instilling Values in Our Children"**
by Michele Forney, Elizabeth Garlock, and Joe Morse

_____ COMPREHENSION CHECK

_____ APPLICATION TWO

_____ **"Message from the Dean"**
by Wayne B. Hamilton

_____ COMPREHENSION CHECK

_____ APPLICATION THREE

_____ **"Entunese Mañana (Tune in Tomorrow)"**
by Lelia Loban Lee

_____ COMPREHENSION CHECK

✪ **INTRODUCTORY CHAPTER ACTIVITY**

Read the following poem carefully. What message is the author trying
to convey? Share your answers with your classmates.

Perception

Misperceptions produce fear
and true perceptions foster love.

You respond to what you perceive,
and as you perceive
so shall you behave.

Everything you perceive is a witness
to the thought system you want to be true.

What you perceive in others
you are strengthening in yourself.

Perception is a choice and not a fact.
But on this choice depends far more
than you may realize as yet.
For on the voice you choose to hear,
and on the sights you choose to see,
depends entirely your whole belief in what you are.

Instruction in perception is your great need.

What would you see?
The choice is given you.
But learn and do not let your mind
forget this law of seeing:
You will look upon that which you feel within.
If hatred finds a place within your heart,
you will perceive a fearful world,
held cruelly in death's sharp-pointed, bony fingers.
If you feel the Love of God within you,
you will look out on a world of mercy and of love.

Learn how to look on all things
with love, appreciation, and open-mindedness.

You have no conception of the limits
you have placed on your perception,
and no idea of all the liveliness that you could see.

Perception can make whatever picture
the mind desires to see.
Remember this.
In this lies either Heaven or hell,
as you elect.

Perception is a mirror, not a fact.
And what I look on is my state of mind,
reflected outward.

— anonymous

Different Perspectives

In Chapter 3 we discussed facts and how people connect them, interpret them, and draw conclusions from them. The accumulation of facts, interpretations, and conclusions combine to form a person's opinions or worldview. Many factors can influence our interpretation of the world around us, account for our most dearly held beliefs, and contribute to the positions we take on controversial issues. These factors include culture, occupation, religion, socioeconomic status, schooling, age, and gender.

We are raised within a cultural setting that may or may not be the same as the dominant Anglo-American culture. We learn about union workers' or management's point of view at the dinner table. Some of us receive in-depth religious exposure, and others little or none. Our families may have so little or so much money that we spend a lot of family time deciding how to spend it. Those of us who are affluent may see the status quo as desirable, while others who have less may advocate political change.

Schools also have the potential to expand our worldviews and prepare us for future roles. If our experience is positive, we may come to value education for itself. If our experience is less than positive, however, we may see it only as a stepping stone to where we want to go, or even as a waste of time.

Age can also influence our personal opinions. Both parents and children will readily acknowledge differences in their perspectives — that is, a generation gap. Parents have one set of opinions regarding responsible behavior, while their children have another. What parents once felt entitled to do as adolescents, they now work diligently to prevent their children from doing.

Do you think gender plays a role in determining how men and women view the world? Is it possible that men and women prioritize values differently, that men value logic and reason over feelings of affiliation or relationships while women prefer the opposite? Are there differences in how men and women confront the notion of debating or thinking critically? There is certainly no conclusive evidence to support this belief; however, some researchers are discussing this hypothesis, as we shall see in Application Four of this chapter.

The Role of Values in Developing Worldviews

Out of the myriad of experiences that form our backgrounds, we develop a set of values. A *value* can be defined as a general principle or concept that is recognized as having worth, or as being "right" action or thought.

For example, honesty, friendship, loyalty, and justice are values that most of us believe in. Values are a powerful foundation for many of our opinions. Of course, terms such as *friendship* and *justice* are ambiguous — that is, unclear in their meaning. We may all believe in them and yet define what they mean very differently.

Does this mean that people of the same gender, age, and occupation who come from the same socioeconomic background and worship at the same temple, church, or mosque will all have the same values? Certainly not. However, the similarity in backgrounds does increase the probability. Having shared many of the same experiences, these people may have come to believe in many of the same values or, more important, come to *mean* the same things when they talk about certain values. One could argue that certain values transcend cultures or socioeconomic class and are part of a set of universal values. For example, we might claim that all people desire to live in a safe and healthy world; however, what that means can vary depending on one's culture. A Navajo Indian and a Manhattan businesswoman might want to create very different environments that they would define as safe and healthy.

What then might account for differences of opinion among people of similar backgrounds? Some of it may be due to differences in personalities. Kim will forever see the half-filled glass as half empty; Pat will always see it as half full. Individual experiences play a significant role in the formation of our opinions. Another key factor is our exposure to others who do not share our opinions. Surrounded by people who believe just as we do, we have little reason to question our beliefs. Being exposed to differing views is challenging. We can either dismiss the ideas as nonsense or listen carefully and try to understand what's behind those views. The result is a valuable opportunity to understand ourselves and others better.

Consider the following two examples.

Example One   Leelay, an Asian friend of yours, announces that her parents have found a young man they think she will want to marry. What is your reaction? In Western culture individual choice is highly valued, and young adults view matchmaking attempts by relatives as intrusive and inappropriate. Because Leelay's traditional Asian upbringing places greater value on extended family cohesion than on individual choice, she expects her family to play a significant role in her choice of a marriage partner.

Does knowing this affect your reaction? Think for a moment, and then list some of the advantages and disadvantages of choosing your marriage partner.

Advantages   ***Disadvantages***

_____   _____

_____   _____

_____   _____

Now list some of the advantages and disadvantages of having your marriage partner chosen for you.

Advantages   ***Disadvantages***

_____   _____

_____   _____

_____   _____

Does being male or female influence your perspective? In what ways?

_____

_____

Example Two   While some of us have been taught that leading "a good life" on Earth will mean eternal life in Heaven, others have been taught that leading a good life on Earth will mean being reincarnated into a better life here on Earth. Some of us assume that a good life means being industrious and achieving success; others assume that it means accepting our personal circumstances and doing our best to fulfill that role.

How then might people from these two different backgrounds view competition or the need for economic progress? List a few of their differences here.

Believers in Heaven   *Believers in Reincarnation*

_____   _____

_____   _____

_____   _____

What are some economic and/or geographic conditions that might influence people's views? For example, how might living in a rich agricultural region influence a person's belief in competition?

_____

_____

⊙ **ACTIVITY BREAK**

This activity asks you to investigate informally how similar your and your classmates' backgrounds are, and then to compare how similar your views are on several issues.

1. Complete the "Class Data Sheet" on page 123. For example, how many members of your class are between the ages of 16 and 19? How many members of the class work full-time and are students? Record class numbers in the appropriate box. Now look at the completed data sheet. Which categories show the greatest similarity? Which categories have the greatest diversity?

2. Poll your classmates on the issues listed in the "Issues Survey" chart on page 124 and record your answers in the "Yes or No" column.

3. Based on the answers recorded on the "Class Data Sheet" and student responses to the issues survey, explain which factors *might* be influencing students' opinions on each issue. Enter these in the "Factors" column of the "Issues Survey" chart.

4. Discuss what general statements you can make comparing students' backgrounds and their views.

Class Data Sheet

Age	Gender	Employment	Cultural Background	Religion	Economic Status
16–19	Male		African American	Buddhist	Wealthy
20–24	Female		Asian	Christian	OK
25–29		Student (part-time)	European American	Hindu	Need More
30s		Student (full-time)	Latino	Jewish	
40s		Homemaker	Native American	Moslem	
50s		Full-time Employment	Biracial	Other	
		Part-time Employment	Other		

Issues Survey

Issue	Yes or No	Factors
1. Should abortion be legal?	_____	_____
		_____
2. Should music lyrics be censored?	_____	_____
		_____
3. Should prayer be allowed in schools?	_____	_____
		_____
4. Should illegal aliens be denied schooling?	_____	_____
		_____
5. Should drug-addicted mothers be prosecuted?	_____	_____
		_____
6. Should the United Nations send peacekeeping troops to ____?	_____	_____
		_____
		_____
7. (Class makes up issue)	_____	_____
		_____
		_____

Reasoned Conclusions

So far we have been looking at how differences in our backgrounds can influence our perspectives on issues. While this offers us some understanding of *why* a person might take a certain stand on an issue, we really haven't *evaluated* the conclusions themselves. Students often shy away from evaluating a conclusion. They feel comfortable with their ideas and readily accept or at least tolerate opposing views and opinions: "Well, that's your opinion; I understand where you're coming from. Hey, tolerance and freedom are two values I believe in, so I have no problem with your views even if they are the opposite of mine."

As we mentioned in Chapter 1, academicians like to examine and evaluate opinions. They do, however, make a distinction between mere preferences and informed opinions. For example, they don't seriously debate issues surrounding preferences, such as "Is mocha almond fudge ice cream better than coffee Heath bar crunch?" or "Should everyone like reggae, rap, or rock?" However, they might be interested in investigating and determining answers to such issues as "Is frozen yogurt really healthier for you than regular ice cream?" or "Is reggae more popular among European-American than African-American listeners?"

Academicians are interested in issues on which people can come to reasoned conclusions. A *reasoned conclusion* can be described as a position taken on an issue that is supported by evidence and/or reasons. In this way arguments can be analyzed for their strengths and weaknesses. The evidence and reasons provided can be examined, first to determine if they are true, and second to establish whether they support the position.

However, going through this process does not guarantee that everyone will agree upon the "right" position. There will always be room for disagreement. Some people will disagree over the interpretation of the evidence; others will use the same words but mean very different things. Some will disagree over the weight certain reasons should be given; and others will stress the importance of one value over another. You will want to keep this in mind as you begin to analyze your own reasoning and that of others.

✪ **DISCUSSION BREAK**

Prepare for class discussion by jotting down brief answers to the following questions.

1. There is no dearth (scarcity) of controversial issues to be found. Every family, profession, and academic discipline has its favorite topics for debate. For example, in criminal justice courses students debate the issues underlying individual deviance and criminal behavior. Educators debate the merits of academic tracking as related to student achievement and self-esteem. Economists debate the benefits to productivity of cuts in capital gains taxes. Mathematicians debate the possibility of determining a finite number of primes. Ecologists debate whether the summer 1988 drought was caused by the greenhouse effect.

    Come up with a list of your favorite debate issues. Write your issues in the form of questions: Was the drought of 1988 caused by the greenhouse effect? Should teenagers be executed? Now share your issues with other members of the class.

2. How significant a role do you think the media plays in changing people's attitudes and values? For example:

    a. What possible effect do soap operas have on viewers' attitudes toward love relationships?

    b. Have advertising campaigns and television programs changed people's views on cigarette smoking?

    c. What impact do you think talk shows have on people's values? Does this lead to greater conformity?

    d. If you do think that the media is exerting a significant impact on establishing social values, should we be concerned?

3. If there is no guarantee that people will reach agreement when they debate different issues, you may ask why we should bother. That's a legitimate question. What *are* the benefits to disagreeing? What role can informal debating play in our personal and professional lives? How important in a person's life is it to be able to disagree, negotiate, and collaborate? (We will return to this topic in Chapter 5.)

Application: Building Connections

APPLICATION ONE

Former students, now parents, were asked this question: What values do you hope to instill in your children? As you read the following responses, look for similarities and differences in the values presented.

Instilling Values in Our Children

This world is a tough place to be in. I hope to see my son learn compassion for others, no matter what their ethnic background may be. He may do anything he likes, but he better be ready to pay the price. I wish I could say this world is kind, friendly, and a great place to be. What I will say to my son is this:

"I cannot lie to you my son. You must be strong and assertive. You must believe that you can do anything. You must concentrate on your goals and strive to achieve them. That is my wish for you, my one son. Don't expect everything to be done for you. You must take responsibility for your actions. You must never do or say anything to anyone else that you wouldn't want done or said to you. Follow these rules and your life should be full of content."

— **Michele Forney**

cliché

synonymous

The values that I wish to pass on to my children sound rather "cliché-ish." I chose the definition of *value* from Webster's Dictionary, which describes value as synonymous with the word *worth*. As the definition of *worth* may suggest a "more lasting and genuine merit, which rests on a deeper intrinsic and enduring quality," I chose to take this as my definition of *value*. Based on that, the values I wish to pass on to my children are trustworthiness, honesty, and kindness.

— **Elizabeth Garlock**

Young women! These are my girls, and if I think of them, what shall I give them? And I end with how shall I protect them? And I'll never protect them. So I give them self-defense and health and love. Oh yes, and peace. I hate this eve of war. I'm scared. And teach them please! I will — truth and justice. Show them the Holy Language. And relax girls. It's what we do sometimes when I tuck you into bed. I talk and breathe and we relax and create a world full of imagery. And we relax and that's what I give.

— **Joe Morse**

COMPREHENSION CHECK

Write brief answers to the following questions.

1. What values do these parents say they hope to instill in their children?

2. Are their values similar or dissimilar?

3. Joe Morse speaks of the "Holy Language." To what value do you think he is referring?

4. What adjectives would you use to describe the differences in tone among the writers?

APPLICATION TWO

Former Dean of Graduate and Continuing Studies Wayne B. Hamilton cautions students to be aware of their preconceptions and the resistance all people have to "letting in" new information. "Be aware that you are not completely open to the things that you are learning." He asks students to challenge themselves and their professors. Read this selection to understand how his examples support "pre-cognitive commitment."

Message from the Dean

BY WAYNE B. HAMILTON

In a column like this, one might expect the usual prattle from a Dean about the "joys of learning," "the search for truth," etc., but I may have to disappoint you on that score. Instead, I want to alert you to some grave, personal dangers as you approach your studies in college.

grave

In the interest of science, and in an effort to make my point here, I refer to two experiments (which you may test for yourself, if you have the right equipment). First, about twenty houseflies are placed in a jar, which is then capped with a lid with holes so the flies have air. The flies cannot escape. After a time (I leave it to you to test how long) the lid may be removed, and the flies will still be unable to escape. Why can't the flies escape? Apparently they have made what some psychologists call a "pre-cognitive commitment" to the limitations of the world as they know it,

and it never "occurs" to them to venture beyond this world.

venture

Second, a baby elephant is tied to a small bush about the size of a Christmas tree by means of a thin green rope about the thickness of a clothesline. The baby cannot escape. And even though much later, as an adult of enormous strength, this same elephant could easily escape by snapping a thick chain tied to a thick tree, it could *not* escape if tied to a small bush by means of a thin green rope. Why not? "Pre-cognitive commitment."

A few years ago, as I recall, some Harvard researchers won the Nobel Prize for their work on pre-cognitive commitment. They explained why such a very small portion, out of the billions of bits of stimuli which surround us, ever enters into our nervous system. Which portion do you suppose gets in? Right: that portion

stimuli

analogy

predetermine

which supports pre-cognitive commitment! We let in that which supports the way we have already perceived the world to be; the rest of the stimuli are kept out!

Now, I would like to draw an analogy (it's only an analogy) and attempt to make my point about the dangers facing you as you approach your studies: your mind and its self-limiting preconceptions will predetermine what you learn here, or anywhere else. Be aware that you are not completely open to the things that you are learning. Know that you will have to suspend some of your preconceptions

if you ever expect to let in anything new. This will be your main work here, and it will be your most difficult work. You will have to change yourself in some fundamental way if you expect to get the most out of your education.

Ask your professors to help you with this. Ask them to recognize that you have some difficult work to do in shedding old ways of seeing things before you can be open to the new things they may be professing. Remind them that, if they think this is easy, they ought to try it themselves.

COMPREHENSION CHECK

Write brief answers to the following questions.

1. How does Hamilton define *pre-cognitive commitment*?

2. Explain how the two experiments are examples of pre-cognitive commitment.

3. Explain the following statement: ". . . your mind and its self-limiting preconceptions will predetermine what you learn here, or anywhere else."

4. What advice does Hamilton offer students who want to break through this learning limitation? What makes following this advice so difficult?

5. What examples of pre-cognitive commitment are you aware of in your life?

"Entunese Mañana" was written by Lelia Loban Lee, a freelance writer whose article first appeared in *Soap Opera Digest*. When she is not writing, Lee is a stained glass artist with a TV in her studio. She writes, "I'm now so hooked on Hispanic soaps that I've almost quit watching our network soaps. If people all over the world watched each other's TV programs, they might not feel so xenophobic [fearful or disliking of foreigners]."

"Entunese Mañana" has no main headings or subheadings to help readers preview the article. The only available clue is the subtitle. Read that now. What two worlds do you think Lee will be addressing? How do you think she will organize her information?

_____

_____

Now read the article to see if your prediction is correct.

Entunese Mañana (Tune in Tomorrow)

BY LELIA LOBAN LEE

Watching Spanish-language soaps is like visiting another world

In English, they're soap operas. In Spanish, they're *historias* or *novelas* (stories). I discovered them when I tuned into the Spanish-language stations Univision and Telemundo to brush up on my rusty, outdated Spanish. (Imagine what your English would be like if you'd learned it from hippies in 1965, and hadn't spoken it since.)

I tuned in to REBELDE (REBEL); MARIA, MARIA; CANTARE PARA TI (I'LL SING FOR YOU); SIMPLEMENTE MARIA; VENGANZA DE MUJER (WOMAN'S VENGEANCE, which uses a Spanish-language version of "Memories" from the musical *Cats* as its theme song); LA REVANCHA (REVENGE); and AMANDOTE II. There are many more including CARRUSEL (CAROUSEL) and other soaps specifically made for children. These programs come from all over the Hispanic world, from as far as Peru and as near as Los Angeles. Most

hiatus

Spanish soaps run every day for only a few weeks or months at a time, then conclude or go on *hiatus*, the way our nighttime series do.

At first, I couldn't understand the dialogue, but the characters and plots seemed so familiar that I could still follow the stories. Soon I began to recognize common phrases. One day, I realized I wasn't just hearing the words anymore. I understood.

Hispanic soaps focus on love and family, the same as Anglo soaps. Even a viewer who can't speak any Spanish will be able to identify the hero, the villain, the earth mother, the loving father, the bitch, the wayward daughter, the meddlesome aunt, the scheming uncle, the headstrong son, the hero's clownish buddy and the fragile innocent — and, of course, the super couple. Murder mysteries, revenge stories and Romeo-and-Juliet romances between members of rival families are as popular in Spanish as they are in English.

Some cultural differences may startle Anglo viewers at first. Men hold hands with men. Women hold hands with women and kiss each other on the lips. Such behavior doesn't suggest homosexuality to Hispanic audiences. And remember the scene in TWIN PEAKS, when Leland Palmer discovered his daughter, Laura, was dead? Anglo viewers didn't quite know how to react to his hysterical sobbing, but Hispanic viewers probably thought, "Finally, a man who acts normal." On Hispanic soaps, men cry as freely as women.

The sex and violence on Hispanic soaps are somewhat less graphic than what is routinely seen on Anglo shows. Although there are plenty of smooches and provocative clothes, sex scenes usually end at the bedroom door. The programs available for viewing in the U.S. aren't a completely representative sampling of Latin American soap operas. ENTERTAINMENT TONIGHT recently reported that audiences in Brazil, for example, expect nudity and sex scenes far too explicit for North American television.

graphic

Characters on Spanish-language soaps discuss morality, sin and their religious beliefs more often than characters on AMC or Y&R. While Anglo soaps don't treat abortion, divorce or illegitimate pregnancy lightly, these subjects get far graver treatment from Hispanic writers. The reason may be that Anglo soaps reach viewers who practice many different religions. The audience for Spanish soaps is so overwhelmingly Roman Catholic that the producers can make nearly all their characters outspoken Catholics without worrying about alienating viewers.

Although Hispanic soaps promote Catholic ideas as best, they also reinforce the "love will find a way" theme familiar to fans of the mixed

---

A Little Lesson in Spanish Soapspeak

In case watching Spanish-language soap operas makes you feel as if you're in another world, we've provided a glossary of phrases, along with their translations, just to get you started.

Spanish: *¿Yo? ¿Embarazada? ¡Imposible!*
English: Me? Pregnant? Impossible!
Real Meaning: I'm at least four months along.

Spanish: *No me importa.*
English: It doesn't matter to me.
Real Meaning: My whole life depends on it.

Spanish: *No hay problema. No se preocupe.*
English: No problem. Don't worry.
Real Meaning: All hell is breaking loose.

Spanish: *No es la verdad. ¿Por qué pienses tu esta tonteria?*
English: It's not true. Why would you think such a silly thing?
Real Meaning: How did you find out?

Spanish: *¡Claro que yo soy el papá del niño de mi eposa!*
English: Of course I'm the father of my wife's baby!
Real Meaning: The kid doesn't look a bit like me. . . .

(Character has just regained consciousness.)
Spanish: *Me siento mejor. Es solamente que yo no he comido desde ayer.*
English: I feel better. It's just that I haven't eaten since yesterday.
Real Meaning: It's probably brain cancer.

---

marriage of Cruz and Eden on SANTA BARBARA. The children's soap CARRUSEL recently showed Hispanic children from different racial and religious backgrounds learning not to taunt each other with ethnic slurs.

Anglo viewers may also notice that the Hispanic entertainment industry sees fashion and beauty differently. Many performers wear blond or red wigs, or bleach their hair. Because many of these Hispanic women have olive or brown skin and many leave their eyebrows dark, the lightened hair is more conspicuous than on Anglo actresses.

Characters dress quite differently on Hispanic soaps, too. Although some Hispanic soap opera characters do dress outrageously, wild styles are not the norm. On a fair number of

conspicuous

Spanish-language soaps, women favor dresses with lots of gathering and ruffles (a style popular for many years among Hispanics that never caught on for long among Anglo women) and men wear shinier fabrics, brighter colors and bolder patterns than their Anglo counterparts.

counterparts

But most Hispanic soap characters wear affordable, department store clothing, in the same fashionable but not extreme styles that middle-class viewers would wear.

Set decoration looks less pretentious on Telemundo and Univision. Offices seem smaller and more like real offices, and homes are more down-to-earth, not like the extravagant palaces of SANTA BARBARA's Capwells or GENERAL HOSPITAL's Quartermaines. Hispanic soap characters don't hide their TVs off-camera. A living room setting often includes a gigantic television in an impressive cabinet, along with other electronic gear of all kinds, including huge console stereos and elaborate telephones. The less-affluent characters seem to furnish their homes from moderate-priced chain stores, such as Levitz and Sears, while furniture in the homes of wealthy characters looks as if it came from Bloomingdale's or Ethan Allen, not from design shows in Italy.

This difference in appearance is probably less a reflection of taste than of money—most Hispanic shows look low-budget. The sets resemble those of network soaps in the United States from the late 1960s. Expect fewer camera angles and more production glitches; however, the acting is so professional, you won't hear many flubbed lines.

glitch

You'll feel right at home during the commercials. Watch for Madge, selling Palmolive in Spanish with a terrible accent. One big difference: Commercials on Hispanic soaps address men and women equally. You'll see ads for baldness cures, automotive services and electronic equipment. Most of the ads are local rather than national. They promote neighborhood restaurants (this is a great way to find out where to get authentic ethnic food), Hispanic civic organizations, language and citizenship classes and professional offices where doctors and lawyers speak Spanish.

Some Hispanic viewers think of soap opera characters as real people, the same way Anglo viewers do. If you watch Univision and Telemundo long enough, the day may come when you can't help understanding a conversation in Spanish on the bus or in a restaurant. Suddenly, you realize you know those people that your neighbors are gossiping so happily about. That's right—they're talking about characters from Spanish-language soaps.

Write brief answers to the following questions.

1. What organizational structure did Lee use to write this article? Explain your answer.

2. Lee assumes her audience knows what a soap opera is. Imagine that you have just met someone who has never seen a soap opera; define *soap opera*. If you do not know what a soap opera is, use the context of the article to help you define it. Why do you think it is called a "soap" opera?

3. What are some of the similarities between Hispanic and Anglo soaps?

4. What are some of the differences between Hispanic and Anglo soaps?

5. What differences does Lee attribute to cultural characteristics of Hispanics and Anglos?

6. What differences does Lee attribute to budget issues?

7. What inference might be drawn about Hispanic soap audiences from the statement "Commercials on Hispanic soaps address men and women equally"?

8. In addition to being entertained, what other benefits does watching Spanish soaps offer its Anglo viewers?

APPLICATION FOUR

Our fourth reading is excerpted from the book *Women's Ways of Knowing*. In this book the authors "examine women's ways of knowing and describe five different perspectives from which women view reality and draw conclusions about truth, knowledge, and authority." They claim that relatively "little attention has been given to modes of learning, knowing, and valuing that may be specific to, or at least common in, women."

This excerpt discusses two kinds of procedural knowledge: separate knowing and connected knowing. For people whose orientation is toward *separate knowing*, understanding ideas is based on a set of separate rules. In contrast, those who engage in *connected knowing* try to understand ideas by developing a relationship between an idea and its speaker. Separate knowers are characterized as developing "techniques for analyzing and evaluating arguments" while connected knowers believe "trustworthy knowledge comes from personal experience rather than pronouncements of authorities." The authors suggest that separate knowing is much more common among males, and connected knowing more common among women.

Read the following passage to understand the types of knowing presented. Do these categories make sense to you? How would you characterize yourself? Are you a connected knower or a separate knower?

Women's Ways of Knowing

BY MARY FIELD BELENKY, BLYTHE McVICKER CLINCHY,

NANCY RULE GOLDBERGER, AND JILL MATTUCH TARULE

Listening to reason "I'll not listen to reason," says a woman servant in Elizabeth Gaskell's novel *Cranford*. "Reason always means what someone else has to say" (1894, p. 242). The women in this chapter, like all the women we interviewed, were wary of other people's words and reasons, because people had battered them with words and reasons. Separate knowers remain suspicious; but as they develop techniques for analyzing and evaluating arguments, they become less vulnerable to attack. Because other people's reasons threaten them less, they are more able to listen to them. They can detect specious reasoning and find rational

specious

subjectivist

grounds for disagreement; but, like hidden subjectivists, they find it difficult to give voice to their disagreement, unless they can couch it in the method. Some said they could argue only with strangers; others said they could argue only with their most intimate friends. In both situations, we think, arguing feels relatively safe because it does not threaten the dissolution of relationships. Some women said, for perhaps the same reason, that they could argue only about things that did not matter; argument was possible only if pointless.

dissolution

In general, few of the women we interviewed, even among the ablest separate knowers, found argument—reasoned critical discourse—a congenial form of conversation among friends. The classic dormitory bull session, with students assailing their opponents' logic and attacking their evidence, seems to occur rarely among women, and teachers complain that women students are reluctant to engage in critical debate with peers in class, even when explicitly encouraged to do so. Women find it hard to see doubting as a "game"; they tend to take it personally. Teachers and fathers and boyfriends assure them that arguments are not between *persons* but between *positions*, but the women continue to fear that someone may get hurt.

congenial

A woman may avoid debates with peers, but her professors force her to construct arguments. Sometimes they invite her to argue with them. Faith, in her sophomore year, said, "Last night, the professor gave us his interpretation of Henry James's *Turning* [sic] *of the Screw*, and after it he said, 'All right. This is my interpretation. You should be ripping it apart. You're sitting there. Come on, start ripping at it.'" The interviewer asked, "Did you?" and Faith replied, "Well, I did a little, but basically I agreed with what he was saying." Faith had not yet learned how to play the doubting game. It does not matter whether you agree with an interpretation or not; you must still try to find something wrong with it. In fact, as Elbow (1973) says, the more believable the interpretation is, the harder you must try to doubt it.

Separate knowing is essentially an adversarial form. If played among peers, the game is fair; but in the "games" the women described, as in Faith's case, the woman was nearly always pitted against an authority, usually a professor and usually male. These were unequal contests. The teacher wields very real power over the student, although masked with genial camaraderie; and it is dangerous for the relatively powerless to rip into the interpretations of the powerful.

adversarial

pit

camaraderie

Teachers, being professionals, are much more skilled than students at playing the game. Daphne, in her sophomore year, said, "It seems like he's up on Cloud Nine, and you're way down on the ground floor, and there's just no way you can get on common ground. A lot of the time I don't agree with his interpretation of the poetry, but I can't come up with anything he would consider worthy of notice."

When we asked Faith to tell us about an important learning experience in her life, she recalled a time when she successfully challenged her seventh-grade physics teacher's assertion that Mount Everest was the highest mountain on earth. This seemingly trivial incident stuck in her mind, she thought, because it taught her that "you don't have to accept people's words." But seven years later Faith continued to wrestle with issues concerning acceptance of teachers' words. "Teachers are in such a powerful position at any level. I think it's important for students not to take everything they hear at face value." But she admitted that she often did, especially in an area with which she was not familiar. Just beginning to trust her own reasoning, she was easily intimidated by displays of brilliance. "Whenever I'm around anyone I perceive as

being very, very intelligent, I'm always afraid of saying something stupid. And so I tend to be silent."

This loss of voice is common, especially when separate knowing is the only voice allowed and especially when that voice is just beginning to emerge. Faith had trouble doubting her teacher's polished interpretations, but she had no trouble doubting her own. Lines from Marge Piercy's poem "Unlearning to Not Speak" come to mind.

> Phrases of men who lectured
>   her
> drift and rustle in piles:
> Why don't you speak up? (1973,
>   p. 38)

Faith believed that the only way people could say something important was by weighing its importance in advance. But how could she help but think before she spoke? She knew her thinking was inadequate; teachers told her so in person and in the margins of her papers. Again, from Marge Piercy's poem,

> You have the wrong answer,
> the wrong line, wrong face . . .
>   (p. 38)

Faith had adopted for herself the standards teachers used in evaluating her thoughts. The "phrases of men who lectured her" reverber-

reverberate

ated inside her head whenever she picked up a pen to write, whenever she opened her mouth to speak. In Piercy's words, "she grunts to a halt" (p. 38).

Although the process of learning can be painful, many students become adept in playing the academic game of separate knowing. Daphne is one of them. As a sophomore, Daphne despaired over writing anything that "the guy on Cloud Nine" could tolerate, but a year later she devised a surefire formula for constructing successful papers. "You take a point of view, and then you address the points of view that might most successfully challenge your point of view. You try to disqualify those." Using this procedure, she consistently received A's on her papers and occasionally reached "common ground" with her teachers, at least to the degree that she could engage in friendly arguments with them. This is not the common ground of genuine colleagues. The teacher has not, in the words of radical educator Paulo Freire, become a genuine "partner of the students," a "student among students" (1971, p. 62). The teachers still wield the power: They write the rules of the game and rate the players' performances. But teachers and students can now speak a common language, and they can at least play at being colleagues.

adept

wield

Separate knowers use these new skills to defend themselves against the authorities in their lives. As students, they use their new skills to construct essays that they submit to authorities for evaluation in an attempt to demonstrate that they have mastered the requisite skills and so defend themselves against the teacher's doubts. In their academic lives students sometimes come to feel like pawns in the doubting game. They are the "something" put on trial to see whether or not "it" is wanting. (And, as we shall see, even when they succeed and are found not wanting, something may seem to them to be wanting.)

pawn

In accepting authorities' standards, separate knowers make themselves vulnerable to their criticism. The authorities have a right to find fault with the reasoning of separate knowers; and since there is nothing personal in their criticism, the separate knowers must accept it with equanimity. On the other hand, separate knowers move toward a collegial relationship with the authorities. Armed with new powers of reason, separate knowers can criticize the reasoning of authorities. Laws, not men, govern the world of separate knowers, at least in theory. Authority is nonarbitrary; it rests on reason rather than power or status. Anyone who speaks with the voice

equanimity

collegial

of reason—even a peasant or a student—has a right to be heard; and anyone who does not, whether a king or a professor, has no right to be heard. Experts are only as good as their arguments. . . .

Connected knowing

Connected knowing builds on the subjectivists' conviction that the most trustworthy knowledge comes from personal experience rather than the pronouncements of authorities. Among extreme subjectivists this conviction can lead to the view that they can know only their own truths, access to another person's knowledge being impossible.

Connected knowers develop procedures for gaining access to other people's knowledge. At the heart of these procedures is the capacity for empathy. Since knowledge comes from experience, the only way they can hope to understand another person's ideas is to try to share the experience that has led the person to form the idea. A college senior, discussing *The Divine Comedy* with us, said, "You shouldn't read a book just as something printed and distant from you, but as a real experience of someone who went through some sort of situation. I tend to try and read the mind of the author behind

empathy

it, and ask, 'Why did he write that? What was happening to him when he wrote that?'"

Connected knowers know that they can only approximate other people's experiences and so can gain only limited access to their knowledge. But insofar as possible, they must act as connected rather than separate selves, seeing the other not in their own terms but in the other's terms. Elbow (1973) calls this procedure the "believing game," and he says it is very hard to play. Although it may be difficult for men, many women find it easier to believe than to doubt. An undergraduate we interviewed said, "I'm not superanalytic. It's easy for me to take other people's points of view. It's hard for me to argue, because I feel like I can understand the other person's argument. It's easy for me to see a whole lot of different points of view on things and to understand why people think those things."

And, while women frequently do experience doubting as a game, believing feels real to them, perhaps because it is founded upon genuine care and because it promises to reveal the kind of truth they value—truth that is personal, particular, and grounded in firsthand experience. This comes through most clearly in their accounts of conversations.

ground

Conversing in the connected mode

A first-year student recalled a "wonderful conversation" with a student from Ethiopia who explained why her people had accepted communism and described the effects of the new regime: "It was great to get another view on it from someone who's right there in the situation and who can see it differently from the American view that communism is bad, although I still feel it is."

We have in our records innumerable reports of conversations like this, especially among students in their first year of college. These conversations differed in both form and substance from the competitive bull sessions mentioned earlier. These young women did not engage in metaphysical debate. They did not argue about abstractions or attack or defend positions. No one tried to prove anything or to convert anyone. The Ethiopian articulated her reality, and the American tried to understand it. They did not discuss communism in general, impersonal terms but in terms of its origins and consequences among a particular group of real people.

The differences between the women's conversation and the male bull session were strikingly reminiscent of the differences Janet Lever (1976) noted between the play of fifth-grade girls and boys: intimate rather than impersonal, relatively informal and unstructured rather than bound by more or less explicit formal rules. Women have been practicing this kind of conversation since childhood.

An alumna recalled spending much of her first year "just sitting around and talking." Having lived in the same small town for eighteen years, she was dazzled by meeting "all kinds of people from all kinds of walks of life from all across the country and the world who have all kinds of different opinions and views of life. That made me really start listening to people and comparing and contrasting views." She began to engage in less facile and more energetic forms of listening, interviewing her new acquaintances. And she discovered that "if you listen to people, you can understand why they feel the way they do. There are reasons. They're not just being irrational."

The reasons mentioned here have to do not with propositional logic but with experience. "Why do you think that?" they ask, meaning not "What were the steps in your reasoning?" but "What circumstances led you to that perception?" This is not like an oral examination in which the respondent must prove that she knows

metaphysical

propositional

what she is supposed to know. It is not like a courtroom interrogation in which the attorney fires off a series of highly specific questions and allows only brief responses so as to elicit only the evidence he or she wants. It is more like a clinical interview. By inviting the respondent to tell her story, without interruption, the questioner allows the respondent to control and develop her own response.

These conversations occur with special frequency whenever women encounter people who hold and practice beliefs that seem exotic, intriguing, bizarre, alien, even frightening. Naomi, for example, was initially shattered when, late in her first year at college, a woman who had become a close friend revealed that she had discovered she was a lesbian. The friend talked, and Naomi listened until she understood.

experiential   If one can discover the experiential logic behind these ideas, the ideas become less strange and the owners of the ideas cease to be strangers. The world becomes warmer and more orderly. Some-

times, but not always, a woman adopts another person's ideas as her own. Through empathy she expands her experiential base; she acquires vicarious (secondhand, firsthand) experience and so expands her knowledge. "What I know," one freshman told us, "is very limited. I've grown up one way, and many people have grown up different ways; and if I don't know what they have to offer, I don't have those experiences."

Connected knowers begin with an interest in the facts of other people's lives, but they gradually shift the focus to other people's ways of thinking. As in all procedural knowing, it is the form rather than the content of knowing that is central. Separate knowers learn through explicit formal instruction how to adopt a different lens— how, for example, to think like a sociologist. Connected knowers learn through empathy. Both learn to get out from behind their own eyes and use a different lens, in one case the lens of a discipline, in the other the lens of another person.

COMPREHENSION CHECK

Write brief answers to the following questions.

1. What is the topic of this selection? In general, what is being said about the topic?

2. How is information in the excerpt organized?

3. How do separate knowers defend themselves against verbal attack?

4. a. What do the authors mean by the "doubting game"?

    b. Why is this term used to describe the academic game of separate knowing?

    c. In general, how do women view this activity?

    d. What makes the "doubting game" unfair for college students with regard to their professors?

5. How do you define connected knowing? What role does empathy play in connected knowing? Why does Elbow describe connected knowing as the "believing game"?

6. How do the authors compare men's and women's conversations?

7. Consider the following statement: "The classroom discussion was awful. The people didn't know how to talk about anything. They didn't know how to share ideas. It was always an argument; it wasn't an idea to be developed or explored." What kind of knowing would you guess the speaker prefers? Why?

What Do You Think?

✪ DISCUSSION QUESTIONS

Prepare for class discussion by jotting down brief answers to the following questions.

1. Are you a person who enjoys arguing or debating? Explain your answer. Under what circumstances do you like to have your ideas challenged? Do you enjoy "arguing" with your friends, your boss, your coworkers, or your instructors?

2. Reread the poem "Perception" in the Introductory Chapter Activity and the "Message from the Dean." Compare the ideas presented in both selections. What ideas do they have in common? What ideas are different?

3. Do you think that women tend to believe what others say and have difficulty being analytical? What are the implications of this for students taking a course in critical thinking? In what way might such a course be more difficult for women? What are discussions like in this and other classes you are taking? Do they support the views of Belenky et al.?

4. What values were stressed in your family? Can you recall a time when you realized that some of your values were different from those of a friend, parent, or instructor? Were any of these differences culturally based? Were you able to discuss these differences? Did these differences lead to conflict?

WRITING ASSIGNMENTS

Select one of the following topics and in a few paragraphs develop a thoughtful written response.

1. Earlier in Chapter 4 we said that while many of us may agree that we want "to live the good life," we might disagree on what we mean by that expression. What do *you* mean by "the good life"?

2. Define a common value such as "freedom of expression," "equal opportunity," "faith," or "human rights."

3. Write about a time when you were extremely homesick or when you experienced culture shock. Explain how these experiences are related to "pre-cognitive commitment."

4. Summarize the differences between Anglo and Hispanic soaps. How do these differences reflect differences in values or a difference in emphasis on particular values in the two cultures?

5. Respond to one of the claims Belenky et al. make about separate and connected knowing. First, explain how the statement is "believable." Then explain why you "doubt" the information.

Exploring Writers' Perspectives

After reading Chapter 5 you should be able to:

- identify arguments found in conversations and expository text
- recognize prescriptive and descriptive arguments
- understand the differences between inductive and deductive reasoning
- define and identify counterarguments
- develop a well-structured argument
- identify several methods for resolving conflicts

CHAPTER OUTLINE AND CHECKLIST

You may use the following checklist in planning your study of arguments. Activities marked with a ✪ are to be completed in class. Some preclass preparation may be required.

CONTEXT FOR LEARNING

✪ _____ **INTRODUCTORY CHAPTER ACTIVITY**

_____ The Prevalence and Packaging of Arguments

_____ Deductive Versus Inductive Reasoning

_____ **GUIDED READING ACTIVITY: RECOGNIZING WRITERS' PERSPECTIVES**

_____ **"The Language of Foreign Trade"** by Leonard A. Lauder

_____ Descriptive Versus Prescriptive Arguments

_____ Counterarguments

APPLICATION: FINDING ARGUMENTS

_____ **APPLICATION ONE**

_____ **"Let TV Cameras Show Executions"** from *USA Today*

_____ **COMPREHENSION CHECK**

_____ **APPLICATION TWO**

_____ **"Don't Let TV Cameras Exploit Executions"** by Sherry Roberts

_____ **COMPREHENSION CHECK**

_____ **APPLICATION THREE**

_____ **"What? Send Women to War?"** from *The New York Times*

_____ **COMPREHENSION CHECK**

_____ **APPLICATION FOUR**

_____ **"Participation and Leadership in Small Groups"** by Cheryl Hamilton and Cordell Parker

_____ **COMPREHENSION CHECK**

_____   What Do You Think?

✪ _____   **DISCUSSION QUESTIONS**

_____   **WRITING ASSIGNMENTS**

_____   Extended Practice

_____   **"Reality Bites for the Baboos"** by Patricia Plaster

_____   **"A Game of Life"** by Lavinia Edmunds

✪ INTRODUCTORY CHAPTER ACTIVITY

Each of the following examples makes an assertion or claim about the way the world, or something in it, is or ought to be. Each assertion is accompanied by a supporting reason. The reason may provide strong evidence for the assertion, or it may seem irrelevant. Your task is to find the assertion and reason(s) given in each of the examples. Ask yourself the following: "What does the speaker want me to believe? What evidence does the speaker offer as proof?" Share your answers in groups of two or three. The first one has been done for you to serve as a model.

Example 1

Additive-free "Perfect Finish" Makeup . . .
For the Glow of Everlasting Romance!

Assertion: *People should buy "Perfect Finish" makeup.*

Reason: *It offers the glow of everlasting romance.*

Example 2

If $6 + 3 = 9$ and $4 + 5 = 9$,
then $6 + 3 = 4 + 5$.

Assertion: _____

Reason: _____

Example 3

Luz: This is ridiculous. I need to take Math for Business Majors in order to graduate and it's only being offered on Tuesdays and Thursdays from 3:30 to 4:45 p.m.

Annette: Oh, I know what you mean. That happened to me last semester. I had to beg and plead with my day-care center to keep Scott until 5:15 p.m. I couldn't get there before then and I barely made it by that time. They made me feel so guilty.

Luz: Yeah, well, that's my problem this semester. Somebody has got to do something. If the state wants me to support myself, then they better come up with ways for me to have my kids taken care of while I'm in school.

Assertion: _____

Reason: _____

Example 4

Students who do well on their SAT or ACT tests will earn high grades in college.
Biff did well on his SAT tests.
Therefore, Biff will earn high grades in college.

Assertion: _____

Reason: _____

Example 5

Demographers predict by the year 2000 our nation's workforce will undergo dramatic changes. According to a study completed by the Hudson Institute for the United States Labor Department, 85 percent of the 25 million workers expected to join the labor force in the next few years will be women, minorities, and immigrants.

Assertion: _____

Reason: _____

The Prevalence and Packaging of Arguments

If someone starts talking about an "argument," what's the first thing that comes to mind? A disagreement or fight? That's one definition of *argument*. Are you familiar with any others? *Webster's New World Dictionary* gives the following definitions:

> **argument** *n* **1** a reason or reasons offered for or against something **2** the offering of such reasons; reasoning **3** discussion in which there is disagreement; dispute; debate **4** a short statement of subject matter; summary

We are concerned with definitions 1 and 2. Students of philosophy refer to reasons as premises and to the position(s) being argued as a conclusion(s). In English composition courses students write essays and are taught to develop a thesis statement (conclusion) with supporting details (reasons). Philosophy students talk about conclusions and premises; English composition students talk about thesis statements and supporting details. Regardless of the terms used the concepts are the same; however, be careful not to confuse the conclusion of a paper with the conclusion to an argument. The first usage refers to the ending of a paper; the second to the assertion in an argument. In the Introductory Chapter Activity you found the arguments in the examples given. Take a moment to check your answers and see if they fit our definition of an argument: a reason or reasons offered for or against something.

From one perspective you could make the case (that is, argue) that every declarative statement has the potential of becoming an argument — from the casual remark "It's a nice day" to the doomsday prediction "The world will destroy itself in the twenty-first century." By themselves, these statements make an assertion about the way things are, but they don't offer any evidence to support their claims. Someone else could easily assert the opposite: "It most certainly is *not* a nice day" or "The world will *not* destroy itself in the twenty-first century." In order to decide with whom you agree, you would need to ask some questions: What evidence supports the existence or nonexistence of "a nice day"? What evidence indicates that the world will or will not destroy itself?

Once evidence is supplied — be it relevant, irrelevant, accurate, or absurd — you have the necessary components of an argument: a conclusion and premises (reasons) that support it.

As our Introductory Chapter Activity demonstrates, arguments come in all kinds of formats: advertisements, conversations with friends and parents, mathematical laws, formal reports. We use arguments to help us explain, prove, persuade, or predict different conclusions.

Of course, these categories sometimes overlap. For example, we often explain in order to persuade: "We can't have the test on Thursday because our research paper is due that day and we won't have time to study." And in some sense all arguments are persuasive because they attempt to influence someone to accept or agree with the conclusion. Be aware of the arguments that surround you in everyday conversations, on television and radio shows, and in the books, magazines, and newspapers you read. Realizing that someone is presenting you with "an argument" that is not necessarily factual allows you to think more critically about what is being said.

Deductive Versus Inductive Reasoning

Consider the following arguments:

Argument 1

Premise 1: All students experience stress in their lives.

Premise 2: Reuben is a student.

Conclusion: Therefore, Reuben experiences stress in his life.

Argument 2

Premise 1: Stress can cause illness.

Premise 2: Reuben experiences stress in his life.

Premise 3: Reuben is ill.

Conclusion: Therefore, stress may be the cause of Reuben's illness.

What's different about the conclusions in Arguments 1 and 2? Argument 1 appears to state an indisputable truth: Reuben experiences stress in his life. But how do we know this is true? We examine the premises or reasons given. If they are true, then the conclusion must also be true. Thus, if all students experience stress in their lives and Reuben is a student, then we can be certain that Reuben experiences stress in his life.

In order to decide whether we should accept the conclusion, we need to consider the validity or truth of the supporting pieces of evidence (that is, the reasons or premises). The conclusion will follow logically from facts that are known to be true, given certain assumptions (see Chapter 3). In other words, if the reasons are true, then the conclusion must also be true. This is an example of *deductive reasoning*. Deductive reasoning uses stated premises to arrive at conclusions that can logically be inferred from them.

Now look at the conclusion in Argument 2: that stress may be the cause of Reuben's illness. It is not stated with absolute certainty; rather, it only suggests that stress *may* be the cause. The link between reasons and conclusion is not unequivocally (without a doubt) determined. There might be other reasons for Reuben's illness.

So how do we determine the truthfulness of this conclusion? We must consider alternative explanations. Our reasoning may lead us to agree that stress is the *most likely* cause of his illness, or it may lead us to reject this conclusion in favor of some other explanation. This is an example of *inductive reasoning*. Inductive reasoning uses premises that strongly suggest that the conclusion is true. In inductive reasoning the conclusion goes beyond the limits of the reasons presented. In other words, the premises don't necessarily guarantee the conclusion, but they should point strongly in that direction.

Our task in evaluating the argument rests in being able to know that the reasons are true and to accept with some confidence that the reasons support the conclusion. In Reuben's case, we would want more evidence before accepting the conclusion. Has Reuben been exposed to any viruses lately? Did he stay out all night in the rain?

The box on page 155 presents a quick overview of the kinds of reasoning we have been discussing. Below are three more arguments. Which arguments are examples of deductive reasoning or inductive reasoning? How do you know?

Example 1

Miaki always tells the truth.

Miaki told me the party starts at 10 p.m.

The party starts at 10 p.m.

Example 2

I sleep better if I exercise before I go to bed.

Eduardo told me he sleeps better on the days he exercises.

Wanda said she sleeps better when she exercises.

Therefore, exercise helps people sleep better.

Example 3

Anyone who gets the right answers to Examples 1 and 2 understands the difference between inductive and deductive reasoning.

I got the right answers to Examples 1 and 2.

I understand the difference between inductive and deductive reasoning.

If you said that Examples 1 and 3 are examples of deductive reasoning and Example 2 indicates inductive reasoning, you are correct. In Examples 1 and 3 the conclusion follows logically from the premises. The form or structure of the argument conforms to the rules of formal logic, and as long as the premises are true, the conclusion is also true. Look at the premises in Examples 1 and 3. Do you think they are true? Explain your thinking. Example 2 is an example of inductive reasoning. Even if the premises are true, the conclusion is not absolutely certain. The premises may provide strong support for the conclusion, but the conclusion is broader than the premises. Look at the premises in Example 2. Do you think they are true? Do they provide strong support for the conclusion? Explain your thinking.

Two Types of Reasoning

Argument Structure:

conclusion/assertion supported by premises/reasons

Deductive Reasoning:

1. If the premises are true, then the conclusion must also be true. The conclusion is certain.

2. The validity of the argument is based on:
   a. the truth of the premises
   b. adherence to rules of formal logic that require that the conclusion follow from the premises

Inductive Reasoning:

1. True premises do not guarantee that the conclusion is true, but they should provide support. The conclusion is not certain.

2. The validity of the argument is based on:
   a. the truth of the premises
   b. evidence that *strongly* supports the conclusion

Another way of distinguishing between deductive and inductive reasoning is to consider the order in which observations and hypotheses are made. An inductive thinker makes several observations in order to develop a hypothesis or draw a conclusion. For example, the speaker in Example 2 has collected data from two of her friends. Based on their comments and her own experience, she comes to the conclusion that exercise helps all people sleep. Notice that the conclusion goes beyond the finite number of cases cited. The speaker hypothesizes that what is true for three is true for all. If she meets Cheryl, who tells her that exercising keeps her awake at night, her conclusion will be wrong. In inductive reasoning your conclusion can be proven wrong, but it can't be proven absolutely right!

A deductive thinker begins with a hypothesis that is known or believed to be true and then makes observations to confirm that he or she is correct. In Example 1 the speaker begins with a hypothesis that he believes is correct — Miaki always tells the truth. He can then conclude that if Miaki says something new, that also will be true. The conclusion will follow from the beginning statement.

The study of deductive reasoning is the focus of formal logic, while inductive reasoning is the focus of informal logic. Deductive arguments can take several different forms, and certain rules are used to evaluate their validity. Courses in formal logic deal with these in depth, and students who are interested in learning more about deductive reasoning should consult J. Cederblom and D. W. Paulson, *Critical Reasoning* (Belmont, CA: Wadsworth, 1982), or G. M. Nosich, *Reasons and Arguments* (Wadsworth, 1982).

In this text we are more concerned with inductive reasoning. Consider all the controversial issues associated with such social topics as crime prevention, medical care, civil rights, sports, and politics. The variables affecting any one of these issues are so numerous and complex that a logically guaranteed conclusion or proof is an impossibility. All we can hope for is a well-reasoned argument where the evidence strongly suggests that the conclusion is true. In order to discuss and argue these issues, we need to develop our inductive reasoning skills.

GUIDED READING ACTIVITY *Recognizing writers' perspectives*

Many of the questions you are asked to answer in various classes require you to give your view and support it with reasons or to state the views of others and give their reasons. Your view backed by reasons clearly conforms to our definition of an argument. Thus, you have already had experience in uncovering arguments. We now want to test your skill on longer texts. For this activity, do the following:

1. Read the following newspaper editorial to determine the writer's conclusion. The conclusion may be stated explicitly in the text, or it may be stated implicitly (that is, not stated directly) so the reader must infer it from the information given. Inferring is a pro-

cess of taking what information has been given and coming to a conclusion. The reader must "read between the lines" in order to find the writer's conclusion.

2. On a separate piece of paper, write the author's conclusion. Another way to state this is to find the author's *thesis*. (*Hint*: If you are having trouble finding the conclusion, ask yourself what topic is being discussed and then what is being said about that topic.)

3. List all the reasons you can find to support the writer's position. Focus on finding the writer's complete argument, not on whether you agree with the writer's position.

4. Look at the results produced by your authors, as well as some comments, when they completed this activity.

(*Note*: This article was written prior to the fairly recent changes in the political map and so contains names that are slightly out of date, such as "West Germany" and "the Soviet Union.")

The Language of Foreign Trade

BY LEONARD A. LAUDER

The debate rages over United States foreign-trade difficulties. But nobody is talking about the one issue that is more disturbing and far more revealing about the underlying problem than our overvalued dollar, closed foreign markets and the other obvious causes of our stunning trade deficit.

Why has no one raised the fact that so many Americans engaged in foreign trade can speak no language but their own? It's getting late in the day to realize that the language of international trade is not English. The language of international trade is the language of the customer.

In part, Japan, West Germany and other successful exporting nations have penetrated foreign markets because they have tried to understand the cultural peculiarities of those markets. Their executives take the trouble to learn the language of the country with which they wish to trade as the first step in gauging demand.

It is self-evident that you can't sell unless there is a demand for the product. It is also self-evident that you can't begin to understand what a people demand if you can't talk to them on their own terms. Their own terms, of course, means their own language.

It is hard to find figures on how many American business executives overseas speak the native tongue; it is certain, however, that virtually all foreign business executives in the United States speak English. S. I. Hayakawa, a former U.S. Senator, estimated a few years ago that there were 10,000 Japanese in business here, all of whom spoke English, compared with 1,000 Americans in business in Japan, of whom perhaps a handful spoke Japanese. That no hard data exist is not surprising. There's not enough interest to gather it.

parochial

The situation today is not better and is probably worse than it was when Mr. Hayakawa made his estimate. As far as business is concerned, our national parochialism is growing worse. A study commissioned by the National Council on Foreign Language and International Studies questioned 1,690 young men and women in 564 business schools working toward their doctoral degrees in business in the spring of 1984.

The study found only 17 percent of these students were taking one or more courses in international affairs and foreign languages. In 1976, that figure was 25 percent. Those surveyed are the people who will one day be teaching in business schools training our future business executives. In an area crucial to the health of business and the United States economy, these future teachers are inadequate.

Meanwhile, we continue to demand that the rest of the world speak English, play by our rules, buy more of our goods. Not in our country, in theirs. From a deficit-inflated dollar to the tongue-tied American executive, our foreign-trade problems are largely a self-inflicted wound.

Next May, the first class will graduate from the Joseph H. Lauder Institute of Management and International Studies at the University of Pennsylvania with an M.B.A. from the Wharton School and an M.A. in international affairs from the School of Arts and Sciences. There will be 51 of these dual-degree-holders, all with a foreign-language proficiency. That same spring, 50,000 more M.B.S. candidates will graduate from the other 563 business schools. In just 13 of those schools are courses in foreign languages and international affairs required for graduation.

American business and business education are not the only guilty parties. The State Department does not require a foreign language to enter the Foreign Service. There are more teachers of English in the Soviet Union than there are students of Russian in the United States. Aside from the coverage given by a few national newspapers, the media's coverage of world affairs is scanty to the point of ridicule. A national survey of high-school seniors to assess their knowledge of international affairs showed recently that 40 percent thought that Israel was an Arab nation.

After World War II, as other nations were rebuilding, the United States was a world player shaping its own terms. The U.S. still has the world's mightiest economy, but it is now one of several mighty economies. We are watching our strength and influence erode before our eyes. Paradoxically, this is happening not from weakness but from arrogance.

Leonard A. Lauder is president of Estee Lauder, Inc., a cosmetics company.

To understand Lauder's arguments, your authors followed a certain process. First, we asked a basic question: What is Lauder's position? That is, what does he want us to believe? Several answers come immediately to mind:

1. He thinks that not enough Americans speak foreign languages.

2. He thinks that American trade and the U.S. economy are suffering because so few Americans speak foreign languages.

3. He believes Americans don't know enough about foreign affairs.

Then, we asked ourselves this question: Are there three different position statements, or can these ideas be combined into one position statement? We came up with one statement, and then went back through the article to look for reasons that might support this position.

Tentative conclusion (thesis) statement

U.S. trade and the U.S. economy are suffering because too few Americans speak foreign languages or know anything about foreign affairs.

Possible reasons

1. Executives in other countries (Japan and Germany) have learned foreign languages, which has helped them better understand the market.

2. If we don't know the language, we will have trouble knowing what the demand for our goods is.

3. Statistics show that few American business graduates are required to know foreign languages.

4. In American business schools, too few students take courses in international affairs.

5. Americans "demand that the rest of the world speak English, play by our rules, and buy more of our goods."

6. The State Department "does not require a foreign language to enter the Foreign Service."

7. Media coverage of world news is very poor.

Next, we asked this question: Are the statements listed here reasons, and do they support the conclusion? In order to answer this question, we had to decide whether each of the seven reasons explained why Lauder believes in his conclusion. If the answer was yes, then it was a legitimate reason. And if all the reasons fit into this category, then we could accept our tentative conclusion. But if the reason did not answer the question "Why?" then we had to consider whether we had the writer's complete thesis or conclusion and whether our statement was a reason. It could have been:

1. background information that told us more about the topic or issue

2. an example or additional information that supported one of the other reasons

3. a piece of information that really belonged to another argument that was not the writer's major focus

Remember that the object is to find reasons that the writer believes support his or her thesis, not whether we agree with them.

Once you have agreed on the substance of Lauder's argument, you can decide whether you agree with it. On what do you base *your* conclusion? (Here it is again, that same old format: statement supported by evidence!)

In Chapter 4, we talked about people's values. Can you make any guesses about Lauder's values? For example, what stand might he take on the English-only movement, which seeks to make English the official language of the United States? How would you expect him to view foreign exchange programs for American students?

Descriptive Versus Prescriptive Arguments

Should women be allowed in combat units? Should boxing be outlawed? Is capital punishment a deterrent to crime? Does watching violence on television make young children more aggressive? Answers to these questions and the reasons provided to support these conclusions constitute two kinds of arguments. One is an argument over how the world *should* or *ought to be*; the other is an argument over how the world *is, was,* or *will be*. The difference between the two kinds of arguments is the difference between how you see the world versus how you think the world ought to be.

Descriptive arguments

Descriptive arguments make claims about how the world is. They describe. For example, they make claims about whether capital punishment is a deterrent to crime, not whether it should be. They decide whether violence on television causes aggression in children, not whether it should. In his article Lauder argues that American trade and the U.S. economy are suffering because not enough Americans speak foreign languages or know enough about foreign affairs. Does this statement reflect how Lauder interprets or "sees" the world, or is he making a statement about how he feels the world ought to be? Because his argument makes a claim about the way things are, it is a descriptive argument, although clearly he hopes that the situation will change.

Some students find it difficult to understand how descriptive arguments can be controversial: "How can people argue over the way things are? They are the way they are." The problem with this line of reasoning is its assumption that reality is a constant, or that people will look at the same event, situation, or facts and interpret them the same way. This is not always the case. For example, some children may consider their parents' requests that they pay rent during the summer months as insensitive and mercenary, while parents may see their actions as a legitimate attempt to develop responsibility and independence in their children.

In Chapter 4, we discussed some of the factors that contribute to the development of individual worldviews. Imagine the possibilities for disagreement when people interpret the definitions, causes, and solutions to social problems! Each one of us looks out at the world through our own "reality filter." That filter is an intertwining of our thoughts, culture, values, knowledge, and experiences. Remember our example in Chapter 4 of Leelay and her parents' interest in choosing a husband for her. Being aware of our own filter and those of others is a valuable critical thinking skill. It is an essential point in being able to accept and not condemn another's viewpoint. Because the filter remains invisible to us most of the time, we accept its interpretations as though they were true. This is an idea we do not want to overlook.

Prescriptive arguments

Prescriptive arguments speak more directly to our personal filters and make claims based on how we think the world ought to be or what people should or should not do. They offer a prescription, like the doctor's remedy for good health, on how to make things better. Prescriptive arguments explain why women ought or ought not to take part in combat or why boxing should be outlawed.

Counterarguments

A commonly used strategy in trying to convince someone of our viewpoint is to explain why opposing views are invalid. We produce reasons that *counterargue* our opponent's reasons, that attack the validity of our opponent's evidence by pointing out false assumptions or errors in his or her reasoning. What's interesting is that we offer counterarguments all the time, often quite unconsciously, when we talk to each other.

See if you can find the counterargument in the following conversation:

> *Jenna:* All I'm saying is that Spike Lee did not give most of the Black characters in *Do the Right Thing* as much depth as he gave Al, the pizzeria owner. We really get to know Al, but we don't really know Radio Raheem. Therefore, the focus of the film gets misplaced on the trashing of the pizzeria, not on the

death of Radio Raheem. People keep forgetting that the violent death of Radio Raheem started the craziness at the pizzeria, not Mookie throwing the trash can into the window. Spike just got caught up in the glamour of the urban scene, and that hurt his film from an artistic point of view. I have some doubts about how responsible Spike has been; I think there will be more tensions between the races because of the way he handled the characters' frustrations.

Shane: I disagree with you. This is one movie; look at all the issues the critics are asking him to address. I think it's a great work of art. And let me tell you, it's a good thing we don't know Radio Raheem that well. Suppose Radio Raheem had been our hero and we had seen him killed? Don't you think *that* would have led to some real violence in the streets? The fact that Spike didn't let us know him in depth shows real artistic responsibility. The film makes people talk, not act. You all should give the man a break.

Jenna's conclusion: _____

_____

Reasons: _____

_____

_____

Shane's counterargument: _____

_____

Jenna's position is that Spike Lee has not acted very responsibly. She argues that because viewers do not get to know Radio Raheem very well, the film's focus shifts to the destruction of the pizzeria. She feels that this may lead to greater racial tension. Shane *counterargues*. He believes that by *not* letting the audience get to know Radio Raheem, they react to the movie with anger and talk but not action. If Radio Raheem had been the hero of the film, then viewers' reactions might have been different.

Writers often try to anticipate the counterarguments of their opponents and refute them within the context of their own writing. They imagine that you, their readers, are "the opponents" in an unspoken debate. In this way they can anticipate your opposition, point out the "errors" in your reasoning, and increase their chances of persuading you to accept their views. They play a version of the "doubting game" mentioned by Belenky et al. in Chapter 4.

Application: Finding Arguments

APPLICATION ONE

The first step in analyzing an argument is finding it. This takes practice. In this Application section we offer you several additional opportunities by including editorials on controversial subjects. There is also an Extended Practice section at the end of the chapter. The class may decide to choose other editorials. All newspapers and many popular magazines contain editorial columns.

For Application One preview the editorial by reading the headline, and then read to find the author's argument. The Argument Outline on page 167 provides you with a format for identifying an author's argument. As you read the article ask yourself "What role does this statement play?"

Is it there to support the author's conclusion (that is, reason)?

Does it explain, elaborate, or give examples to support a reason (that is, supporting evidence)?

Is this statement a claim that is the focus of the article and for which reasons are provided (that is, conclusion)?

As you determine the role of the different statements fill in the appropriate spaces in the Argument Outline. You may find a reason before you find the conclusion, and not all statements are conclusions, reasons, or supporting evidence. Authors provide readers with background information they think is necessary to understand their position. They find creative ways to introduce their issues. They may also repeat their conclusions for emphasis or provide solutions for problems. They may even get sidetracked and add irrelevant material. Once you have found the argument, determine what kind is being presented. Is this a descriptive argument where the author attempts to persuade you about how the world is, was, or will be? Is it a prescriptive argument that seeks to convince you or prescribe to you how the world ought to be? You may also want to use the chart as you work through the Comprehension Check questions.

Let TV Cameras Show Executions

FROM *USA TODAY*

If a San Francisco TV station gets its way, viewers across the USA could watch executions from the comfort of their own living rooms.

KQED, a public television station, is suing California officials to get cameras a view of the gas chamber. If the suit succeeds, the spectacle will be shared with television audiences across the nation.

In Virginia, meanwhile, a condemned killer named Joseph Savino recently asked to have his execution televised. His case is under appeal.

Televised executions surely could be gruesome.

The May execution in Florida of Jesse Tafero took four minutes. Witnesses said Tafero's eyebrows were singed and sparks flew from the metal band around his head.

In California's gas chamber, condemned killers have torn loose their straps in futile attempts to escape the approaching gas.

futile

In Texas, the 1988 execution of Raymond Landry by lethal injection took 24 minutes because fluid leaked.

That violence disgusts many, including 200 letter writers to KQED and the columnist writing across this page. But it is not sufficient reason to keep the public in the dark.

Television offers a 20th century means of informing a 20th century debate about life and death.

Today, witnesses routinely attend executions so the public will be represented. Television cameras let all who wish be the witnesses.

Journalists routinely attend executions so the public can be told what happened. A television camera is just another way of telling the story.

Cameras commonly peer into nearly every aspect of the justice system. Cameras in the death chamber would provide a view of that system's ultimate act.

There isn't even much reason to fear an orgy of sensationalized execution on TV.

KQED says it will not broadcast an execution live. It will present it as part of a broader, late-night program on the death penalty.

Others will take different approaches, but the evidence suggests sensationalism will be scarce. Three years ago, when a Pennsylvania state treasurer shot himself to death on camera, no major network, and few local stations, aired the portions of the tape showing the actual shooting.

Nor is one's opinion of capital punishment an issue. People on both sides want TV.

Death penalty advocates say TV can help make the death penalty a deterrent to violent crime. Savino agrees. That's why he wants his execution televised.

Death penalty opponents hope the spectacle will so disgust the public that it will turn against capital punishment.

Television may at last give the nation a means of finding out who is right.

Today, more than 2,300 people await their fate on death rows in 36 states. Most will die late at night, out of sight.

Many would like to keep it that way.

But those who want to see the results of society's decision to kill its criminals should have that right, no matter how gruesome the spectacle.

COMPREHENSION CHECK

Write brief answers to the following questions.

1. What topic is being discussed? What is being said about the topic?

2. What background information on the topic does the author provide?

3. What kind of evidence does the author present to support the view that "televised executions surely could be gruesome"?

4. Which reasons are elaborated on by the author? Be specific and explain what information is provided to support the reasons. Which reasons are presented without further follow-up? How does this strengthen or weaken the author's argument?

Argument Outline

Conclusion: _____

Reason 1: _____

_____

Supporting evidence: _____

_____

Reason 2: _____

_____

Supporting evidence: _____

_____

Reason 3: _____

_____

Supporting evidence: _____

_____

Reason 4: _____

_____

Supporting evidence: _____

_____

Kind of argument: _____

APPLICATION TWO

Again, preview the editorial by reading the headline, and then read to find the author's argument. Is it descriptive or prescriptive? For this reading, again, complete an Argument Outline chart (see page 167), and then answer the Comprehension Check questions.

Don't Let TV Cameras Exploit Executions

BY SHERRY ROBERTS

GREENSBORO, N.C.— Every Sunday, during my *formative* years, there were gladiator movies on television after church. While my mother fried chicken in the kitchen, I watched enough sword-fighting, lion-roaring and Christian-crunching to put anyone off her feed.

It was as if the gladiator movies were part of the Sunday service: Here were those poor Christians getting it again, suffering, dying for their faith. But at age 9, the *subliminal* sermons passed me over. I dug the action. The Christians' struggle to escape death by *panthera leo's* incisors — now, that was entertainment.

So, it is not easy for me to say we shouldn't televise the executions of death-row inmates. I have all this bloodthirsty history. I'm also a journalist.

For almost half my life, I've done my bit for Edward R. Murrow, Lois Lane and Woodward and Bernstein. I don't sign petitions. I'm pleasant when sources slam the door in my face. And, under extreme *coercion* from the city desk, I've chased ambulances, tornadoes and fire trucks.

The First Amendment is under my skin.

But I also believe in something pondered more often in journalism school classrooms than newsrooms: responsible journalism. Can the public's right to know be satisfied without further contributing to the desensitizing of our culture? Are the news media responsible for the way they present the news as well as for its accuracy? In other circumstances, can a reporter justify wrecking an innocent life for the sake of a story?

How responsible is a lawsuit filed by a San Francisco public television station making a public affairs program on capital punishment (a hot issue in this year's California gubernatorial race), seeking to bring cameras to an execution?

formative

subliminal

coercion

The station admits, if it wins the case, it's opening a can of potential exploitation. Doesn't our society have enough worms?

Is this another case of individuals fighting for their rights just for the sake of fighting, then absolving themselves of the responsibilities that inherently come with rights?

There are 2,300 people on U.S. death rows, and 270 more are added every year. If we permit televising executions, we could program almost nightly entertainment.

Maybe television producers could schedule the daily "frying" between the lottery and home videos of children tearing the wings off butterflies. Considering man's historic fascination with the spectacle of public execution, the ratings would soar.

The insensitivity and cruelty of humans can never be underestimated. When murderer Ted Bundy was electrocuted, Floridians cheered and turned off their electrical appliances to boost the charge.

Televised executions today or gladiator sports in ancient Rome: It is still "death for public edification." Education? That's entertainment, folks.

COMPREHENSION CHECK

Write brief answers to the following questions.

1. What topic is being discussed? What is being said about the topic?

2. What is Roberts trying to convey in the first four paragraphs of the article?

3. How would Roberts define "responsible journalism"?

4. Which reasons are elaborated on by Roberts? Be specific and explain what information is provided to support the reasons. Which reasons are presented without further follow-up? How does this strengthen or weaken Roberts's argument?

APPLICATION THREE

The editorial "What? Send Women to War?" includes several counter-arguments. Read the editorial to see how they are used to support the author's position. Then complete an Argument Outline chart (see page 167) and use it to help you answer the Comprehension Check questions.

What? Send Women to War?

FROM *THE NEW YORK TIMES*

Capt. Linda Bray led an attack in the Panama invasion, apparently the first time that a woman has commanded American forces in battle. But she was acting as a Military Police officer; women are still barred from combat roles in the armed forces. Since women like Captain Bray already serve with distinction in danger zones, isn't it time to allow them into combat too? A careful experiment could clarify a difficult issue.

Very few regular armies have allowed women to serve in combat, so there's little hard evidence to go on. The issue reaches deep into the relations between the sexes and is fraught with politics and prejudice. The debate goes like this:

The purpose of an army is to win wars, not promote equality. History shows that human factors like group cohesion, far more than weapons, determine victory. Women would erode group cohesion because they distract men, who by instinct or culture would seek to protect them, and because they cannot enter into the male bonding process by which the esprit of combat units is built up.

Before President Truman's order of 1948, group cohesion was also used as an argument against integrating black soldiers into white units. Once integration was imposed, the argument was found to be meritless.

Women lack the physical and psychological stamina to endure the stress of prolonged combat. Few women can easily carry the 100 pounds of equipment that infantry soldiers now take into combat.

Modern combat depends far less on brute strength and more on skills like the ability to operate complex weapons. A certain degree of strength is necessary, but there's no more reason to exclude women from combat on this ground than from police and fire departments. Why not let both sexes be judged by the same objective standards?

fraught

cohesion

esprit

brute

Women who are taken prisoner are likely to be abused and raped.

Men are abused and raped too.

To date, the arguments against allowing women in combat have prevailed. Almost all the world's regular combat troops are exclusively male. Canada recently opened combat roles to women, but only one woman has qualified. In Israel in 1948, women fought in the Haganah units but they were later prohibited from combat service.

The United States, to fill the ranks of the all-volunteer army, now has a force that is 11 percent female, but women are barred from combat roles. Women officers in particular are keen to lift the ban because it impairs their chances of promotion. But most older

impair

officers and those experienced in combat probably oppose the idea of letting women into combat. So far, Congress does too.

Military institutions differ designedly from civilian ones. The past discrimination against black soldiers was based on nothing more than white prejudice. The case against putting women in combat has some objective validity. That's all the more reason to put the question to an honest test, as in the four-year trial program suggested by Representative Pat Schroeder of Colorado.

An army should reflect the values of its society as much as possible, and when it comes to the role of women in this society, those values are changing by the day.

designedly

objective

COMPREHENSION CHECK

Write brief answers to the following questions.

1. What topic is the author discussing? What point does the author make regarding the topic?

2. Which of the reasons presented are counterarguments?

3. How would you interpret "objective validity" in the sentence "The case against putting women in combat has some objective validity."

4. What values do you think the author is referring to in the last paragraph?

APPLICATION FOUR

So far in this chapter we have tackled issues related to the U.S. foreign trade deficit, televised executions, and women in combat. The editorial writers present their views and sometimes support their positions by counterarguing their opponents' reasons. Underlying each editorial is the presentation of ideas with the intent to persuade. Students employ this same technique in essay exams, compositions, and research papers. The emphasis is on making the strongest case and then turning it over to an instructor for evaluation. The focus is not on dialogue or on an exchange of ideas; rather, there is an implied competitiveness in this debatelike format.

But what if the goal of presenting one's views is to develop a collaborative plan of action? The process of arguing and counterarguing is more than an exercise. It's a means to an end. In classroom activities you are often asked to exchange ideas, interact with one another, and work together to produce a finished project. The goal is to express your views, resolve any conflicts, and make decisions. This same collaborative process is an important part of the work world.

Our final reading, excerpted from a textbook on business communication, focuses on methods of conflict resolution used in the business world. Preview this passage by skimming the headings and noting how the information is organized.

Participation and Leadership in Small Groups

BY CHERYL HAMILTON AND CORDELL PARKER

Methods of resolving conflict

In addition to being flexible in choice of leadership style, a good leader is effective at resolving conflicts among group members. Any group that meets for any length of time is bound to have conflict of some kind. Kreps points out that

"Interpersonal conflict provides organization members with important feedback about potentially problematic situations." The success of the group often depends on how the conflict is handled. In developing your conflict resolution

resolve

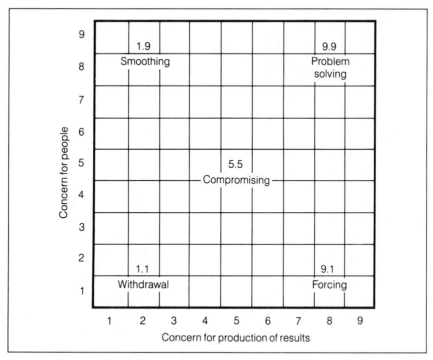

Figure 10.3 Conflict grid (Adapted by special permission from *The Journal of Applied Behavioral Science*, "The Fifth Achievement," by Robert R. Blake and Jane Syrgley Mouton, Volume 6, Number 4, p. 418, copyright 1970, NTL Institute.)

skills, you should determine (1) the strategy you feel most comfortable using, (2) the strategy the group members prefer, and (3) when each strategy is the most productive. There seem to be five main strategies for coping with conflict. Thomas calls them avoidance, accommodation, competition, compromise, and collaboration. Blake and Mouton call them withdrawal, smoothing, forcing, compromise, and problem solving, as illustrated in Figure 10.3, the conflict grid.

As the grid illustrates, the way you deal with conflict depends on where you place the most concern — people or production of results. Which of the following methods of handling conflict best describes the way you typically resolve conflict? the ways your boss or employees resolve conflict?

1. **Withdrawal/avoidance.** This person
   a. Maintains *neutrality* at all costs; views conflict as a worthless and punishing experience

    b. Removes self either physically or mentally from groups experiencing any type of conflict; stays away from any situation that might possibly produce conflict

    c. Feels little concern for people or production of results but great desire for noninvolvement

    d. Tends to lead in a closed management style

2. **Smoothing/accommodation.** This person

    a. Feels a high concern for people regardless of the production of results and, therefore, tries to smooth over or ignore conflicts in an attempt to keep everyone happy

    b. Believes that surface harmony is important to maintain good relationships and receive personal acceptance; has motto "If you can't say anything nice, don't say anything at all"

    c. Views open conflict as destructive; gives in to the will of others if necessary

    d. Tends to lead in a hidden management style

3. **Forcing/competition.** This person

    a. Views production of results (usually his or her own personal goals) as much more important than people and, therefore, sees nothing wrong with using force when necessary

    b. Views conflict as a win–lose situation or as a contest-of-power situation — one person must fail so the other can succeed; no possible compromise

    c. Has great respect for power and will submit to arbitration only because the arbitrator's power is greater   *arbitration*

    d. Tends to lead in the blind management style

4. **Compromising.** This person

    a. Believes that everyone should have an equal chance to express opinions

    b. Tries to find a solution that everyone can live with

    c. Uses voting or other methods of compromise as a way to avoid direct confrontation; believes that a high-quality solution is not as important as a workable or agreeable solution

    d. Tends to lead in the open management style

5. **Problem solving/collaboration.** This person

    a. Gives equal consideration to people and production of results

    b. Views conflict as beneficial if handled in an open manner; lays all cards on the table

    c. Guides group through the basic problem-solving procedure

    d. Attempts to reach a consensus agreement; willing to spend a great deal of time and effort to achieve it   *consensus*

e. Tends to lead in an open management style

Conflict strategies: When to use them

There are certain times when the five conflict strategies are productive and other times when they are best avoided.

Withdrawal (avoidance) may be the best response to conflict in the following situations:

- Issues really are trivial
- Parties lack the communication skills necessary to prevent destructive escalations
- Potential losses from an open conflict outweigh possible gains
- There is insufficient time to work through the issue adequately

The drawback to handling conflict by avoidance is that the confrontation is usually only delayed or transferred to another issue.

Smoothing (accommodation) may be the best response when:

- The issue is minor
- The damage to the relationship would harm both parties
- A temporary reduction in conflict is needed to give time for additional research or information
- Tempers are too hot for productive discussion

The drawback to handling conflict by accommodation is that it only temporarily solves the problem — it is like putting a Band-Aid on a serious cut.

Compromise may be the best response to conflict when:

- Both parties stand to gain
- An "ideal" or "quality" solution is not required
- Time is short
- A temporary solution is needed for a complex problem (a later problem-solving discussion will be held to determine the best solution)
- The parties in the conflict are equals

The drawbacks to handling conflict by compromise are that everyone loses something and the best solution is probably not reached.

Forcing (competition) may be the best response to conflict in the following situations:

- A decision or action must be immediate
- The parties in the conflict expect and appreciate the force and power necessary in a win–lose situation
- The combatants recognize the power relationship between themselves

combatant

The drawbacks to handling conflict by force are that the real cause of the conflict is usually not resolved, and because of the unmanaged emotions of the losers, the solution may be only temporary — when the losers gain more power, they may reinstate the conflict.

Problem solving (collaboration) is especially useful in handling conflict when:

- Members are trained in problem solving
- The parties have common goals that need the cooperation of all to be achieved
- The conflict arises from misunderstandings or communication breakdown

The drawback to handling conflict by collaboration is that it may not be successful when the parties have different values or goals. For example, a person who feels that conflict should be resolved in a competitive manner has goals and values completely opposed to the "everyone wins" view of the collaborator. Another important drawback to the problem-solving strategy is that it usually requires a long time.

The success of the five conflict strategies can be analyzed by dividing them into three categories.

- **Win–Lose** (only one party achieves objective). Forcing and voting are win–lose strategies.
- **Lose–Lose** (neither party achieves objective, or both get only a small part of what was wanted). Compromise, arbitration, smoothing, and avoidance are examples of lose–lose strategies.

- **Win–Win** (all parties receive acceptable gains). Problem solving and consensus are examples of the win–win strategy.

Although all of these methods can be used to handle conflict, the most productive and satisfying method over the long run is that used by the democratic problem solver. When conflict is handled correctly, it can be very productive.

Imagine that you are the leader of a task force and that you are striving to use the problem-solving method of handling conflict. Under your guidance, all facts and opinions are openly discussed. But after a long and tedious discussion, the group cannot reach an agreement. Half of the group prefers solution A, while the remaining members insist on solution B. How will you handle the problem?

Many leaders would urge the group to compromise. If this also failed, they would then probably turn in anger to the forcing method or employees not only would be unhappy with the wasted time and the leader's decision, but would probably be beginning to lose trust in a leader who so easily switched from the democratic to the authoritarian style.

Of course, sometimes it is impossible to reach a consensus agreement, and compromise or even force is necessary to reach a solution. However, keep in mind that settling for just *any* solution could be worse than no solution. Group members who are told that they can make the decision and then find that the decision is taken away from them will probably view this action as punishment.

If you find yourself leading a group that seems to have reached a stalemate — that is, the problem-solving method is impossible — try the following procedure before yielding to compromise:

1. Clarify the situation to the group. Include such comments as "The group seems to have reached an impasse. Further discussion along the same lines would be a waste of time. Obviously, a new approach is needed."

impasse

2. Urge the group to set the two conflicting solutions aside temporarily and to pretend they do not exist.

3. Guide the group to seek new solutions through brainstorming or the two-step nominal group technique (review the rules for each of these procedures in Chapter 9). Once a new list has been created, have the group evaluate these solutions and select the best one.

4. Guide the group in comparing the original two solutions with the new solution to see which of the three is now the best. Usually, the new solution is more creative and effective than either of the original conflicting solutions and is selected by the surprised group members as the best solution.

This four-step procedure is not a compromise, because no concessions are required to reach a consensus agreement. The group members believe that the new solution is better than the original solutions and usually wonder why they did not think of it sooner. However, if a consensus is still not possible, the conflict will have to be resolved by compromise, mediation, or even force of some type.

[NOTE: Footnotes have been deleted.]

COMPREHENSION CHECK

Write brief answers to the following questions.

1. What factors should be taken into consideration when developing conflict resolution skills?

2. What is the purpose of Figure 10.3? What are the key points illustrated by the chart?

3. How is information in this reading organized?

4. What examples can you come up with to illustrate the five approaches?

5. What kind of chart can you draw that will include the advantages and disadvantages of the five approaches?

6. How would you describe the conflict strategy preferred by Hamilton and Parker?

What Do You Think?

⊛ **DISCUSSION QUESTIONS**

Prepare for class discussion by jotting down brief answers to the following questions.

1. What is your view on the issue of televising executions? You may refer to the Argument Outline charts you developed for the two related editorials, as well as add other reasons of your own. Be sure to follow the guidelines for good discussions developed in Chapter 1.

2. Keeping in mind the framework presented in the Application Four reading, how are conflicts resolved in your family? Between you and your friends? Roommates? Professors?

3. Do different cultures approach conflict resolution differently? Is your answer based on personal experience? Exposure to the media? Stereotypes about a particular culture?

4. Are there gender differences in the way women and men like to resolve conflicts? Explain your answer giving examples. How do you account for these differences? What portion of your reasoning is based on personal experience? What part on scientific data?

5. Can you think of a situation where the problem-solving strategy led to a "win–win" situation? Can you think of examples from history that illustrate "win–lose" or "lose–lose" results?

WRITING ASSIGNMENTS

Select one or more of the following topics and in a few paragraphs develop a thoughtful written response. Completing topics 1 and 2 will help you evaluate how well you have understood the concepts presented in this chapter. Topics 3 and 4 focus on extending your reasoning skills to include negotiation and conflict resolution.

1. Now it's your turn to write an editorial. For this editorial you will not be required to do any research at the library. Choose a prescriptive argument and, relying on your own background knowledge, make a convincing case. Follow these steps to complete your essay:

    a. *Decide on a position.* Make sure that it responds to a prescriptive issue. (*Hint*: If you are having trouble thinking of a controversial topic, ask yourself: "What are the topics that I usually argue about with myself, parents, or friends? Do I argue about rules and regulations, curfews, or class attendance policies? Do I like to debate politics, religion, cases of sexual harassment, discrimination, sports, relationships, or careers?" Flip through a newspaper or magazine and see if any issue catches your attention. Listen to other people and see what they argue about.)

    b. *Prepare an argument outline.* To do this, first state the conclusion. Then identify reason 1 and give some examples and/or additional explanation. Do the same for reasons 2, 3, 4, and so on.

    c. *Write an introduction.* Introduce your reader to the topic. Provide any necessary background information the reader might need to understand your issue. Make the introduction as interesting as possible. You may want to end your introduction by stating your position or thesis. Look back at some of the editorials you have already read and see how writers organized their ideas.

    d. *Write the body of your paper.* Follow your argument outline: Present each of your reasons and elaborate on your reasons by giving additional facts or supporting examples.

    e. *Write a conclusion.* The conclusion should pull your thoughts together. Sometimes the conclusion is a short paragraph that states in strong terms the point (position) you are trying to make.

    f. *Be creative.* Experiment with style, vocabulary, and tone, but be sure to include the ideas from your argument outline.

    g. *Write a headline (title) for your editorial.*

2. Once you have completed your editorial, exchange essays with a classmate. Find the argument in your classmate's essay and prepare an argument outline. Does your outline match his or hers? Finally, compose a counterargument that could be used to refute the view presented.

3. Write an essay describing your own negotiating (conflict resolution) skills. You might recount one particular incident or cite several examples of strategies you have used to resolve conflicts. Be sure to incorporate information from the text.

4. You have been asked to write a script for a leadership training video aimed at corporate employees. The purpose of the tape will be to demonstrate the advantages and disadvantages of the various approaches to resolving conflicts. Develop a script for one or two of the approaches described in Application Four.

Extended Practice

Two additional articles are included in this section to provide you with further practice in dealing with arguments. "Reality Bites for the Baboos" is written by Patricia Plaster, editor of a college newspaper. "A Game of Life" by Lavinia Edmunds is from the Johns Hopkins magazine. Familiarize yourself with the questions for the selection prior to reading.

SELECTION ONE

The author of "Reality Bites for the Baboos" writes about the misconceptions Baboos (Baby Boomers) have about Generation Xers — a label often attributed to the generation of young people currently aged 13 to 33.

1. What argument(s) is (are) being made?

2. What evidence is provided to support the argument(s), and what evidence is provided to support the reasons?

3. What view does the author have of Baby Boomers?

4. Are there any values in conflict between the two groups?

5. Do you agree with the author's view of the Baboos? Generation Xers? Give reasons to support your conclusion. (Here you are developing your own argument.)

6. What kind of an argument is the author making?

Reality Bites for the Baboos

BY PATRICIA PLASTER

Within the past year or so there has been a lot of talk about "Generation X." What does this mean? To people who have decided that this label describes Americans from age 33 to age 13, it means drug-addicted, whiny, white, Kurt-Cobain-idolizing slackers from broken homes, who buy anything presented in a slick Madison Avenue MTV-style commercial. In other words, Baby Boomers (Baboos) have decided that this is an accurate depiction of this age group.

Drugs have been around for generations before the Xers. So, why is there so much concern about what is going on now? In the twenties there was alcohol, in the fifties there was the emergence of pot, in the sixties there was LSD, the seventies PCP, the eighties cocaine and now substances like ecstasy. Drug usage may stem from the modern American ideal of medicating whatever is wrong with you. Can't sleep because your brain is (gasp!) thinking? Well, here's an assortment of over-the-counter sleeping pills.

Second, considering all that this generation is inheriting from the Baboos, some complaining seems warranted. They just don't want to be reminded of the mess they have created with the environment, the federal deficit, overpopulation, the economy, the sharp racial class stratification, AIDS, various post–Cold War crises in Africa and Central America, and the "Me" ideology. The list could go on, but it won't to save this commentary from being labeled as yet another expression of the "Xers whine." Basically the Baboos don't want to hear it. They're trying to forget about the negative impact they've had on society and relax in their Lazy Boys. They don't want to hear a group of people in their twenties—young, eager and full of questions—demanding some answers and accountability for the state of the world that they see. And since they do not want to take responsibility for society's maladies, they respond by attacking the questioner rather than the questions.

This so-called Generation X is by no means "white." This is the first generation in history to have grown up in integrated schools. Of course there is still more than enough racism to go around, but in this generation racism has not been institutionalized. There is also greater racial diversity by population figures than any other previous generations. According to the June 6, 1994, issue of *Newsweek* the Baboos are 77% white whereas the Xers are 70% white.

There is little truth to Kurt Cobain being "the" epitome of Xers. Personally I have rarely listened to Nirvana's music and Cobain is no hero of mine. It was sad when he died, but it is inaccurate to claim that a heroin addict with a death wish is an icon that defines Xers.

The worst of all of the labels that the Baboos have given the Xers is "slacker." This is the worst because it only describes a small portion of the generation. The majority are currently in the workforce making valid and essential contributions to society; however, this is easily overlooked because the Baboos don't want to admit that they are even partially wrong. More people between ages 18–34 voted in 1992 than had since 1972. That's slacking? Who do they think are flooding the Peace Corps offices with applications? Who do they think are participating in the Americorps program? It's the Xers. If that's what they call slacking, then the Baboos desperately need to re-evaluate their definition.

Lastly, the worst misconception of Xers is that we will buy anything that is presented with a slick commercial. In fact we're the generation that has been so heavily bombarded by product commercials that the federal government has had to legislate advertisers. So there is no easy sale here, my friend. Xers want quality, not good advertising.

If the Baby Boomers are willing to transfer the reins of power and accept that it is now our turn to begin taking over, the transition will be a lot smoother and there will be a lot less name calling.

SELECTION TWO

"A Game of Life" by Lavinia Edmunds is a version of the lifeboat dilemma described in "Open Letter to Salman Rushdie" included in Chapter 3. In this article the choices deal with who should be selected for a needed heart transplant.

1. Your task is to decide the order in which you would select the organ candidates and defend your choices. Your choice and your reasoning are arguments.

2. The last two paragraphs of the article can be found on page 353. Read these to determine how the United Network for Organ Sharing (UNOS) is required to make its choices. How do your reasons for selection compare with UNOS rules? Which argument is "better"? Explain your answers.

A Game of Life

BY LAVINIA EDMUNDS

In what order would these patients be given hearts?

The United Network for Organ Sharing (UNOS) was designed to be as fair as possible. But no matter what the policies are, as long as one person is waiting, they won't seem fair enough. Distributing the inadequate supply of organs becomes a version of the lifeboat dilemma. And with the organ shortage growing more critical, harder decisions must be made. The following "patients" are composites from actual cases: For our purposes consider them to live in the same region and have the same blood type and weight; none has any medical alternative to a heart transplant. If you had to make the decision, in what order would you give them available hearts?

Sally Smith, 23, has congenital coronary artery disease and is unable to walk without having difficulty breathing. She is a brilliant PhD student at a university with a transplant center. If she doesn't obtain a heart within the year, her physicians say, she will die. Covered by health insurance, she has been on the waiting list 11 months. Her prognosis after transplant: better health than ever in her life.

Five years ago, Maria Long had her first heart attack and was forced to quit her job cleaning houses. Al-though expected to die three months ago after another heart attack, she has managed to stay alive and is now out of the hospital. She has saved money for the one-hour flight to the transplant center. Her church is collecting money for the operation.

Howard Chatsworth, 48, a house painter, has been confined to a hospital intensive care unit since his heart attack last month. His heart is working at 18 percent of its capacity. His name, body weight, and blood type entered the UNOS computer two weeks ago. His doctors give him two more months to live provided that he does not strain himself. The father of four children, grandfather of two, he lives about 200 miles from a transplant center and is covered by his health insurance. His morale and condition are worsening as his wait continues. Already his chance of survival after transplant has diminished to 50 percent.

Alexio Rodriquez is a wealthy 53-year-old physician from Mexico who has friends at a transplant center. Recently he moved nearby, got on the waiting list, and took a part-time job. He has enough money to pay for the operation and promises to donate a library to the hospital, should he live. Prognosis after transplant: excellent.

Cindy Johnson, 18, had been going to local public school as normal, although since birth she has not been able to participate in sports. After growing weaker, unable to walk up steps, she was advised to have open-heart surgery to repair a valve. When her doctors opened her up, they discovered that her heart had deteriorated and their only option was to replace it. Without a transplant, she will die within hours. Her doctors sewed her back up and kept her on a bypass machine in intensive care, in the hope that a donor would be found. Doctors believe she could survive and live a normal life if a heart is found immediately.

Billy Forbush, a 16-year-old from Massachusetts, has moved to a motel near the transplant center to wait for a heart. The operation is not covered by insurance, and his family cannot afford it. His doctors say he can survive for another year without a transplant. He has been on the waiting list for two weeks, and his doctor says he has about a 60 percent chance of survival after a transplant.

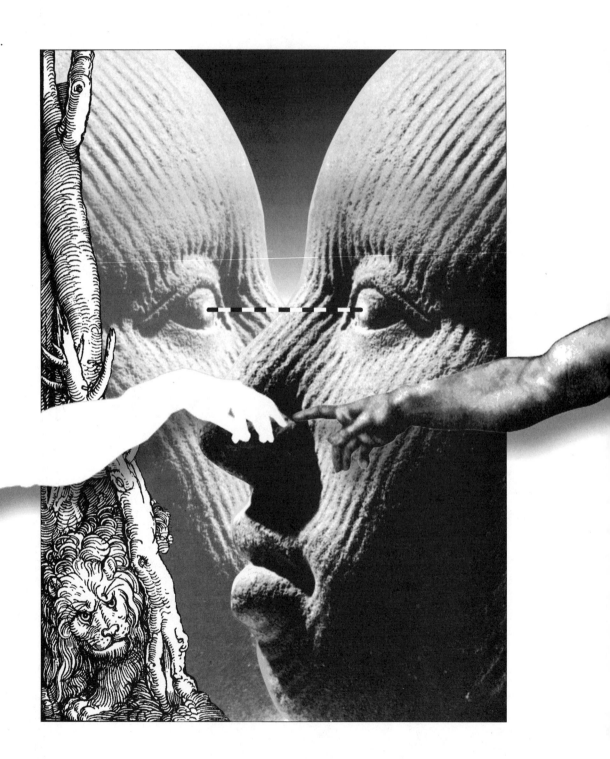

CHAPTER 6

Exploring the Unspoken: Finding Assumptions

After reading Chapter 6 you should be able to:

- define a "sound argument"
- recognize the role assumptions play in analyzing arguments
- identify assumptions used in conversations and arguments
- discuss the origins of assumptions
- complete a written analysis of an argument

You may use the following checklist in planning your study of assumptions. Activities marked with a ✪ are to be completed in class. Some preclass preparation may be required.

CONTEXT FOR LEARNING

✪ _____ **INTRODUCTORY CHAPTER ACTIVITY**

_____ Analyzing Arguments

_____ Two Kinds of Assumptions

✪ _____ **ACTIVITY BREAK**

_____ The Origins of Assumptions

✪ _____ **DISCUSSION BREAK**

APPLICATION: CRITIQUING AN ARGUMENT

_____ **APPLICATION ONE**

_____ **Student Arguments**

_____ **COMPREHENSION CHECK**

_____ **APPLICATION TWO**

_____ **"When Jobs and Family Care Clash"** by Cal Thomas

_____ **COMPREHENSION CHECK**

_____ **APPLICATION THREE**

_____ **"The Structure of the Universe"** by Michael A. Seeds

_____ **COMPREHENSION CHECK**

_____ What Do You Think?

✪ _____ **DISCUSSION QUESTIONS**

_____ **WRITING ASSIGNMENTS**

_____ Extended Practice

_____ **"Even Prisoners Must Have Hope"** by Richard Stratton

_____ **"Are Lotteries a Ripoff?"** by Amy Bayer and John W. Merline

✪ INTRODUCTORY CHAPTER ACTIVITY

For each of the photographs on this page develop a brief (one-paragraph) story describing what is occurring. Share your work with other students.

Belinda Rain/Documerica

U.S. Geological Survey

Were your stories similar to theirs? List on the board some of the interpretations that were made by the class. On what were the interpretations based?

Your ability to make interpretations depends on certain unstated beliefs called *assumptions*. For example, your interpretation that the men in the rowboat are friends is based on the assumption that this is the kind of activity friends engage in. Your own experience may reinforce this assumption.

Choose one of your stories and list several assumptions you made in order to write the story.

_____

_____

_____

_____

Analyzing Arguments

Assumptions play a significant role in the process of understanding and evaluating arguments. In the previous chapter we discussed deductive and inductive reasoning (see the box on page 155). We learned how to identify an argument—conclusion and reasons—and how to distinguish between prescriptive and descriptive arguments. But how do we know whether we should accept an argument as correct? The term often associated with "a good argument" is "a sound argument." One definition of *sound* is "to be free from flaws or defects." In this case a sound argument is one that does not contain any errors in its reasons or conclusion. But how does one check for errors?

Testing for soundness

To test the soundness of an argument, we must ask two questions: (1) Are the reasons true? and (2) Do they support the conclusion? People often interchange the terms *soundness* and *validity*. Strictly speaking, *validity* refers only to the logic of the reasons. When we discuss only the validity of an argument, the reasons must be true or assumed to be true.

Conway and Munson in their book *The Elements of Reasoning* explain validity this way:

> Validity is a matter of the support a set of premises lends to a conclusion. It is a question of whether a certain relationship holds between premises and conclusion. (*If* we grant the premises, *must* we grant the conclusion?) Hence, validity does not require the premises of an argument to be true. Yet if they are true and the argument is valid, the conclusion must be also true.

Recall our example about Biff in Chapter 5:

> Students who do well on their SAT or ACT tests will earn high grades in college. Biff did well on his SAT tests. Therefore, Biff will earn high grades in college.

Is this a valid argument? If we assume that the reasons are true, then does the conclusion follow logically? In this case the answer is yes. According to the rules of deductive reasoning, the conclusion follows logically from the reasons:

> All A's (students who earn high scores on their SAT or ACT tests) are B (will earn high grades in college). Since Biff is an A, then B will apply to Biff also.

Is this a sound argument? The test for soundness involves true reasons and validity. We have already established the validity of the argument and now must decide whether the reasons are true. The argument will be sound only if the reasons themselves are true. Maybe we don't believe that people who earn high scores on the SAT or ACT exams will be successful in college. We may know someone whose scores were high but who is on academic probation. Maybe the Biff we know didn't earn high SAT or ACT marks. Under these circumstances, even though the argument is valid, we don't believe the reasons are true. Therefore, we reject the argument as unsound.

Analyzing the reasons

In the Biff example we looked at validity first. However, it usually makes more sense to consider the truth of the reasons first. Obviously, if the reasons aren't true, there is no point in continuing the analysis. Let's take a more in-depth look at answering the two questions that determine soundness.

Question 1: Are the reasons true?   Perhaps a better question to ask is whether the reasons are *probably* true — that is, are they facts? In areas where you have a great deal of knowledge, expertise, or personal experience, the task of knowing whether a reason is true is easier than if you don't know anything. For example, if you are a college student attending a large institution, you are in a better, although not foolproof, position than a corporate executive to evaluate the following statement, quoted in Deloughry's article in *The Chronicle of Higher Education*:

> "The typical undergraduate at a large state university studies one to two hours a day, spends an average of 12 hours a week at drinking parties, attends college primarily to pursue career goals, and has little loyalty to or respect for the large bureaucratic university."

Or suppose your friend Bing tries to convince you that there is life on Mars because six Martians came to his house for dinner last night. You might legitimately question the truth of his reason — as well as his sanity. However, if the evidence provided was data from a recent study based on satellite information, you might find it more difficult to refute the claim and be more willing to accept the reason as a fact. Then again, if you had a Ph.D. in astronomy and had been working at NASA for the past five years, you might question the data and ultimately reject the findings.

In Chapter 10 we will discuss some ways that nonexperts can question research and statistical findings. What we are suggesting now is that as you analyze reasons, you probably won't be able to know with 100 percent accuracy whether the reason is true. You will have to rely on your knowledge and common sense as well as the advice of experts in the field.

Wise writers provide evidence to support their reasons and thus strengthen their chances of convincing others of their conclusions. For example, people who support capital punishment often claim that capital punishment deters crime, but unless they provide additional evidence to back up their reason, opponents can simply argue that it doesn't. Here the reason offered is nothing more than an assertion — a claim about the way the world is. In order for you to accept the reason as true, you would want to know what's behind the statement.

When someone offers reasons that coincide with your own unstated beliefs or assumptions, it is very easy to accept them without question. Be careful not to fall into that trap. Likewise, if you are making an argument, you may assume that everyone will automatically agree with the reasons you provide and therefore feel there is no need to back up your statements. For example, people often quote religious teachings in support of their positions and are surprised when others do not recognize them as being the final authority.

Question 2: Do the reasons support the conclusion? Read the following dialogue and consider Melvin's argument.

> *Melvin:* Hey Mom, can I borrow your car this Friday night?
>
> *Mom:* What!? My new sports car? Are you kidding?
>
> *Melvin:* Come on, Mom, I've never had an accident. Besides, did you see my grades for this semester — all A's and B's. Haven't I been taking out the trash all week?
>
> *Mom:* Forget it. When you can afford to buy a car you can drive mine.

If you were to chart Melvin's argument the way you learned in Chapter 5, it might look like this:

Conclusion: Melvin should be allowed to borrow his mother's new sports car Friday night.

Reason 1: He's never had an accident.

Reason 2: His grades are all A's and B's.

Reason 3: He's been taking the trash out all week.

Is this a sound argument? Let's assume that we are Melvin's mother and we know that Melvin's reasons are true: He has never had an accident, his grades are good, and there's no trash to be found in the house. Should we accept Melvin's conclusion? To answer this question, we must decide whether the reasons support his conclusion.

What assumptions is Melvin making in his argument? We must ask ourselves: "How is never having had an accident related to borrowing the car? What do high marks or taking out the trash all week have to do with borrowing the car?" From Melvin's perspective his reasons are linked to or support his conclusion. But the link is not stated explicitly and takes the form of an unstated belief or assumption. Can you determine what unstated belief links his first reason to the conclusion? What about the unstated beliefs for his second and third reasons? If we accept the assumptions, then we will agree that the reasons *do* support the conclusion, and if we have accepted the reasons as true, we will conclude that the argument is sound.

Let's consider Melvin's assumptions:

Assumption 1: A good driving record is an asset when it comes to borrowing someone else's car.

Assumption 2: The intelligence and effort used to get good grades will be useful in driving or entitle one to certain privileges.

Assumption 3: Taking the trash out is an act of responsibility that is transferable to borrowing the car.

What is your view? For our part, we can understand the relationship between being a good driver and being allowed to borrow a car: Chances are nothing will happen to the car. We find it difficult, however, to see how good grades and taking out the trash are relevant. The skills required to get good grades aren't necessarily the skills that make a person a good driver, and the amount of responsibility involved in taking out the trash pales in comparison with the responsibility required to sensibly control a car. We believe reasons 2 and 3 are not valid and therefore consider the argument to be unsound. (However, we do recognize that emotional appeals to mothers often work, making logic irrelevant!) What is your analysis?

To recap, the way to determine whether the reasons support the conclusion is to find the assumption(s) behind them and decide whether you agree with them. The assumptions are usually unstated. Writers rarely state them explicitly; however, they are the glue that "attaches" the reason to the conclusion. Assumptions are unseen but play a powerful role in determining the validity of an argument.

Two Kinds of Assumptions

Students sometimes have difficulty locating assumptions. Therefore, it may be helpful to understand two different kinds of assumptions and to practice finding them. The characteristics of the two kinds are quite similar to those of descriptive and prescriptive arguments.

Descriptive assumptions

Consider the following dialogue:

> *Bryan:* Where were you last night?
>
> *Clarence:* What do you mean?
>
> *Bryan:* I mean I was at the library at nine o'clock as usual and you weren't there.
>
> *Clarence:* So?
>
> *Bryan:* Well, you were there Monday and Tuesday night.

What does Bryan believe, but not say, that leads him to be surprised that Clarence isn't at the library on Wednesday? Bryan's argument is that Clarence will be in the library on Wednesday because Clarence was there on Monday and Tuesday. What is the link that ties his reason to his conclusion?

Bryan believes that if Clarence does something two days in a row, he will do it again on the third day. This unspoken (implicit) statement is an assumption. What is your opinion of Bryan's assumption? Do you believe that because someone does something two days in a row, it is reasonable to assume this pattern will continue the third day? Why?

Because the assumption is an implicit statement about how the speaker sees the world or how the speaker thinks the world operates, we call this a *descriptive assumption*.

Prescriptive assumptions

Consider this dialogue:

> *Melinda:* Did you see that newspaper article, the one on capital punishment?
>
> *Carey:* Do you mean the one that gives the statistics showing how capital punishment is administered unfairly?
>
> *Melinda:* Yeah, they say that the law is administered unfairly and is racially biased.
>
> *Carey:* In that case, they ought to abolish capital punishment.

Carey comes to the conclusion that capital punishment should be abolished because it is unfair. What is the link between abolishing capital punishment and its being unfair? It is the belief or value assumption that we should not do things that are unfair. If a person does not hold this value — if she believes that it is all right, at least under certain circumstances, to do things that are unfair — then she would not find Carey's reason a valid one. Because the assumption is a statement of how Carey thinks the world ought to be, it is called a *prescriptive assumption*.

Linking conclusions and assumptions

As you can see, the terms *prescriptive* and *descriptive* have similar meanings when applied to assumptions or arguments. Descriptive arguments try to defend a perception of how the world is, was, or will be, and often draw on unstated beliefs about the status of the world (that is, descriptive assumptions) to link their reasons to conclusions. Prescriptive arguments propose a vision of how the world ought to be and often rely on unstated beliefs about how the world should be (that is, value assumptions) to link their reasons to conclusions.

Read the following dialogue and find the position, reason(s), and assumption. Can you figure out what kind of an assumption is being made?

> *Tomeekeo:* Great, the weather forecast said there'll be two feet of snow tonight.
>
> *Tala:* Fantastic, no school tomorrow.
>
> *Tomeekeo:* I won't even bother to set the alarm.

Both speakers come to the conclusion that there will be no school tomorrow. The reason they give is that the forecast is for two feet of snow. What assumption are both women making that leads them to believe that if there are two feet of snow, there will be no school? It is a descriptive assumption about how their world operates. They believe that if there is a lot of snow, the roads won't be plowed, driving conditions will be hazardous, and college officials will be compelled to cancel school. This may be true, and their past experience may make this assumption reasonable. However, if it stops snowing by midnight, crews may be able to clear the roads and classes will not have to be canceled.

When evaluating an argument, it makes sense to analyze the assumptions before accepting the reason as valid. Accepting the assumption that links the reason to the conclusion means you believe that the reason supports the conclusion. In short, assumptions are the links between reasons and conclusions that make the reasons supportive proof for the conclusion. When you want to evaluate an argument, examine the assumptions underlying the reasons. To find the assumption ask yourself "What must I also believe if I want to use reason X to support the conclusion?"

✪ **ACTIVITY BREAK**

Assumptions can be tricky to find. It is difficult to find what isn't there! Understanding the assumptions in an argument can hold the key to resolving a dispute or clarifying differences. Knowing the assumptions allows the participants to focus on the key sources of disagreement. Clarifying assumptions can lead to greater understanding among the disagreeing parties even if it cannot guarantee agreement. Our students are always amazed to realize that many of their daily disagreements are more easily understood by focusing on "what's behind the facts" (the assumptions) than on what the facts are.

For the following dialogues or statements, write (1) the conclusion, (2) the reasons, and (3) the assumptions. Use the following format to complete the activity.

Conclusion: _____

Reasons: _____

Assumptions: _____

Dialogue 1

Sandra: Did you see the new statistics about the numbers of people who may be exposed to AIDS?

Edward: Yeah, and the TV networks are refusing to allow ads for condoms even though the Surgeon General says it can help prevent the spread of the disease.

Sandra: In my opinion, the networks are acting stupid. They ought to show the ads.

Dialogue 2

Tania: That course is so boring!

Gerry: I agree. I can't understand what the professor is talking about.

Dialogue 3

Neha: I remember that article we read last semester about health clinics in high schools.

Lance: The idea was that these clinics would also make information available about birth control.

Neha: Well, they really need to do something because the number of teenagers getting pregnant is increasing dramatically.

Dialogue 4

Daniel: Businesses should be allowed to fire people if they smoke cigarettes.

Belinda: Studies show that employees who smoke are sick more often than those who do not.

Dialogue 5

Paul: Athletes should maintain a 2.0 average to play sports. College is supposed to be for academics, not sports.

Dialogue 6

Donia: Core courses should be eliminated. I'm planning on being a business major, so what do I need with a course in biology or sociology?

Michael: I agree. It's a waste of our time. Students don't learn much in courses that they aren't interested in.

Dialogue 7

Jenna: Anybody who wants a job can get one. Just look at all the want ads in the newspaper!

The Origins of Assumptions

The Introductory Chapter Activity asked you to make up stories to go with some photographs. We suggested that you could do this rather easily by relying on assumptions you have made about your world. Since you are well on your way to becoming a critical thinker, you are probably wondering how one develops a set of assumptions: Where do they come from, and how do you know when you have "acquired" a new one? Value assumptions are the result of all the factors we discussed in Chapter 4: culture, religion, education, socioeconomic class, gender, age, and so on. But we also make descriptive assumptions about the way we think the world is. For example, you may believe that teenagers have not altered their sexual habits due to AIDS, most people are honest, and America is a democracy. This relates to our discussion of "reality filters" in Chapter 5.

Some students ask us: "Aren't assumptions bad? Isn't it wrong to make assumptions?" The answer is not a simple yes or no. We can't help but make assumptions about our world and our lives. Otherwise, we would be in a constant state of anxiety. Since nothing could be taken for granted (that is, assumed), we would always be wondering what was going to happen next: Will the mail be delivered today? Will a friend's telephone number be changed tomorrow? If we didn't have a shared set of assumptions, we wouldn't know how to interpret the actions and statements of those around us. Most of our assumptions are an outgrowth of our daily lives including our exposure to the larger world through schooling and the media. There is an inevitability about having assumptions. The important point is to be aware of your assumptions and decide for yourself if they are accurate.

⊙ **DISCUSSION BREAK**

As you read the following list of questions, you will realize that there are no hard-and-fast answers to any of them. We will return to some of the issues raised in these questions in Chapter 7. For now, prepare for class discussion by jotting down short answers to the following questions.

1. Do some kinds of reasons seem more credible or believable to you? For example, do research findings tend to convince you more than

examples? Does personal experience hold more weight for you than expert testimony? Explain your answers. Are your answers justifiable?

2. Arguments are judged according to their logic or reasonableness. Should reasonableness always be the basis of our beliefs and decisions? What place, if any, should emotions have in persuading us to accept or reject an argument?

3. We've talked about the relationship of reason to truth, and yet "truth" seems to come from knowledge and experience. Does this mean that there is no such thing as a universal truth?

4. Think about some of the descriptive assumptions you make about your life, for example, about a college degree, sports, fraternities and sororities, politics, children, the economy, or your future. Many of your assumptions may take the form of how you hope the world will be. Are you taking steps to ensure that your predictions will come true? Are you planning to continue your studies in graduate school? Are you putting in the study time needed to make sure you will receive your undergraduate degree?

5. Can you recall a time when you felt you were prejudged? What inaccurate assumptions were being made? When have you made stereotypic assumptions about someone? What are some ways to counteract stereotyping?

Application: Critiquing an Argument

APPLICATION ONE

Read the following passages to understand the students' arguments presented in "Student Arguments." Complete the topic and conclusion sections of the "Analyzing Arguments" chart on page 203. Then record any reasons presented and determine what assumptions the writers have made. That is, what unstated beliefs must they hold in order for their reasons to support their conclusions?

Student Arguments

Equal money for women's sports

Money in athletic programs in schools and colleges should be equal for men and women. It is time to admit that women are being dis-
arena criminated against in the sports arena. They don't receive the same opportunities or funds to help them develop their abilities because men have taken the lion's share of the cash. Schools deny women their fair share of advanced-level coaching, and they seldom receive the same number of awards, honors, scholarships, press coverage, and public acclaim that is reserved for male athletes. In the interests of equality, it is time for a change.

—anonymous student

Surrogate motherhood: Babies for sale

Surrogate motherhood is the practice of bearing a child on behalf of another woman. In the United States this practice has become a highly publicized and controversial issue.

infertility   Many married couples who desire to have children but can't do so because of infertility or other medical complications resort to surrogacy. The process begins with a formal agreement, usually handled
prospective by a lawyer or a clinic, between a married couple and the prospective surrogate mother.

No, surrogate motherhood should not be legal. I feel it is ethically and morally wrong for a woman to carry a child who she intends to sell at the time of delivery. In this aspect, surrogacy is like prostitution, because in both situations, the woman is selling her bodily services for a fee. In addition, how can you place a monetary value on human beings? If society allows this type of behavior, "things" will get out of hand.

—Tabitha Guess, student

Boxing should not be outlawed

First of all, boxing provides lower-income children with an opportunity to rise above their economic status. In many instances, it keeps kids away from drugs, drinking, and crime because it gives them something constructive to do with their time. Yes, boxing is violent, but it is each person's choice to participate. There is a possibility that someone may get brain damaged, but people don't see the strategy or all the work that goes into a match. Boxing is an art form, like karate or judo. I agree that the AIDS issue in boxing is serious. However, this can be solved by having all amateur and professional boxers tested regularly for AIDS.

constructive

— Dan Mathers, college boxing student

COMPREHENSION CHECK

For each of the passages complete the third column of the "Analyzing Arguments" chart by giving *your* view (that is, evaluation) of the assumption. Do you agree with this assumption? What evidence do you have to support your viewpoint?

Analyzing Arguments		
Topic: _____		
Conclusion: _____		
Reasons	Assumptions	Your Evaluation of the Assumptions
_____	_____	_____
_____	_____	_____
_____	_____	_____
_____	_____	_____

Read the following editorial "When Jobs and Family Care Clash," by Cal Thomas, vice president of the Moral Majority. Pay particular attention to the kinds of evidence presented: personal anecdotes of famous people, statistics, research studies, and popular movies.

When Jobs and Family Care Clash

BY CAL THOMAS

LYNCHBURG, Va. — "It can be hard because kids don't understand. When I'd leave, little Al would get mad and not talk to me. But I have to be happy too. I wouldn't be a happy mother if I was staying home as a housewife."

That is Valerie Brisco-Hooks, the Olympic gold-medal runner, speaking to a *New York Times* interviewer. She is not alone in her belief that motherhood is a hurdle that must be jumped to find real fulfillment.

The Labor Department says that nearly half of the nation's married women with children one year old or younger are in the labor force. The figure jumped from 24 percent in 1970 to 46.8 percent by the end of 1984.

While some of these women must obviously work to survive, others work for different reasons. Regardless of the reason, the impact on families, particularly children, is severe.

Psychologist James Dobson, who advises the White House and the Pentagon on family life, says a child may suffer permanent emotional damage from an exhausted lifestyle when there is no full-time homemaker in the house.

Numerous studies have shown that children who are shuttled from one baby sitter to another are different than they would be otherwise. Research has consistently demonstrated that the mother–child relationship is especially vital during the first three years of life and that there is no substitute for the bonding that occurs between generations during that time.

shuttle

vital

The Harvard preschool study revealed that a child's future intellectual capacity and emotional security are largely dependent on the quality of mothering occurring when the child is young.

Numerous studies have found, notes Dobson, that children "thrown into group situations too early" incline toward peer-dependency and insecurity as they move through childhood.

Dobson believes that mothers who have a choice about whether to work should ask themselves several questions:

1. To whom shall I submit the task of guiding the unfolding process of development during the years when dramatic changes are occurring in my children?

2. Who will care enough to make the investment if every day my husband and I are too busy for the job?

facility

3. What group-oriented facility can possibly substitute for the individual attention and love my child needs?

4. Who will represent our values and beliefs and be ready to answer our child's questions during his peak period of interest?

Says Dobson, "I worry about a nation that calls homemaking unrewarding, unfulfilling and boring."

The 1909 White House Conference on Children had it right when it concluded, "Home life is the highest and finest product of civilization."

It was in the 1920s that a new ideology of "social parenting" began to take shape in America. This has led us to the "modern family," no better represented than in the movie "Irreconcilable Differences."

ideology

In the film, Casey Brodsky, age 10, is divorcing her parents. Says Casey, "If I'm not going to be totally nuts when I grow up, I'd better get out while I still have a chance." Mom and Dad are so involved with personal ambitions that they don't have the time and energy to give Casey the warmth and affection that all children need. In the end they realize this and make a new start. In real life not everyone comes to such a realization.

As we relentlessly pursue "happiness," we would do well to remember what C. S. Lewis wrote: "We have no right to happiness. We have only an obligation to do our duty." It is in doing that duty that ultimate happiness is to be found.

COMPREHENSION CHECK

Write brief answers to the following questions.

1. What topic is the editorial discussing?

2. What major point is being made about the topic (that is, what is the author's conclusion)?

3. What reasons or evidence are presented to support this conclusion?

4. What *kinds* of evidence are presented?

5. What assumptions does Thomas make in his argument?

6. Which assumptions do you accept? Reject? Explain your reasoning.

7. What other value assumptions might Thomas hold?

APPLICATION THREE

Although the final reading in Chapter 6 does not deal with any current social issues, it does underscore the significance of assumptions in scientific thought. The selection comes from a college astronomy text-book. Preview this reading by skimming the headings and graphics. Next, read through the entire selection to understand the importance of assumptions in cosmology (the study of the universe), and answer the first set of Comprehension Check questions. Then, read to understand the specific information being presented, and answer the second set of Comprehension Check questions. Use the Comprehension Check questions 1–4 for Application Two to guide your reading.

(*Note*: In Chapter 2 we discussed several misconceptions about reading. We suggested that readers needed to keep their purpose for reading in mind. The following selection contains some technical information that may be difficult to understand if you do not have much interest in or background information about astronomy. Use your analytical skills to follow the logic of the information the second time you read the article.)

The Structure of the Universe

BY MICHAEL A. SEEDS

cosmology

geometry

infinite

We begin our study of cosmology by considering the most basic property of the universe — its geometry. By understanding the geometry of space-time, we will see how we might discover whether the universe is infinite or finite.

Why does it get dark at night?
We have all noticed that the night sky is dark. However, reasonable assumptions about the geometry of the universe can lead us to the conclusion that the night sky should glow as brightly as a star's surface. This conflict between observation and theory is called *Olbers' paradox* after Heinrich Olbers, a Viennese physician and astronomer who discussed the paradox in 1826.

paradox

However, Olbers' paradox is not Olbers'. The problem of the dark night sky was first discussed by Thomas Digges in 1576 and was further analyzed by such astronomers as Johannes Kepler in 1610 and Edmond Halley in 1721. Olbers gets the credit through an accident of scholarship on the part of modern cosmologists who did not know of previous discussions. What's more, Olbers' paradox is not a paradox. We will be able to understand why the night sky is dark by revising our assumptions about the nature of the universe.

To begin, let's state the so-called paradox. Suppose the universe is static, infinite, eternal, and uniformly filled with stars. (The aggregation of stars into galaxies makes no difference to our argument.) If we look in any direction, our line of sight must eventually reach the surface of a star (Figure 15-1). Consequently, every point on the surface of the sky should be as bright as the surface of a star, and it should not get dark at night.

aggregation

Of course, the most distant stars would be much fainter than the nearer stars, but there would be a greater number of distant stars than nearer stars. The intensity of the light from a star decreases according to the inverse square law, so distant stars would not contribute much light. However, the farther we look in space, the larger the volume we survey. Thus the number of stars we see at any given distance increases as the square of the distance. The two effects cancel out, and the stars at any given distance contribute as much total light as the stars at any other distance. Then given our assumptions, every spot on the sky must be occupied by the surface of a star, and it should not get dark at night.

intensity

square

Imagine the entire sky glowing with the brightness of the surface

   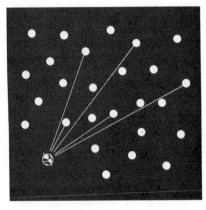

a   b

Figure 15-1   (a) Every direction we look in a forest eventually reaches a tree trunk, and we cannot see out of the forest. (b) If the universe is infinite and uniformly filled with stars, then any line from earth should eventually reach the surface of a star. This predicts that the night sky should glow as brightly as the surface of the average star, a puzzle commonly referred to as Olbers' paradox. (Photo courtesy Janet Seeds.)

of the sun. The glare would be overpowering. In fact, the radiation would rapidly heat the earth and all other celestial objects to the average temperature of the surface of the stars, 1000 K at least. Thus we can pose Olbers' paradox in another way: "Why is the universe so cold?"

Olbers assumed that the sky was dark because clouds of matter in space absorb the radiation from distant stars. But this interstellar medium would gradually heat up to the average surface temperature of the stars, and the gas and dust clouds would glow as brightly as the stars.

Today cosmologists believe they understand why the sky is dark. Olbers' paradox makes the incorrect prediction that the sky should be bright because it is based on two incorrect assumptions. The universe is neither static nor infinitely old.

In Chapter 13 we saw that the galaxies are receding from us. The distant stars in these galaxies are receding from the earth at high velocity, and their light is Doppler-shifted to long wavelengths. We can't see the light from these stars because their light is red-shifted, and the energy of the photons is reduced to levels we cannot detect. Expressed in another way, the universe is cold because the photons from very distant stars arrive with such low energy they cannot heat up objects. Although this explains part of the problem, the red shifts

celestial

medium

static

photons

of the distant galaxies are not enough to make the sky as dark as it appears.

The second part of the explanation was first stated by Edgar Allan Poe in 1848. He proposed that the night sky was dark because the universe was not infinitely old but had been created at some time in the past. The more distant stars are so far away that light from them has not reached us yet. That is, if we look far enough, the look-back time is greater than the age of the universe, and we look back to a time before stars began to shine. Thus the night sky is dark because the universe is not infinitely old.

This is a powerful idea because it clearly illustrates the difference between the universe and the observable universe. The universe is everything that exists, and it could be infinite. But the observable uni-

verse is the part that we can see. We will learn later that the universe is 15 to 20 billion years old. In that case, the observable universe has a radius of 15 to 20 billion lightyears. Do not confuse the observable universe, which is finite, with the universe as a whole, which could be infinite.

radius

The assumptions that we made when we described Olbers' paradox were at least partially in error. This illustrates the importance of assumptions in cosmology and serves as a warning that our commonsense expectations are not dependable. All of astronomy is reasonably unreasonable — that is, reasonable assumptions often lead to unreasonable results. That is especially true in cosmology, so we must examine our assumptions with special care.

COMPREHENSION CHECK

Write brief answers to the following questions.

First reading

1. What role did assumptions play in Olbers' explanation of why the night sky should be bright?

2. What incorrect assumptions were made about the universe?

3. Why is it often a mistake in the study of cosmology to base assumptions on commonsense expectations and observations?

Second reading

1. Olbers' reasoning led him to believe that although the night sky was dark, it should be bright. This discrepancy was called Olbers' paradox. What was his reasoning?

2. What piece of information does the author assume the reader knows (that is, what causes the day sky to be bright)?

3. In your own words, why does the night sky get dark?

What Do You Think?

DISCUSSION QUESTIONS

Prepare for class discussion by jotting down brief answers to the following questions.

1. Compare surrogate motherhood with sperm banks. Are the issues the same? Can you support one without supporting the other?

2. In Chapter 6 we have touched on issues related to women in sports, women as surrogate mothers, and working women. Keeping the information presented in these selections in mind, how do you respond to the argument that women today are under too much pressure to perform?

3. With so much emphasis being placed on "women's concerns," are men being neglected?

4. How would you define *men's liberation*?

5. In what way is the night sky magical?

6. If looks can be deceiving, how can people protect themselves from being duped?

WRITING ASSIGNMENTS

With your instructor select the writing assignment(s) the class will complete. Assignments 1–3 give you additional practice in analyzing a portion of an argument. Assignment 4 asks you to write a critical analysis of an entire editorial.

1. Look back at the argument outline for "Let TV Cameras Show Executions" in Chapter 5. Select three major reasons to analyze: Do you believe the reason is true? Explain. Does the writer provide any support for the reasons? Does this support convince you that the reason is true? Be careful not to confuse your task. At this point your job is to decide whether or not you *believe* the reasons. Later you will decide whether to accept or reject the whole argument. Write out your answers and share them with members of the class.

2. Return to the editorial you wrote at the end of Chapter 5. (If you have not written an editorial, you might do so now or select another editorial; in either case, you will need to have an argument outline from which to work.) Reread your editorial to see if you supported any of the reasons with additional information: an example, statistical data, research findings, expert testimony. Analyze your reasoning. How strong an argument do you think you have made?

3. Create two dialogues of your own or write down two dialogues you hear. Make sure each dialogue contains at least one argument. Write down the arguments in each dialogue.

4. You are now ready to critique an argument by evaluating its strength. Select an editorial — either one from this text or one of your own choice — and complete the following steps:

    a. Read the editorial to find the author's argument. Keep in mind that your task is to analyze the writer's argument, not to agree or disagree with the conclusion. What does this mean? In the first instance, you are being asked to evaluate the *reasoning* abilities of the writer. In the second instance, you are being asked to agree or disagree with the writer's conclusion.

b. List the author's position statement and reasons.

c. Analyze the writer's argument by doing the following: (1) Decide whether the reasons are true, (2) find the assumptions behind the reasons, (3) decide whether you agree with the assumptions and be able to explain your decision, and (4) assess the overall strengths and weaknesses of the argument.

Some students find it helpful to put their answers in chart form such as the one below. To illustrate, we have filled in the blanks for our sample argument dealing with Melvin and his mother's car.

Analyzing Arguments

Topic: *borrowing car*

Conclusion: *Melvin should be allowed to borrow mother's car*

Reason 1	Assumption 1	Evaluation of Assumption
no accidents	*driving record as asset*	*perhaps valid relationship*

Reason 2	Assumption 2	Evaluation of Assumption
good grades	*grades useful to driving*	*irrelevant*

Reason 3	Assumption 3	Opinion of Assumption
takes out trash	*shows responsibility*	*irrelevant*

Overall assessment: unsound argument

---

d. Compose an essay in which you evaluate the strength of the argument. Your essay should include an introduction that discusses the issue and relates to the controversy. Remember that the focus of your paper is the writer's reasoning skills. Your thesis is a statement about either accepting or rejecting the writer's argument. The body of the paper uses the information from your chart to explain your analysis. The conclusion sums up your position regarding the writer's reasoning skills. You may also now include any additional information or personal opinions concerning the controversial issue.

The "Optional Essay Format" box on pages 214–215 outlines one possible format for your paper. Following the format will ensure that you include all the parts of your paper. The drawback, however, is that it is formulaic.

Optional Essay Format

"Essay Title"

Introductory Paragraph: In the introduction to your essay, you can include background information and a statement of the issues involved. It's important to capture the reader's interest at this point.

Body of Essay: In the body, which may consist of one or several paragraphs, list the reasons and discuss the underlying assumptions. Then assess the validity of the assumptions. The following sample paragraph shows how the body can be organized.

The article ___(title)___ written by ___(author)___, deals with the issue of ___(topic)___ and takes the position ___(conclusion)___. The author provides several reasons to support his/her position and makes several assumptions. For example, ___he/she___ states ___(give reason)___. The assumption behind this reason (OR the writer assumes) is ___(give assumption)___. In my view, this assumption is correct/incorrect because ___(give reasons)___.

You can use this format for all the important reasons. Again, give the reason and the assumptions, then explain why you do or do not accept the assumption. Be sure to point out ambiguous terms and how they affect the author's reasoning.

The author's reasoning suffers because of his/her use of ambiguous terms. For instance, ___(give examples)___.

Is the issue about two values in conflict where one value carries more weight with the author? If so, explain what the value is and whether you agree with the author.

Concluding Paragraph: Here you summarize your analysis of the author's argument, as well as offering supplemental information or giving your own opinion of the issue. For example:

> In conclusion, I accept/reject the author's argument because ____(give reasons)____ .

Possible reasons might include the following:

The evidence is (is not) very convincing. (Explain.)

The author relies too much on personal experiences that may not be typical of all people. (Explain.)

I don't agree with the author's value assumptions. ____(State your belief and give alternatives.)____

The evidence is weak but I have the same values as the author. ____(Offer better reasoning. Explain.)____

The author is a personal friend of mine and paid me to support him or her.

Extended Practice

Two additional articles are included in this section to provide you with further practice in evaluating arguments. Familiarize yourself with the questions for the selection prior to reading.

Preventing crimes and punishing criminals are popular political themes today. Some politicians call for a "three strikes and you're out" policy; others say money and resources should be focused on prevention. Although statistics report actual decreases in the most violent types of crimes, many people feel less secure and more frightened. In "Even Prisoners Must Have Hope" Stratton makes his argument.

1. Does Stratton present a valid argument?

2. What kinds of evidence does he present?

3. What value conflict is embedded in this issue?

Even Prisoners Must Have Hope

BY RICHARD STRATTON

Opinion: Getting tougher is a mistake

I did eight years in federal prison for smuggling marijuana. I was punished, I was demeaned and I was scared. I waded through sewage backed up from toilets. I lived in overcrowded cells. I saw men brutally beaten. It could have been worse: it could have been pointless. I wasn't condemned to idleness. I wasn't denied a place to exercise, a television to watch, an education to embrace. By the time I left prison, I had earned a bachelor's degree, written a novel, mastered enough law to get out early. Now I have a wife, two sons, a job and a message: don't make prisons more miserable than they already are.

For all the lip service once paid to rehabilitation in this country, imprisonment in America is about nothing but punishment, and punishment is the intentional infliction of pain by those in power upon the less powerful. In the United States we equate justice with vengeance; we embrace the theory of "just deserts" for criminals and deviants. Instead of improving the harsh conditions that create crime and violence, which might restore peace and harmony to our society, we inflict more pain, more punishment, thus creating more crime and more violence.

The get-tough-on-crime attitudes of the '80s have given us rampant, desperate inner-city crime and violence in the '90s. If we continue with our vengeful attitude toward criminals (poor minorities, the mentally ill, those who have nothing to lose), the violence will only get worse until there is an all-out war between the haves and the have-nots. Do I overstate? Maybe. For the moment, most violent felons attack people who live near them, who look like them, who share the same social class. Will the crime stay confined? I saw the hate festering in the American gulag all during the '80s. Now I am watching it spill into the streets.

Today's politically motivated campaigns to make prison conditions even harsher are so wrongheaded it scares me — not because I fear the conditions but because I fear the rage and violence that will ricochet back at society. The only prison programs that have consistently been proven to reduce recidivism and temper violence are the education and counseling programs designed to help prisoners make positive changes in their lives. Prisoners who seek out some sort of education while in prison have a very low recidivism rate. Yet we have eliminated Pell grants for prisoners and have cut

back or discontinued other highly effective programs.

To do justice, to break the cycle of violence, to make America safer, prisons need to offer inmates a chance to heal like a human, not merely to heel like a dog. Society is right to expect that prisons will promote respect for the dominant culture and our laws. But how? To paraphrase Malcolm X, a man who has nothing to lose is a dangerous man. Take away what rights prisoners have and no one will be safe — not the guards, not the police, not even the other prisoners.

Prisoners, no matter how heinous their crime, have a right to our compassion and understanding, just as their victims have a right to restitution and to healing, just as society has a right to be protected. Prisoners have a right to hope, they have a right to opportunities that will enable them to change the behavior that led them to crime, and they have a right to reenter society after they've done their time. Prisoners have a right to become welcome members of society instead of brutalized and brutal outcasts.

Stratton is the editor of Prison Life, a bimonthly magazine.

In "Are Lotteries a Ripoff?" Bayer and Merline pose the question, present their evidence, and leave the conclusion up to the reader. As you read this article notice how the authors organize their argument and the kinds of evidence they present to support their position. Begin to think about the assumptions and values behind their argument.

1. What is the authors' argument?

2. What kinds of evidence do they present?

3. Find two examples of counterarguments. What makes them counterarguments?

4. What assumptions do the authors make? What is your view of these assumptions? (Notice that here you are beginning an analysis of the reasons.)

5. Discuss any ambiguous terms the authors may have used.

6. Do the authors present a sound argument? Explain.

Are Lotteries a Ripoff?

BY AMY BAYER AND JOHN W. MERLINE

In more than 28 states, governments are selling lottery tickets with much the same zeal that Procter & Gamble utilizes to sell soap.

In all, states spent nearly $200 million last year advertising one of the few items they sell: lotteries.

This heavy promotion of state-run lotteries has had its intended effect. From 1982 to 1988, lottery revenues increased a staggering 288%. Per capita spending on lotteries in states that sponsor the games increased from $39 in 1982 to $89 in 1988. Americans spent about $17 billion last year chasing after jackpots that sometimes exceeded $50 million.

Recent polls reveal that Americans support lotteries three to one. North Dakota is so far the only state where voters have rejected a move to establish a lottery, while voters in Iowa, Florida, and California approved lotteries over the objection of their governors and many state legislators.

C. Gray Bethea, vice president of Scientific Games, the largest manufacturer of lottery supplies, explains that lotteries are popular because they are "inexpensive entertainment with none of the sordidness some people associate with gambling. And for those who want to play a game of chance, the lottery is a heck of a lot more accessible than Atlantic City or Las Vegas."

However, if consumers knew more about how states run lotteries, fewer might be inclined to favor them.

Lowest Odds

Compared with other forms of legal (and in some cases illegal) gambling, lotteries represent the worst bet for gamblers.

Lotteries have the lowest odds of winning of any form of gambling. The primary reason is that, on average, only about half the money bet on lottery tickets is ever returned to winners. States are in the business of running lotteries to reap the profits, and, in the typical case, take half the revenues right off the top.

On average, 16% of gross lottery sales goes to pay for the administration and promotion of the games. About 35% of the money raised by lottery sales goes into the states' budgets. This means that, on average, less than half of the money bet on lotteries is paid out to bettors — the lowest payout, so far as can be ascertained, of any form of gambling. In some cases, it's even worse for bettors. According to the Indiana Fiscal Policy Institute, New York paid only 39% of lottery receipts back in winnings, and Kansas only 44%, in 1988.

To put this in perspective, consider the average payout rates of other forms of legal gambling:

Craps 98%

Roulette 95%

Slots 75–95%

Jai Alai 85–87%

Horses 83–87%

Lotteries 49%

States cut themselves a bigger break here than they allow other forms of legal gambling. For instance, according to Rick Rolapp, spokesman for the American Horse Council, state governments mandate, on average, a payout for parimutuel wagering on horses of about 80%.

The odds of winning a Lotto jackpot, like the $70 million pot won in April 1989 in Illinois, can range from one in 2 million to one in 17 million, according to Terri La Fleur, senior editor of *Gaming and Wagering Business* magazine. The typical odds are one in every 5 million times. To put this in perspective, the average person is eight times more likely to be hit by lightning than he is to win a million dollar jackpot.

How Much Is a Million?

And, even if you should win, there are some hidden problems. What is also not commonly understood by lottery players is how the state pays out its jackpot. Contrary to popular belief, the Lotto millionaire does not go home with a check for $1 million in his pocket. Here's how it works:

The winner receives a check for $50,000, the first of 20 payments spread out over 20 years. From this amount, the IRS automatically deducts 20% in federal income tax. State and local tax is also deducted. The total received after 20 years is technically $1 million, but in actuality much less when taxes and inflation are factored in. That $1 million ends up looking more like about $560,000 in real money.

Who Promotes Them?

Lotteries have been around for centuries. The ivy-covered buildings of Harvard, Yale, and Princeton were financed in part with lottery dollars, as were some of the 13 original colonies, and battalions in the Revolutionary and Civil Wars. But never have lotteries been so heavily promoted as today.

Lotteries are put on the ballot by voter referendum and passed by popular vote. But rarely is the referendum a product of a citizen grassroots movement. Instead, most lottery referendums are promoted by state legislators and the lottery industry. Legislators who favor lotteries are looking for a new revenue source without the political cost of a tax increase. The lottery industry, which is dominated by Scientific Games Inc., stands to gain whenever new states approve the games.

An Alternative to Taxes?

Many states now view lottery money as "painless taxation." According to the National Conference of State Legislators, the lottery is now "the predominant new revenue source for state government."

In 1988, lotteries brought $375 million into Florida, $435 million into Massachusetts, $543 million into Illinois, and $725 million into New York. All told, 1988 lottery ticket sales pumped $6 billion into state coffers.

However, lottery profits don't represent a large portion of state budgets. On average, lotteries account for only about 2% of total state revenues in those states with the games, according to the U.S. Census Bureau. They have not proved an effective alternative to new taxes, and many states that passed lottery referendums have subsequently raised state taxes.

In Massachusetts, which is facing one of the worst budget crises in recent history, the state legislature in July 1989 passed a bill to extend the state's daily numbers game to Sunday — an extra day of play that would bring another $20 million a year into the state treasury. But at the same time, Massachusetts passed a record $500 million income tax increase.

The same is true for Illinois, where income taxes were raised 20% in 1988 even though lottery revenues rose more than 20%. And, according to *The New York Times*: "New York's game began amid increases in the sales tax and personal and corporate income taxes in the administration of Governor Rockefeller. Washington state's lottery came with the package of tax increases in 1982, when the state was hard-pressed for cash."

A Fiscal Shell Game?

Lotteries are sometimes sold to the public as benefitting certain governmental enterprises such as education, conservation, the arts, etc. According to the Indiana Fiscal Policy Institute, 51% of the states with lotteries dedicate lottery revenues to more or less specific purposes; 8% earmark lottery revenues specifically for education. The remaining states place revenues into their general fund.

The Florida lottery was established with the promise that profits would go into the state education budget. And in California, a 1986 teachers' strike ended in part because teachers were offered raises paid for with lottery profits.

In Virginia, lottery money is directed to community colleges, mental health facilities, park services, etc. And New York's lottery raised more than $848 million last year for education.

The earmarking system has been both a boon and a bust. Ideally, lottery funds make possible the nice but not necessary public programs that state governments otherwise could not afford. But in practice, lottery funds targeted toward specific programs sometimes end up supplanting rather than supplementing general fund money for a program.

Such was the case in Florida last year, when lottery funds were simply substituted for general funds in the education budget.

"It's a fiscal shell game," says Florida education lobbyist Mario Batista. "The voters approved the lottery thinking education would get a real boost, but instead the state just budgeted that much less for education. More money came into the state, but there was no net gain for education."

Another critic is California education superintendent Bill Honig, who says that California schools are "in worse shape" financially because lottery money has given lawmakers and taxpayers the false impression that education needs less public funding.

A Regressive Tax?

While advocates promote lotteries as harmless entertainment and a palatable supplement to taxes, critics view them as simply an alternative form of taxation, and one that is regressive at that.

Many regular players are those least able to afford it, and tickets eat up a larger share of poor people's income than the income of wealthier players.

Most studies indicate that the average lottery player is middle class and that the poor are no more likely to buy lottery tickets than are others. However, lottery wagers do consume a greater share of poor players' incomes.

In California, poor lottery players spent an average of 1.4% of their income on the games, while those making more than $50,000 a year typically bet less than 0.1% of their income, according to a study by the state Senate. A study by economist Daniel Suits found that, in Michigan, the proportion of income spent on lottery tickets declined 12% for every 10% increase in income.

Similarly, a Duke University study found that the poorest third of households bought more than half of all weekly lottery tickets sold.

A 1988 study of Michigan lottery records conducted by the *Ann Arbor News* cautioned that lotteries offered a particularly raw deal for the poor: While Michigan lottery dollars were disproportionately provided by inner-city residents, a greater share of the profits was channeled to wealthier school districts outside the city.

Still, few arguments against lotteries sway the determined bettor, and the games remain a popular, voluntary form of entertainment. "No one is going into the ghetto forcing poor people to play," says Ralph Batch of the Public Gaming Research Institute. "The people wanted lotteries and only the people who want to play, play."

As Iowa Lottery Commissioner Edward Stanek puts it: "Playing the lottery is a form of recreation that's no more harmful for most people than going to the movies or going bowling."

A Substitute for Illegal Gambling?

Lotteries are frequently sold as a way both to raise revenues for state governments and, at the same time, dry up the illegal numbers racket. The state makes the rather tortured argument that "people are going to gamble anyway, so better for the state to get the money than organized crime." As Nelson Rose, professor of law at Whittier College, notes: "If making money is the goal, why doesn't the state own restaurants, or open its own brothels?"

In any case, it is not clear that the lottery has been successful in supplanting illegal numbers games. According to Larry DeBoer, writing for the Purdue University Center for Tax Policy Studies: "There is wide disagreement about the impact of state lotteries on the illegal numbers game." The Public Gaming Research Institute has estimated that one-third of state numbers players are drawn from illegal games, while New Jersey officials estimate that illegal business fell by 15% due to the state lottery.

However, as DeBoer notes, there is some evidence that the operation of the state numbers game increases illegal sales. "For one thing," he points out, "in several states illegal operators have begun taking bets on the state's daily number. Police officials in Washington, D.C., believe that this practice increases the illegal take by one-third. One reason for this increase is that advertising for the state games is in effect advertising for all numbers games. The existence of the legal game may create new bettors without drawing older customers from illegal operators."

According to *Gaming and Wagering Business* magazine, gross revenues for illegal numbers gambling increased an estimated 25% from 1982 to 1988.

Part of the explanation for the continued success of the illegal numbers game is that it offers some gamblers a better deal than the state-run version. According to G. Robert Blakey, writing in *The Journal of Social Issues,* illegal games frequently offer better odds, higher payout, cheaper tickets, and faster drawings than the state-run lotteries. In addition, illegal numbers games have runners who will come to your door to collect tickets and pay back winnings, unlike lotteries, where the patron must travel to the nearest store selling tickets. "About the only advantage of playing a legal game," Blakey notes, "is that it is legal."

Exploring Errors in Reasoning

After reading Chapter 7 you should be able to:

- identify several common reasoning fallacies
- recognize these fallacies when reading
- avoid making common reasoning errors in writing

You may use the following checklist in planning your study of common reasoning errors. Activities marked with a ✪ are to be completed in class. Some preclass preparation may be required.

CONTEXT FOR LEARNING

✪ _____ INTRODUCTORY CHAPTER ACTIVITY

_____ Understanding Fallacies

_____ Common Fallacies

✪ _____ ACTIVITY BREAK

_____ Fallacies in Context

APPLICATION: DETECTING ERRORS IN REASONING

_____ APPLICATION ONE

_____ **Student Dialogues**

_____ COMPREHENSION CHECK

_____ APPLICATION TWO

_____ **Nike Advertisement**

_____ COMPREHENSION CHECK

_____ APPLICATION THREE

_____ **"Arguing Family Style"** by Elisabeth V. Ford

_____ COMPREHENSION CHECK

_____ APPLICATION FOUR

_____ **"The War on (Some) Drugs"** by Stephen Jay Gould

_____ COMPREHENSION CHECK

_____ What Do You Think?

✪ _____ DISCUSSION QUESTIONS

_____ WRITING ASSIGNMENT

✪ **INTRODUCTORY CHAPTER ACTIVITY**

Each of the following statements contains a common error in reasoning called a fallacy. On a piece of paper write the number of each statement and jot down your analysis of the statement. Ask yourself, "Why shouldn't I believe what is being said?" Discuss your answers with a partner. Together, select from the list of fallacies on pages 228–229 the one that seems to best describe the error your analysis revealed, and enter the appropriate letter in the space provided. How successful do you think you were? We will go over the answers as we explain the different fallacies.

_____ 1. I don't see why I can't take steroids, since many professional athletes do.

_____ 2. For want of a nail, the shoe was lost;
For want of a shoe, the horse was lost.
For want of a horse, the rider was lost;
For want of a rider, the battle was lost.
For want of a battle, the kingdom was lost!
All for the want of a nail!

_____ 3. How long have you hated your mother?

_____ 4. We need to do something about the rising number of teen pregnancies because their numbers are increasing dramatically.

_____ 5. He who is not with me is against me.

_____ 6. *Professor*: If you don't want to flunk the course, you'd better not miss my class on Wednesday.

_____ 7. Improved reading is related to arm length. Data show that people with longer arms read better than those with short arms.

_____ 8. That singer is wicked.

_____ 9. *Phong*: Learning English has been difficult. I've had to work twice as hard as others to get my work done on time. Consequently, I haven't been able to get a part-time job. I was hoping the school could give me a scholarship.

College dean: Well, you're lucky to be here; you've had an opportunity that others just haven't been able to have. I always say it's important to count your blessings.

_____ 10. Professor Clark is always preaching the importance of organizing your thoughts in an essay, but why should anyone believe her? Her lectures are totally disorganized!

_____ 11. I don't drink, do drugs, or have sex. I think I should be allowed to stay out as late as I want.

_____ 12. *Famous actress*: If I eat pitted prunes, don't you think you should?

_____ 13. I find the smell of perfume and cologne as obnoxious as people's cigarette smoke. If they are going to ban smoking on airplanes, then they should also ban people from wearing perfume.

_____ 14. *Politician*: We will not tolerate naked aggression. No country has the right to invade a defenseless neighbor. Of course, our invasion of Panama was different. That invasion was morally justifiable.

_____ 15. A positive attitude will lead to success.

Fallacies

a. ambiguity (confusion over definition of word)

b. circular reasoning (begging the question)

c. equivocation (changing definitions)

d. appeal to authority

e. two wrongs make a right

f. argument by force

g. attacking the person (*ad hominem*)

    h. irrelevant reason

    i. fallacy of the continuum (slippery slope: chain of events leading to disaster)

    j. questionable analogy

    k. questionable cause (*post hoc*)

    l. either/or dilemma (false dilemma)

    m. evading the issue

    n. necessary but not sufficient condition

    o. loaded question (statement makes a questionable assumption)

Understanding Fallacies

A fallacy refers to an error in reasoning that may result from a faulty line of thought or from some distortion or distraction created by the *language* of the argument. Most of the time, fallacies are errors, although some types of fallacies can provide supportive evidence for an argument. We will point those out as we proceed.

In Chapter 6, we discussed the role of assumptions in evaluating arguments. Recall that assumptions are the unstated beliefs of the writer and function as the "glue" that joins a particular reason to a conclusion. It is important to find a writer's assumptions in order to evaluate the soundness of the argument. And even if you believe the reason to be true, you will reject the reason if you don't accept the assumption underlying it. In this circumstance, the reason might be true, but it will not support the conclusion.

This chapter discusses fifteen common errors in reasoning. (In Chapter 10, you will learn a number of statistical fallacies associated with research studies.) Based on your work in the Introductory Chapter Activity, you may have decided that you already know how to detect many of them. Obviously, it is more important that you *understand* the error than whether you know the name of the fallacy. Keep in mind that although a fallacy is described as an error in reasoning, there are times when a fallacy may make sense.

Common Fallacies

While not exhaustive, the following list will introduce you to the more common fallacies. As you read this section, compare your answers from the Introductory Chapter Activity to the ones given, and keep track of the number you got "right."

Two wrongs make a right

_____ *e*   1. I don't see why I can't take steroids, since many professional athletes do.

The speaker in this example believes that doing something "wrong" can be defended or supported by evidence that someone else is already doing it. This approach is a favorite defense of children: "Why can't I _____? William, Ralph, Dwayne, Theo, and John-Boy can!" Parents are not above using the same reasoning strategy themselves when confronted with objectionable behaviors: "Why do you need that earring? You don't see me or your father or William, Ralph, Dwayne, or Theo wearing one, do you?" Or the more subtle approach: "Honey, I just heard Vanessa got married. And didn't Debra, Loren, Madeline, Clarissa, and Tania all get married last year?"

A variation on the "two wrongs make a right" fallacy uses the actions of the speaker to avoid addressing the speaker's argument: "How can you tell me it's important to finish my degree when you quit school?" or "Why should I listen to your advice? You've never been an alcoholic."

Fallacy of the continuum (slippery slope)

_____ *i*   2. For want of a nail, the shoe was lost;
For want of a shoe, the horse was lost.
For want of a horse, the rider was lost;
For want of a rider, the battle was lost.
For want of a battle, the kingdom was lost!
All for the want of a nail!

The fallacy of the continuum focuses on a chain of events where once the first step is taken the rest are predictable. As in our example, these events may at first have a minor impact but eventually lead to important consequences. Another way of looking at the fallacy is to consider the notion of "degrees." At what point does short hair become long? At what point does a good ball player become a great one? At what point is an ice cube melted water? In each case, no one would dispute a difference between the two phenomena, yet they might disagree as to the exact point one becomes the other. The issue is not that a difference exists, but when that difference occurs.

The fallacy of the continuum does not necessarily mean that the argument is bad. After years of dismissing the effects of small changes, for example, physicists are now trying to wrestle with the implications of small changes at one point in time resulting in major changes later. James Gleick's book *Chaos* discusses this concept. For instance, if a butterfly flaps its wings in New Delhi, will it create a tornado in Kansas? The important thing is to consider each of the possible steps in a "slippery slope" to determine its validity.

Loaded question

___o___   3. How long have you hated your mother?

Here, the question is asked in such a way as to assume the listener has already answered another question. It leads the listener to an answer based on an implied assumption. In this example, the question assumes that the listener hates his or her mother. Similarly, "Shall I bring the tapes to the party?" is a loaded question if you haven't already been invited. And "Your boyfriend must enjoy going skiing with you" is a loaded statement if you haven't already told the speaker that you have a boyfriend.

Circular reasoning (begging the question)

___b___   4. We need to do something about the rising number of teen pregnancies because their numbers are increasing dramatically.

The conclusion — that something must be done about the rising number of teen pregnancies — is supported by one reason: Their numbers are increasing dramatically. The reason merely restates the conclusion. Nothing new has been added.

Circular reasoning brings the listener back to where he or she started. The conclusion is supported by itself: "I like mocha ice cream because it's the ice cream I prefer to eat." These examples are obvious, but when writers extend their reasoning over several paragraphs and alter the words, though not the content, it becomes more difficult to recognize the fallacy. Breaking the argument into its component parts and then asking yourself whether the reason is new information that *supports* the conclusion or merely *restates* it will help pinpoint examples of circular reasoning.

Either/or dilemma (false dilemma)

___*l*___   5. He who is not with me is against me.

This argument presents the conclusion in such a way that there are only two alternatives when, in fact, there may be other options. Here's another example that may sound more familiar: "Either stay in school or be a bum." In the first example, the listener has only two options: one, agree totally with the speaker, or two, be totally opposed to the speaker. Similarly, in the second example, the listener can either continue to get a formal education or plan on living on the streets. Surely there are countless other possibilities than these two.

The either/or dilemma is one to which we are all susceptible. Much of our own decision making revolves around considering only two perceived choices. We box ourselves in with either/or ultimatums when actually there are several alternatives in front of us. A good rule of thumb is to stop and question yourself every time you hear an either/or statement: Is there an alternative you're not considering?

The examples presented thus far provide alternatives that represent extreme choices, but the fallacy of false dilemma can also offer simplistic solutions to complex problems. Consider the statement "We can stop inflation by either raising taxes or tightening the money supply." The state of our economy depends on so many political and economic variables that it is naive to assume that the president or Congress (through taxes) or the Federal Reserve Board (through monetary policy) will be able to cure economic ills with one sweeping measure. It would be helpful to know, for example, what kind of taxes might be legislated or how restrictive the money supply might be. Also, identifying why inflation is high would help determine the best policy.

Argument by force

_f_   6. *Professor*: If you don't want to flunk the course, you'd better not miss my class on Wednesday.

The professor's implied position is that you must attend class on Wednesday because if you don't you may flunk the course. While missing one class might mean that a student would flunk the course, it is highly unlikely. Here the argument is based on the possibility of extreme consequences. The listener is being asked to accept the conclusion on the basis of potentially dire consequences. Puritan ministers, for example, used to threaten eternal damnation to congregation members who violated any of the church's prohibitions.

Argument from pity is a variation on the argument by force in which the argument is based on an appeal to emotions, not reason: "Don't leave me; I'll die."

Is appealing to the listener's emotions wrong? Do we want to advocate a world in which we disregard emotions? Perhaps the problem arises when an argument appeals *only* to the listener's emotions and offers no valid reasons to support it.

Questionable cause (*post hoc*)

___k___   7. Improved reading is related to arm length. Data show that people with longer arms read better than those with short arms.

The fallacy of questionable cause incorrectly attributes consequences to a particular cause. In this example, reading ability is attributed to longer arm length (that is, arm length is correlated with reading ability). While longer arm length does often accompany improved reading skills, that is more a function of age than evidence of a relationship between the two variables. A sixteen-year-old's arm is certainly longer than a four-year-old's, and most sixteen-year-olds read better than four-year-olds. However, the key to improved reading ability is related to factors other than arm length.

Here is another example. An informal study at a four-year college showed that the grade point averages for single mothers were higher than for women with no children. Therefore, women who want to do well in college ought to become mothers. What's wrong with this reasoning?

Ambiguity

___a___   8. That singer is wicked.

This statement is ambiguous on several counts. We are not sure of the definition of "wicked." (We will assume that we can't hear the intonation of the speaker, which can often give us clues to meanings.) Does "wicked" mean "not good"? Even if it does, we still haven't gotten very far. Is the speaker referring to the singer's personality? His behavior? If so, what personality or behavior traits constitute "wicked"? Or does "wicked" mean "good" as it is used in popular lingo? And if so, what does "good" mean: Kind? Religious? Competent? Funky?

Does our example define *ambiguous*, or have we been ambiguous? An ambiguous argument contains terms whose meanings are not clear or that can be interpreted in a variety of ways. In order to evaluate someone's argument, the listener must be clear on the definitions of the terms being used. Consider the following examples:

> MEXICO. Experience all of Puerto Vallarta for so little! Savor the magic of Mexico's beautiful Pacific coast in Puerto Vallarta . . . at special Worldex Travel Center's bargain rates!

> DOWNTOWN. New Listing. ADORABLE 5-room cottage with that "Cozy Country Look." Like new inside and out. Has 1 and 1/2 baths, 2-car garage, and a yard that needs a little love. WONDERFUL BUY!

Both examples have a buyer in mind, but their arguments to buy (that is, their sales pitches) rest on a series of ambiguous claims. In order to decide whether to accept the arguments, the potential buyer would be wise to resolve the ambiguities.

Evading the issue

_m_   9. *Phong*: Learning English has been difficult. I've had to work twice as hard as others to get my work done on time. Consequently, I haven't been able to get a part-time job. I was hoping the school could give me a scholarship.

College dean: Well, you're lucky to be here; you've had an opportunity that others just haven't been able to have. I always say it's important to count your blessings.

In this example, the college dean avoids discussing Phong's request for a scholarship by trying to change the subject. She evades the issue by suggesting that Phong is lucky and perhaps should be satisfied with the way things are. The reasons Phong should or should not receive a scholarship are not addressed. Evading the issue is a common ploy of some politicians: If they don't like the question they're asked, they simply answer the one they want to.

Attacking the person (*ad hominem*)

_g_   10. Professor Clark is always preaching the importance of or-
        ganizing your thoughts in an essay, but why should anyone
        believe her? Her lectures are totally disorganized!

Here, the speaker attacks the person as a means of dissuading others
from believing Professor Clark's argument. The fact that Professor Clark
is not organized is not a valid basis for neglecting to organize one's
thoughts in an essay. Professor Clark's ideas should be evaluated on
their own merit. However, in this example, our speaker refuses to accept
the ideas of someone who does not "practice what she preaches."

There is a similarity between the fallacy of attacking the person and
the fallacy of irrelevant reason. Obviously, attacking an idea because of
some personality trait or behavior of the debator is an irrelevant reason
and says nothing about the soundness of the argument.

Irrelevant reason

_h_   11. I don't drink, do drugs, or have sex. I think I should be
        allowed to stay out as late as I want.

This argument offers irrelevant reasons to support its conclusion. Reasons related to staying out late (for example, "I'm old enough to make
this kind of decision" or "I'd like to stay until an event is over rather than
leave in the middle") are more relevant than the ones offered. Drinking,
doing drugs, and having sex can be accomplished during the day as
well as at night. Coming home at a given time is unrelated to those
activities.

Appeal to authority

_d_   12. *Famous actress*: If I eat pitted prunes, don't you think you
        should?

We are constantly bombarded with celebrities telling us which hotel
chain to frequent, which credit card to use, what coffee to drink, or
which politician to support. These kinds of appeals to authority make

bad arguments. Often the "expert" or "authority" speaks out on a topic that is unrelated to his or her realm of expertise (if any).

Consider this statement: "The Surgeon General has determined that cigarette smoking is harmful to one's health and may cause cancer." Clearly, the Surgeon General is warning the public against smoking. The background that qualifies a person to be Surgeon General may also qualify him or her as an expert or an authority in the health field. In this case, the fallacy of appeal to authority represents a perfectly sound argument, but even in cases where the experts are qualified, they often disagree. Hence, the common advice is to seek "a second opinion." Appeal to authority makes a good argument only when the experts all agree.

Questionable analogy

_j_   13. I find the smell of perfume and cologne as obnoxious as people's cigarette smoke. If they are going to ban smoking on airplanes, then they should also ban people from wearing perfume.

In this example, the speaker is comparing her annoyance with having to smell cologne to others' irritation with cigarette smoke. But are the fragrance of cologne and the "fragrance" of cigarette smoke comparable? What are the consequences of breathing in cologne versus breathing in cigarette smoke? The conclusion of the argument is based on a false analogy; the argument falsely compares two situations.

Equivocation

_c_   14. *Politician*: We will not tolerate naked aggression. No country has the right to invade a defenseless neighbor. Of course, our invasion of Panama was different. That invasion was morally justifiable.

Technically, *equivocate* means to "mislead, deceive, or confuse" with words. For example, suppose your professor asks the class if they have completed the research assignment. Peter responds that he was at the library last night, and when the instructor asks if he found any relevant journal articles, Peter says that he was looking in the periodical section. Peter has not really answered the questions, but has responded in such a way as to perhaps deceive an unseasoned instructor.

In logic, the definition of *equivocation* has a more specialized meaning. To equivocate means to switch the definition of a key term in an argument. In quiz example 14, the politician defines *invasion* as naked aggression and in the next breath claims that it is morally justifiable. By shifting the meaning of *invasion*, he alters his position in the middle of the argument.

Here's another example. Imagine you're worried about financing graduate school. You talk matters over with your father who promises to help support you. You send him a copy of your first semester's tuition bill and follow up with a phone call. He asks you why you sent him the bill. You respond by reminding him of his offer to help support you. He laughs and says, "Oh, I don't mean *that* kind of support; I was talking emotional support!" Given the context in which your father first offered to "help support" you, you believed he was defining support as financial assistance. At the last minute, it appears that he has "redefined" the term.

Necessary but not sufficient

_*n*_   15. A positive attitude will lead to success.

People may agree that a positive attitude is important for success. They may even believe it is essential to success. But is it enough to *guarantee* it? It may be necessary but it might not be sufficient. What about hard work? Education? Training?

Consider the following example. All cows eat grass. Bessie eats grass. Therefore, Bessie is a cow. While it may be true that all cows eat grass and Bessie eats grass, the fact that she eats grass is not *sufficient* to prove that she is a cow.

We've discussed all the fallacies in the Introductory Chapter Activity. How well did you do in matching fallacies to statements? Those of you who got 12–15 right should congratulate yourselves. Those of you who got 9–11 right did fairly well, but should review carefully the questions you missed. If you scored below 8, however, you need to study the examples and explanations carefully.

✪ **ACTIVITY BREAK**

Find the errors in reasoning in the following examples. Be sure you can explain your answers.

1. You can't believe what she says; she's just looking out for herself.

   _____

2. Where there is a will, there is a way.

   _____

3. When can I see you again?

   _____

4. Vandals broke the wiper motor on my car, so I had to buy a new motor. But while I was installing the new wiper motor it broke down. I was so frustrated that I threw my wrench. The wrench bounced across the seat and smashed through the rear passenger's window, and I had to buy a new window! It just goes to show you that once something goes wrong everything else will too!

   _____

5. As your coach I am telling you, it's either my way or the highway!

_____

6. I've decided that we will make all our decisions by consensus —
after all, majority rules.

_____

7. I think you should give me a break. I didn't want to have to mention
it, but I'm not the only one who turns in papers late.

_____

8. You should add a little spice to your life!

_____

9. If we put our heads together we'll do better because two heads are
better than one.

_____

10. She has so much academic potential, she couldn't be an alcoholic.

_____

Fallacies in Context

Thus far we have been looking at isolated examples of errors in reasoning. In real life, things get much more complicated. Friendly conversations, impromptu debates, and talk show discussions are prime sources
for uncovering fallacious reasoning. They are particularly good sources
because, for the most part, people don't pay as much attention to their
reasoning when they speak as when they write. They don't have as much
time to think through their positions, and they have fewer opportunities
to revise their arguments. They often find themselves reasoning by the
verbal "seat of their pants." By contrast, the process of writing encourages authors to work through the logic of their arguments _before_ going
public.

Application: Detecting Errors in Reasoning

APPLICATION ONE

The following "argumentative" dialogues were written by students. As you read, look for errors in reasoning.

Student Dialogues

It's Sunday afternoon, and Larry and Nelson have just finished watching a track meet.

Nelson: I don't think they should've allowed Ben Johnson back into the Olympics.

Larry: Why? I don't feel that way at all.

Nelson: He still has drugs in his system.

Larry: How can you say that? You don't know if he's still on drugs. Everyone is entitled to a second chance. Besides, everybody knows that all athletes use drugs and just don't get caught.

Nelson: That's a pretty big assumption to make. How can all athletes be on drugs? It's their right to take drugs, if they want to. Do you drink coffee?

Larry: Yeah, so what?

Nelson: Coffee's a drug, and no one is stopping you.

— **Carole Bowe**

A group of students, all under twenty-one years of age, are sitting in a dorm room discussing different topics and the issue of premarital sex comes up.

Kelly: Hey Alex, do you think that a person should have sex before marriage?

Alex: Well, I think having premarital sex is just like drinking; you shouldn't do either.

Kelly: Are you kidding? Sex, drugs, and rock and roll is the American way!

Alex: Well, maybe in Springfield, but in other parts of the state, sex is only shared between two people bonded in holy matrimony.

Kelly: Stop being such a prude! No one gets married these days without having sex first.

Alex: You can believe what you want to, but we'll see who gets AIDS first.

— Cindy Osgood

It's mid-February, and St. Patrick's Day is approaching. The manager of the school cafeteria has ordered St. Patrick's decorations to be put up around the cafeteria. Even though more than half of February, Black History Month, has passed, no decorations have been put up for it. The manager has said students could put up decorations if they got the materials themselves. Some students are upset.

Carole: It's not fair. I hate these prejudiced people!

Edith: It happened in high school and junior high school. You should be used to it by now.

Carole: Why should we have to put up with it? If the white students don't have to pay for their holidays, why should we have to pay for ours?

Edith: I'm not worried about them not having black, red, and green colors up. I'm living in a white society, and I'm staying here. As long as I'm getting my education, I don't care what these people do.

Carole: How can you say that? If they can have their cultural identity come out, why can't we have ours? I asked him if he could put up stuff for St. Patrick's Day, why couldn't he put things up for Black History Month.

Edith: This is something we should be used to by now; so if you're not going to do something about it, stop talking about it!

— Kimberhly Hopkins

At the end of class Kareem is upset at having to write yet another essay involving critical thinking. He decides to voice his opinion to his professor.

Kareem: I think doing the essays in Critical Thinking class on the sample dialogues is unnecessary.

Professor Rasool: Why do you think doing these essays is unnecessary?

Kareem: First of all, I'm not learning anything by doing these dialogues. They're just useless because they're not going to help me later on in my career.

Professor Rasool: Well, Kareem, you may think you're not going to use it later on in your career, but I can bet you that at some point in your career, these essays are going to come in handy.

—anonymous

COMPREHENSION CHECK

For each of the dialogues, check your understanding by outlining the speakers' arguments. Use the format of conclusion, reasons, and assumptions to outline each speaker's argument. Then examine their reasons for possible errors. Remember, it is more important that you understand the error in reasoning than the name of the fallacy. Be prepared to discuss your answers.

APPLICATION TWO

Advertisements are good places to look for potential fallacies. Read Application Two to discover what argument is implied; be sure to read all the text.

Nike Advertisement

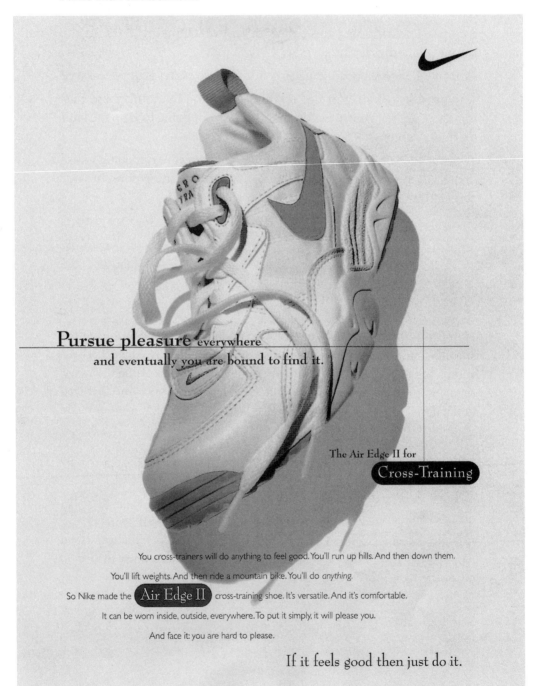

COMPREHENSION CHECK

Find the argument(s) implied by Nike. What kinds of evidence are presented? Are reasons explained or supported? What values are embedded in the advertisement? Are these values important to you? Explain any errors in reasoning you may find. Is the argument valid? This advertisement appeared in *Bazaar* magazine. What influence might the anticipated audience have on the message presented? How might the ad read if it were to appear in a different publication? Explain your answer.

APPLICATION THREE

There are probably as many different ways to argue or debate in a family as there are families! Elisabeth Ford is an English major at Yale University. She wrote this essay in response to the question "What are family arguments like at your house?" In this essay, she describes the uses and abuses of logic employed in family arguments.

Arguing Family Style

BY ELISABETH V. FORD

In my family most of our important communication is conducted by means of arguing and debate. From an early age all of us children were trained in the art of debate, which was a fun game at the beginning. But as we got older, our arguments began to reveal hidden complexity and meaning. We were constantly learning more about the logical structures and the family politics that we had to negotiate our way around. I can see now that an argument has many different meanings in various situations, and we learned techniques for every type.

reveal

The first type of argument we became acquainted with as children was the one-sided argument in which one person tries to get something out of another. Whether the object was a new pair of shoes or a confession of guilt, the strategy was the same. This type of debate usually takes place between a child and a parent, with the child at the *supplicant* end. Adults always have easier ways than debates to get what they want from their kids, and more *subtle* ways to get what they want from each other. The logic we used was one of convenience. The strategy was to hammer the point in with minor variations until the adult *conceded*. Thus these debates were strictly *circular*, and assuming that your opponent didn't have as much of a stake in the transaction as you did, it was easy enough to wear him down given a little time. The argument invariably was won by the most *persistent*.

More difficult to master was the two-sided argument, which is probably the most elegant of the types we use. In this type, both parties care about the issue, which can range from an impersonal question of national politics to an emotionally relevant one of family rights and privileges. It doesn't matter what the subject is; it's given that it's a serious one, and demands formal, *flawless* logic. These are the most *linear* of our debates, the most rigidly structured. But though they always seem on the surface to be hinged on the soundness of our reasoning, there are certain assumptions that can always affect the outcome. The types of arguments that we children can use, for instance, are more limited than they are to my parents. The underlying assumption (at least on their parts) that because of their experience they have more knowledge of any given subject than we do can put us at a disadvantage. When we hold equally sound contradicting opinions, it's always theirs, the voice of experience, that *prevails*. In this and other ways the powers of logic are no match for the power of interpersonal politics.

In other situations, logic plays an even less significant part. Since so much of our communication is conducted through debate, we often use the medium for purposes other than those for which it's intended. An argument can become an easy, if confusing, way to air general emotions and complaints that we're uncomfortable talking about openly. In these the *ostensible* subject bears no necessary rela-

supplicant

subtle

concede

circular

persistent

flawless

linear

prevail

ostensible

tion to the real issue. The surface topic isn't the focus; there is no focus really. Logic is all but ignored as we pry past each other's words to get at the meanings behind them. This type of exchange can rotate frequently and drastically without warning.

The logic in our arguments can be structured or not, present or absent, but no matter how it manifests, it is always a tool we use for our purposes. Logic makes no demands on us, and is always subor-   subordinate
dinate to our needs. Desire and emotion always take precedence in our relations, and thus our logic is one of strict convenience, to be bent and twisted as we like. It's a useful tool in our relations with each other, but in all of its forms it is no more than our tool.

COMPREHENSION CHECK

Write brief answers to the following questions.

1. What topic is being discussed?

2. What is being said about the topic?

3. What kinds of arguments occur in Ford's family?

4. In general, what role does logic play in their arguments? How does it function in each of the different kinds of arguments?

5. What fallacies appear in Ford's essay?

APPLICATION FOUR

Our final reading, by noted paleontologist Stephen Jay Gould, is excerpted from an article that appeared in *Dissent* magazine. The article focuses on dichotomies — divisions of things into two parts or groups. Gould argues that society is "driven to think in dichotomies" and that "our current drug crisis is a tragedy born of a phony system of classification." Read the selection, keeping an eye out for the main reasons he offers to support his conclusion.

The War on (Some) Drugs

BY STEPHEN JAY GOULD

Categories often exert a tyranny over our perceptions and judgments. An old joke—perhaps it even happened—from the bad old days of McCarthyism tells of a leftist rally in Philadelphia, viciously broken up by the police. A passerby gets caught in the melee and, as the cops are beating him, he pleads, "Stop, stop, I'm an anticommunist." "I don't care what kind of communist you are," says the cop, as he continues pummeling.

dichotomy

assert

arbitrary

We seem driven to think in dichotomies. Protagoras, according to Diogenes, asserted that "there are two sides to every question, exactly opposite to each other." We set up our categories, often by arbitrary division based on tiny differences; then, mistaking names for moral principles, and using banners and slogans as substitutes for reason, we vow to live or die for one or the other side of a false dichotomy. The situation is lamentable enough when the boundaries are profound and natural; if cows declared war on chickens, we might deplore the barnyard carnage, but at least the divisions would be deep, and membership by birth could not be disputed. But when humans struggle with other humans, the boundaries are almost always fluid and largely arbitrary (or at least a cu-

lamentable

carnage

rious result of very recent historical contingencies).

Our current drug crisis is a tragedy born of a phony system of classification. For reasons that are little more than accidents of history, we have divided a group of nonfood substances into two categories: items purchasable for supposed pleasure (such as alcohol) and illicit drugs. The categories were once reversed. Opiates were legal in America before the Harrison Narcotics Act of 1914; and members of the Women's Christian Temperance Union, who campaigned against alcohol during the day, drank their valued "women's tonics" at night, products laced with laudanum (tincture of opium).

I could abide—though I would still oppose—our current intransigence if we applied the principle of total interdiction to all harmful drugs. But how can we possibly defend our current policy based on a dichotomy that encourages us to view one class of substances as a preeminent scourge while the two most dangerous and life-destroying substances by far, alcohol and tobacco, form a second class advertised in neon on every street corner of urban America? And why, moreover, should heroin be viewed with horror while

intransigence

scourge

chemical cognates that are no different from heroin than lemonade is from iced tea perform work of enormous compassion by relieving the pain of terminal cancer patients in their last days?

Consider just a few recent items rooted in our false classification.

1. A *New York Times* editorial describes methadone as a drug that "blocks the craving for heroin." You might as well say that a Coke blocks the craving for a Pepsi. Methadone and heroin are both opiates, but methadone is legal as a controlled substitute for heroin (fine by me; I think they both should be controlled and decriminalized). We permit methadone because some favorable features lead to easier control (oral administration, longer action, and a less intense high), but methadone is a chemical cousin to heroin.

2. Representative Charles Rangel (Dem., N.Y.), implacable foe of legalization, spurns all talk about this subject as the chatter of eggheads. In 1988, in a *New York Times* op-ed piece, he wrote, "Let's take this legalization issue and put it where it belongs — amid idle chit-chat as cocktail glasses knock together at social events." Don't you get it, Mr. Rangel? The stuff in the glasses is as bad as the stuff on the streets. But our classifications permit a majority of Americans to live well enough with one while forcing a minority to murder and die for the other.

3. Former surgeon general C. Everett Koop, who was hired by Reagan to be an ideologue and decided to be a doctor instead, accurately branded nicotine as no less addictive than heroin and cocaine. Representative Terry Bruce (Dem., Ill.) challenged this assertion by arguing that smokers are not "breaking into liquor stores late at night to get money to buy a pack of cigarettes." Koop properly replied that the only difference resides in social definition as legal or illegal: "You take cigarettes off the streets and people will be breaking into liquor stores. I think one of the things that many people confuse is the behavior of cocaine and heroin addicts when they are deprived of these drugs. That's the difference between a licit and an illicit drug. Tobacco is perfectly legal. You can get it whenever you want to satisfy the craving."

We do not ponder our methods of classification with sufficient scrutiny — and have never done so. Taxonomy, or the study of classification, occupies a low status among the sciences because most people view the activity as a kind of glorified bookkeeping dedicated to pasting objects into preassigned spaces in nature's stamp album. This judgment rests on the false premise that our categories are given by nature and ascertained by simple, direct observation. Nature is full of facts — and they are not distributed isotropically, so nature does provide some hints about divisions.

scrutiny

taxonomy

ascertain

imposition

plethora

imbibe

vicious

mayhem

But our classifications are human impositions, or at least culturally based decisions on what to stress among a plethora of viable alternatives. Classifications are therefore theories of order, not simple records of nature. More important, since classifications are actively imposed, not passively imbibed, they shape our thoughts and deeds in ways that we scarcely perceive because we view our categories as "obvious" and "natural."

Some classifications channel our thinking into fruitful directions because they properly capture the causes of order; others lead us to tragic and vicious errors (the older taxonomies of human races, for example) because they sink their roots in prejudice and mayhem. Too rarely, in our political criticism, do we look to false taxonomies, particularly to improper dichotomies, as the basis for inadequate analysis.

Our drug crisis is largely the product of such a false dichotomy. At the moment, hundreds of thousands of drug users live in tortured limbo, driven to crime, exposed to AIDS, and doomed (at least statistically speaking) to early death. Millions of others suffer palpably from the deeds of the addicted—experiencing violence, robbery, or simple urban fear that steals the joy from life. Billions of dollars go down the rathole to enrich the entrepreneurs or to try to stem the plague by necessarily ineffective interdiction. The politics of several nations in our hemisphere are corrupted, the cultures of whole peoples severely compromised.

William Jennings Bryan once argued that we were about to crucify mankind on a cross of gold. Are we not now significantly lowering the quality of American life for everyone, and causing thousands of deaths directly, by basing our drug policy on something even worse—a false and senseless classification?

COMPREHENSION CHECK

Write brief answers to the following questions.

1. What topic is being discussed?

2. What is being said about the topic?

3. What fallacy of reasoning does Gould say America is guilty of?

4. How would you paraphrase the following statement: "More important, since classifications are actively imposed, not passively imbibed, they shape our thoughts and deeds in ways that we scarcely perceive because we view our categories as 'obvious' and 'natural'"? Give an example that illustrates this occurrence.

5. How do "improper dichotomies" influence our arguments?

6. Do you agree that our drug crisis is the result of a false dichotomy? Explain your answer.

What Do You Think?

❖ DISCUSSION QUESTIONS

Prepare for class discussion by jotting down brief answers to the following questions.

1. Recently, the California state legislature passed a sales tax on snack food while "regular" food products remained untaxed. How can reasonable guidelines or categories be set up to implement this law? Explain your answer.

2. Advertisers sell products based on convincing consumers that their products offer distinctive features — ruffles on potato chips, for example. Take a product, such as toothpaste, athletic shoes, or candy bars, and list a number of distinctions used to sell this product. In your opinion, which categories represent significant differences in the products?

3. Is logic an effective tool in arguing with your family or friends? Why or why not?

4. Do you agree with Gould's view that "we set up our categories, often by arbitrary division based on tiny differences"? You might consider the categories that develop for different groups on campus: commuters versus residents, traditional students versus nontraditional students, engineering students versus liberal arts students. Give examples from your own experiences.

WRITING ASSIGNMENT

Now it's your turn. As best as you can remember it, write down a conversation or argument that you recently participated in or overheard. Then analyze it for possible reasoning errors. To do this, you'll need to find the position statements of the speakers and their reasons. Use the "Speakers' Arguments" chart to help you. Consider the assumptions behind the reasons and look for errors in the reasoning. Finally, in a few paragraphs, evaluate the overall strengths and weaknesses of the speakers' arguments.

Speakers' Arguments	
Speaker A	**Speaker B**
Position: _____	*Position*: _____
_____	_____
Reasons: _____	*Reasons*: _____
_____	_____
_____	_____
_____	_____
Assumptions: _____	*Assumptions*: _____
_____	_____
_____	_____
_____	_____
Errors in Reasoning: _____	*Errors in Reasoning*: _____
_____	_____
_____	_____
_____	_____

Extending Thinking Skills

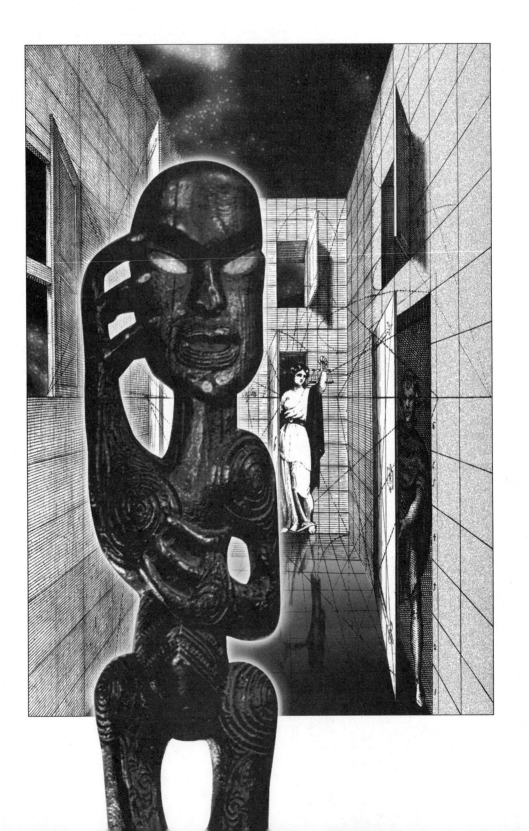

CHAPTER 8

Making Decisions and Solving Problems

After reading Chapter 8 you should be able to:

- define what a problem is
- recognize the role problems play in people's lives
- complete a strategy for problem solving
- appreciate the need for creativity in problem solving

You may use the following checklist in planning your study of decision making and problem solving. Activities marked with a ✪ are to be completed in class. Some preclass preparation may be required.

CONTEXT FOR LEARNING

✪ _____ **INTRODUCTORY CHAPTER ACTIVITY**

_____ Perspectives on Problems

_____ Understanding Problems: Cause and Effect

✪ _____ **ACTIVITY BREAK**

_____ **"Is Food Relief Helpful or Harmful?"** by G. Tyler Miller, Jr.

_____ Strategies for Solving Problems

_____ Creativity in Problem Solving

✪ _____ **DISCUSSION BREAK**

APPLICATION: SOLVING SOME PROBLEMS

_____ **APPLICATION ONE**

_____ **"Setting Limits: The Key to Working, Studying and Parenting"** by Carol Wilson

_____ **COMPREHENSION CHECK**

_____ **APPLICATION TWO**

_____ **"Human, All Too Human"** by Michael Blumenthal

_____ **COMPREHENSION CHECK**

_____ **APPLICATION THREE**

_____ **"Returning Bones of Contention"** by John Elson

_____ **COMPREHENSION CHECK**

———   **APPLICATION FOUR**

———   **"Wildlife and Plants: Preserving Biological Diversity"**
by Daniel D. Chiras

———   **COMPREHENSION CHECK**

———   What Do You Think?

✪ ———   **DISCUSSION QUESTIONS**

———   **WRITING ASSIGNMENTS**

✪ **INTRODUCTORY CHAPTER ACTIVITY**

On a piece of paper, list five national or global problems in need of solutions. Write the problems in the form of a question, and be specific. For example: How can we find ways to cut down on the amount of trash our society produces? or How can we effectively deal with increasing numbers of drug abusers? Next, list three school or community problems. For example: What can students do to make staying on campus over the weekend more exciting? or How can we decrease the amount of crime in our vicinity? Finally, list two personal problems. For example: How can I continue to play ball and pass my courses? or How can I stop worrying about money all the time? Share your list with a few classmates and save it for a future activity.

Perspectives on Problems

A friend walks up to you, looks you straight in the eye, and says, "You've got a problem." You groan, your heartbeat quickens, your body tenses, and depending on how severe you imagine the problem to be, you start feeling guilty, angry, and fearful. This is the typical response of some-one who believes that problems always spell T-R-O-U-B-L-E, that problems are inherently BAD. A corollary to this belief is that the fewer problems in one's life, the better. One of the consequences of this kind of thinking is that people focus on ways to ward off, if not totally eliminate, problems from their lives. Rather than learning how to solve or resolve problems, people develop strategies for avoiding or denying them.

Perhaps problems are an inherent part of our lives. As Master Dogen in Schloegl's *The Wisdom of Zen Masters* observes: "The flower petals fall though we love them, the weeds grow though we hate them — that is just how it is." If it is true that problems will persist like Master Dogen's weeds, then strategies other than avoidance and denial may be wiser. Is it possible that the quality of our lives is directly dependent upon our attitude and approach toward solving our problems? Before we answer this question, however, we need to ask: What exactly is a problem?

Defining problems

A simple definition that minimizes the negative aspects of problems is that a problem signals a desire or need for change. Here, we have avoided defining problems as "challenges" because challenge has the connotation of heroic effort or achievement against the odds. Now this may be appropriate in some situations, but if you are already exhausted, worried, and buried under the weight of the problem, you may find it difficult to summon that superhuman effort. Better to remind yourself that problems mean you want to make a change and that the change initially might be a minor one. Solving problems then becomes an exercise in developing and implementing a plan for change, a blueprint.

Convincing others of their problems

According to our definition, the person who wants change is the one with the problem. However, that person often spends a great deal of time trying to convince others that the problem is theirs.

Consider the following example. Joel wishes Tabitha would be more communicative and share more of her thoughts and feelings. Tabitha says she feels things but doesn't always need to put them into words. Joel tells Tabitha she has a problem and should see a counselor. Who has the problem? The person who wants change. What change does Joel want? More communication and sharing. If Joel is unable to convince Tabitha to change, he may decide he has to solve his problem by breaking off the relationship. This may or may not create a problem for Tabitha.

Often, people let their values decide who has the problem. Joel values open communication, and because Tabitha doesn't, he feels she has the problem. In fact, Tabitha isn't distressed about her style of communication. She doesn't place a high value on verbal expressions of feelings. Joel can try to persuade her to accept his point of view and thereby convince her of her shortcomings, or he can decide whether he wants to be in a relationship with someone who doesn't share his belief in communication. This is his legitimate problem.

But problems don't always arise between parties who share power equally and who are equally free to assume a "take it or leave it" attitude. Consider the problems that can arise between parents and their children. Suppose Hala accuses her parents of never listening to her side of the story; since she is the oldest in her family, she automatically is considered responsible for fights with her brother. While she may indeed sometimes strike him first, she never is allowed to explain the events that led up to the incident — events she feels would prove that her brother was at least equally responsible for what happened. Hala wants her parents to listen to her, so according to our definition she is the one with the problem, because she is the one who wants the change. But the relationship between her and her parents isn't the same as that between Tabitha and Joel. If Hala can't convince her parents that they have a problem, she will have to live with it. Her options are more limited than Joel's.

Convincing the public of their problems

In the public arena, many nonprofit organizations and ecology-minded groups spend considerable time and money trying to convince us that we have problems with teen pregnancy, drugs, the environment, and so on. They are often successful. For example, five years ago few people believed that the ozone layer had any bearing on their lives. After the release of recent reports indicating a rise in skin cancer, many people have become concerned about the potential dangers of a depleted ozone layer. Likewise, many large businesses, who ten years ago only listened politely to requests for affirmative action, now find themselves working frantically to meet the needs of an increasingly diversified work force.

Problems related to culture

As the previous examples suggest, getting people to recognize a problem as their own is a first step to action. Thus, much problem solving may start with making people see they have a problem. This can be very difficult, however, especially when cultures disagree on what behaviors or situations should be considered as "problems." For example, being late is a problem only if your culture places a high value on punctuality, as Western cultures do but Middle Eastern cultures do not. Can you think of other examples?

Let's consider the concept of problems being defined by culture a little more closely. Do we have so many problems in the West because our culture views change as good? Most of us may believe that modern advances in medicine, transportation, communication, and production have meant progress, although we may not agree as readily to a definition of *progress*. If there is a more efficient way to accomplish something, then we want to do it. More choices mean progress. Those who question the notion of change are called old-fashioned, backward, and perhaps uncivilized.

Our logic goes something like this: Westerners like change. Solving problems means change. Therefore, westerners like solving problems. If it is true that westerners like solving problems, then they will find them to solve! Put another way, if we did not believe that change was evidence of progress, would we recognize so many situations as problems? If we lived in a culture that revered the past, as some traditional African cultures did, would we be more content with the status quo and thus have fewer problems?

Understanding Problems: Cause and Effect

A common reaction to identifying a problem is to ask "How did I get here?" What caused this problem? How did it get to be a problem? What will happen if I do nothing or if I try to solve it with Plan x, y, or z? Why certain events happen or why certain problems exist and what will happen as a result of them is characteristic of cause-and-effect relationships. Explaining events in terms of cause-and-effect relationships can be helpful in understanding problems. From this perspective, a cause is often seen as "the problem" with the effect being the consequence of what happens next.

Cause-and-effect relationships are often complicated and function as a chain of causes and effects. One event may be a cause in situation A and the effect in situation B. For example, Tabitha's communication style may be due to her upbringing. Her upbringing is the cause; her lack of communication is the effect. But if Joel ends the relationship because of Tabitha's lack of communication, then communication becomes the cause and ending the relationship becomes the effect. Let's imagine that once Tabitha realizes that Joel is gone, she buys six self-help books on interpersonal relationships and learns how to be more expressive. How would you describe the chain of causality here? Any idea of how our "story" might end?

Causes	*Effects*
Tabitha's upbringing	not very communicative
lack of communication	Joel ends relationship
Joel ends relationship	Tabitha reads six self-help books
Tabitha reads books	She becomes more communicative

✪ **ACTIVITY BREAK**

Looking at problems and solutions as cause-and-effect relationships allows us to see their interconnectedness and the sequence or progress of events. Of course, it is important not to attribute cause when there is none. You may recall the fallacy of questionable cause in which improved reading ability was linked erroneously with arm length. Another fallacy that considered cause was fallacy of the continuum (slippery slope). Turn to page 230, and map out the chain of events.

Read the following passage, and map out the different chains of cause and effect. Which of these causes would be described as problems? Which effects could be called solutions? (*Hint:* It may be useful to start with overall solutions and work backward.)

Is Food Relief Helpful or Harmful?

BY G. TYLER MILLER, JR.

Most people view food relief as a humanitarian effort to prevent people from dying prematurely. However, some analysts contend that giving food to starving people in countries where population growth rates are high does more harm than good in the long run. By encouraging population growth and not helping people grow their own food, food relief condemns even greater numbers to premature death in the future.

Biologist Garrett Hardin has suggested that we use the concept of *lifeboat ethics* to decide which countries get food aid. He starts with the belief that there are already too many people in the lifeboat we call Earth. If food aid is given to countries that are not reducing their population, this adds more people to an already-overcrowded lifeboat. Sooner or later, the boat will sink and kill most of the passengers.

Large amounts of food aid can also depress local food prices, decrease food production, and stimulate mass migration from farms to already-overburdened cities. It discourages the government from investing in rural agricultural development to enable the country to grow enough food for its population on a sustainable basis.

Another problem is that much food aid does not reach hunger victims. Transportation networks and storage facilities are inadequate, so that some of the food rots or is devoured by pests before it can reach the hungry. Typically, some of the food is stolen by officials and sold for personal profit. Some must often be given to officials as bribes for approving the unloading and transporting of the remaining food to the hungry.

Critics of food relief are not against foreign aid. Instead, they believe that such aid should be given to help countries control population growth, grow enough food to feed their population using sustainable agricultural methods, or develop export crops to help pay for food they can't grow. Temporary food aid should be given only when there is a complete breakdown of an area's food supply because of natural disaster. What do you think?

Strategies for Solving Problems

Solving a problem involves going through a process that can involve keen analytical skills as well as an awareness and appreciation of the emotions attached to the problem. If the solution to a problem is essentially a blueprint for change, then a variety of plans and their consequences must be carefully considered. This takes time. Jumping at a solution or convincing yourself that the solution is an either/or dilemma only increases the likelihood of good intentions leading to disastrous outcomes.

Solutions are easy to come by; there may be as many solutions to a problem as there are interested people. *Good* solutions are harder to find. It is important to understand the cause-and-effect relationships between problems and solutions. The following six-step process gives you an effective method for solving problems. Going through each of the steps will enable you to explore the problem from various vantage points. As you read through the steps, keep in mind the list of problems you developed in the Introductory Chapter Activity. The box on pages 266–267 presents a completed chart as a model. It uses the problem-solving format to answer the question "How can I get myself to stick to a regular exercise schedule?"

Method for Problem Solving

1. *Define the problem.* Be specific. Define the problem in terms of a question. For example, phrase the problem as "How can we find ways to cut down on the amount of trash our society produces?" rather than saying "We have a problem with trash in our society."

   (*Note:* Steps two and three can be reversed.)

2. *Gather background information on the problem.* This information may come from library research, personal knowledge, interviews, or other sources. Your goal is to bring together any information that will be useful in coming to a solution.

   a. *Relevant facts.* What is the history of the problem? How urgent is the problem? What solutions have been tried in the past?

   b. *Significant feelings.* Is this a problem that generates strong feelings among people? What are your feelings and on what are they based?

3. *Present possible solutions.* What are the advantages or disadvantages? For example: Is the plan easily implemented? Is it manageable? Does it require enormous amounts of energy,

money, or willpower? Who will benefit most from the proposed solution? Will some groups be unfairly burdened? Is the plan cost effective? Are there hidden variables that haven't been accounted for? Is the solution compatible with personal and cultural values? Can the plan be implemented within a reasonable time frame? Can success be evaluated? (For this step, use the brainstorming techniques described in the section "You and Creative Thinking" on page 7 and reviewed in the section "Creativity in Problem Solving" below.)

4. *Review options with a friend or colleague.* What kind of feedback on your solutions do they offer? Do they agree with your analysis of the solutions?

5. *Decide on the best course of action.* Having completed steps 1–4, you are now in a position to recommend a particular solution, to make an informed choice and defend that choice.

6. *Develop a plan of action.* This may mean developing a timetable for implementation, setting target dates, delegating tasks, and establishing short-term goals.

Creativity in Problem Solving

A common technique used to "free up" the mind is brainstorming. (See also the section "You and Creative Thinking," on page 7.) This strategy employs a kind of free association in which a group of people recount (or write down) everything that they think of on a specific topic, problem, or situation. The goal is to generate as many ideas as possible around the issue without evaluating their worthiness. Later, the brainstormers go back and review and assess the information. At this point, good reasoning skills are important. This approach has also been used effectively by "think tank" organizations in trying to solve national problems.

Sample Problem-Solving Outline

1. *Problem*

   How can I get myself to stick to a regular exercising schedule?

2. *Background Information*

   a. *Relevant facts*:

      I am always planning to exercise, but don't seem to have the willpower to follow through. I think that it's impossible to find a regular time to exercise because my schedule is so irregular. I secretly fool myself by thinking that because I'm not overweight, I'm physically fit. I've tried other forms of exercise and although I don't love aerobics, I don't hate doing it.

   b. *Significant feelings*:

      I like the way I feel after doing aerobics. I feel very guilty when I say I'm going to do them and then I don't.

3. *Possible Solutions*

Solution	Advantages	Disadvantages
#1 join aerobics class	regular time set by someone else have company while exercising more variety	costs money if I don't go I'll feel like a failure might have to be social when I'm not in the mood

#2

| make a chart of my weekly schedule and find workable times | meet flexibility needs of my schedule | no one there to check up on me to see if I do it

boring to exercise alone |

#3

| find time to do aerobics with my daughter | have someone to exercise with | it will be hard to coordinate our schedules |

4. *Options*

I talked my options over with a good friend. She said it looked like exercising itself wasn't enough of a reward for me. She suggested I build in different rewards for myself. Rather than spend the money on an aerobics class, she suggested that I buy a few aerobics tapes to give myself more variety.

5. *Best Course of Action*

I've decided to go with option 2, but include my friend's suggestions. I'll rent a few tapes from the library before I buy any. I plan on having three tapes. I don't know what reward I want at the moment so I think I'll pay myself $2 every time I exercise. I like the plan because I won't waste any money. I will have a variety of exercise tapes, and I'll have a realistic schedule. While I'm exercising I'll be thinking about the money I'm "earning."

6. *Plan of Action*

By this Friday: complete chart of activities
Saturday and Sunday: borrow a few exercise tapes from the library
Monday: begin exercise schedule, put money in jar

If change is the only constant in our future, we can anticipate having to solve many problems. Change produces anxiety, and as Roger Heyns, president of the William and Flora Hewlett Foundation, cautions, "If you're really scared, then the simple answer is going to be better than the complicated answer." However, oversimplifications, he says, don't work in a world where "we've got all this ambiguity."

How will people and nations develop the capacity to solve a never-ending flow of complex problems? In order to succeed it will be necessary to prepare a world community that can think critically and creatively, that can deal with complexity and ambiguity, and that can maintain flexibility and yet be capable of making and implementing decisions.

✪ **DISCUSSION BREAK**

Prepare for class discussion by writing brief answers to the following questions. Then, following the guidelines presented in Chapter 1, conduct a group discussion focusing on these questions. Be sure to prepare for the discussion, choose a facilitator, and, after the discussion, evaluate both the group's and your performance.

1. Recall a recent problem that you attempted to solve. What steps did you take? Did you have all the information you wanted or needed to find a solution? What was the outcome?

2. Provide examples of how disagreement over the causes of a problem can lead to advocating different solutions and outcomes.

3. How does unequal distribution of power in our society affect how different ethnic groups view problems related to race, gender, and socioeconomic class?

4. Think of an international incident where problems arose because of differences in cultural assumptions. What cultural misunderstandings made solving the problem more difficult? Explain your answer. How can we avoid these pitfalls in the future?

Application: Solving Some Problems

APPLICATION ONE

One of the most difficult problems that students must solve is how to balance their academic and social lives. For some, having too much time is a burdensome luxury. For students who always plan to do the work "later," later seems to come at midnight the night before the assignment is due. And for those students who are also athletes, parents, or employees, schoolwork becomes a logistical nightmare. In this reading, a single mother and student describes how she has tried to tackle this problem.

Setting Limits: The Key to Working, Studying and Parenting

BY CAROL WILSON

Being a single mother is very hard, especially when your child depends on you most of the time. I find it difficult to give my daughter the quality time she deserves and still do a good job at work and school.

I have found that in trying to improve myself educationally and financially I have had some negative reactions from my family and friends. An example is my daughter's father who thinks I shouldn't work so hard because I'm always tired. My daughter is also upset because sometimes I cancel our plans to do something together. Working hard keeps me away from my friends and causes tension between us. They take it personally that I don't spend as much time with them as I used to. By the time I do get some time to myself, I just want to rest.

At work I now try to make things a little easier by deciding what has to be done immediately and what can wait. For example, if it is not mandatory for me to stay and work late, I leave at the appropriate time. In the past, I tried to stay as long as I could to make more money, but I have found that's not always the best thing to do.

mandatory

Because I don't have as much time with my daughter as I would like, I try to do more things with her when we are together. We go to the zoo or out to dinner, read books and do projects. By doing this more often I find her to be happier and I feel less guilty about leaving her.

My study time is also limited. Most of the time I study after my daughter has gone to bed. Every other weekend when she's with her father, I spend most of my time in the library.

I think the experience of being a working mother and going back to school has made me a stronger person and has also made me realize that I can do a lot of things I set my mind to.

COMPREHENSION CHECK

Write brief answers to the following questions.

1. What reactions has Wilson experienced as she tries to juggle school, work, and parenting?

2. How does she describe her problem?

3. In what ways has she tried to solve her problem?

4. How does she evaluate her experiences as a working mother and student?

APPLICATION TWO

In "Human, All Too Human," which appeared in the *New York Times*, the author describes a situation in which good intentions led to bad consequences. Preview the article by reading the headline and the highlighted sentence. As you read, be thinking about the problem-solving technique described in this chapter.

Human, All Too Human

BY MICHAEL BLUMENTHAL

extinction

disembark

frenetic

aerial
predator

Isla Espanola, Galápagos Is. If the road to hell is paved with good intentions, an episode in man's interaction with nature I recently witnessed may be further evidence that the road to species extinction is composed of the same materials.

Disembarking onto the beautiful white sand beach of Gardner Bay on the most southern island in the Galápagos, a group of seven travelers and myself, with our naturalist guide, made our way along the beach. We were searching for the large nests in which the eggs of Pacific green sea turtles incubate and hatch.

Most of the hatchlings, which may grow to be as large as 330 pounds, emerge in April and May in a frenetic life-and-death scramble toward the sea, before an intimidating arsenal of aerial predators can reduce them to a satisfying hors d'oeuvre.

It was getting close to dusk, the time at which — if the young turtles are to escape — one of the hatchlings must make a first, tentative foray into the open air to test whether it is safe for its dozens of siblings to follow.

After passing by several large, bowl-shaped nests which showed no signs of activity, I came to a nest in which there was the gray head of a tiny sea turtle hatchling. Signaling to my companions, I watched the tiny reptile hold motionless, its head perhaps a half inch out of the sand.

As the others came over to join me, we heard — no doubt attracted by our presence — a sudden rustling in the brush behind us, as a hood mockingbird, sensing an early evening meal, approached.

"Just be quiet and watch," our young Ecuadorian guide cautioned as the mockingbird moved to within inches of the hatchling's head. "He's going to attack."

Slowly, the mockingbird edged closer to the opening and began pecking at the hatchling's head, trying to pull it onto the beach.

A flotilla of gasps echoed from my companions. "Aren't you doing to *do* something?" a voice demanded of

flotilla

An attempt to help a baby sea turtle wreaks havoc on the species.

---

our guide, who simply held his fingers to his lips. "This is the way nature works," he cautioned us. "We should just be quiet and watch."

"I'm not going to sit here and watch this happen," objected a mild-mannered vegetarian from Los Angeles.

"Why don't you listen to him?" I pleaded. "There's a reason nature works this way. We shouldn't interfere."

"If it weren't for humans," one of our other shipmates, an editor at National Geographic, lectured me, "they wouldn't be endangered to begin with."

"*I'll* do something about it if you won't," her husband added as an additional warning to our guide.

This cacophony of humanists (clearly the right word for that condition) noisily shooed the mockingbird from its scrumptious-looking meal. Reluctantly, our guide pulled the hatchling out of the hole to help it on its way seawards.

What happened next, however, caught everyone, our guide included, by surprise. Rather than one rescued hatchling scurrying to safety, dozens upon dozens of dark gray baby sea turtles—having received a false signal that it was safe—poured out of the nest and began paddling, like a madly retreating army, toward high tide.

The folly, the utter destructiveness, of our group's interference became unmistakably clear. Not only had the hatchlings emerged under the mistaken impression that it was safe to do so, but their mad rush was taking place moments too early—in the still-clear light of dusk which allowed no hiding from the eager scavengers

shoo

scavenger

for whom our intervention must have seemed a gift from the gods.

Within seconds, the air was dense with delighted frigate birds, boobies and swallow-tailed gulls. A pair of Galapagos hawks landed wide-eyed on the beach and a growing flock of mockingbirds eagerly followed their desperately-paddling evening meal down the beach.

"Oh, God," I heard a voice behind me, "Look what we've done!"

"I knew I shouldn't have let you talk me into it," seconded our guide, having returned too late to the convictions of his original wisdom.

By now, the terrestrial and aquatic slaughter of the dozens of hatchlings was well underway. Our young naturalist, madly trying to compensate for having disobeyed his own better instincts, grabbed a baseball cap and filled it with hatchlings. Wading into the ocean, he released the baby turtles into the water, wildly waving the hat into the air to frighten off the armada of frigate birds and boobies whose evening meal had so conveniently been served up to them.

By the time it was over, the celebratory cries of dozens of well-fed predators filled the air. Two hawks stood silently on the beach hoping to catch a final, straggling morsel. The air grew still, as one imagines it might after a large conflagration. All that could be heard was the sound of the tide beating against the white sands of Gardner Bay.

morsel

conflagration

Heads down, my group walked slowly—each in his separate silence—along the beach. It was almost dark, the time of day at which hatchlings, undisturbed by would-be benefactors, will try to make their way toward the sea, toward life. Suddenly, there seemed to me to be a perfect stillness among this all-too-human group.

Something, I think, very much like the sound of humility.

benefactor

COMPREHENSION CHECK

Write brief answers to the following questions.

1.   What is the setting for this article?

2.   What background information does the author give about green sea turtles?

3.   Briefly, what is the article about?

4.   How does the author create interest?

5.   Where did the "problem solvers" go wrong?

6.   Map out the chain of cause and effect described in the article.

7.   What message is the author trying to convey with his story?

APPLICATION THREE

Keep in mind the following questions as you read the *Newsweek* magazine article "Returning Bones of Contention": Which culture is having a problem? What is the problem? What arguments are made by the two groups? How is the problem resolved? Think about the meaning of the article's subtitle: "A bitter debate over spiritual values and scholarly needs."

Returning Bones of Contention

BY JOHN ELSON

A bitter debate over spiritual values and scholarly needs

Arriving at work one day, a Wasp lawyer for Washington's Smithsonian Institution finds a carton on her desk. She is stunned. Inside the box are some clumps of dirt and a note proposing that the contents — the remains of her grandparents, freshly dug up from a New England cemetery — be put on display by the museum. The sender is a part-Navajo conservator at the institution, furious that such a fate has befallen the bones of his ancestors.

epitomize

That grisly episode (from Tony Hillerman's novel *Talking God*) is fictional, but it epitomizes the tensions in a dilemma that confronts curators, anthropologists and those Native Americans who angrily oppose them. To many scholars, and to much of the museum-going public, the Indian bones and burial artifacts are valuable clues to humanity's past. But to many Indians, these relics are sacred and the archaeologists who have appropriated them no better than grave robbers.

artifact

appropriate

Last week the Smithsonian signed a landmark agreement with leaders of two national Indian organizations that both sides hope will help defuse the issue. The institution, which has 18,500 human remains and thousands of other burial artifacts, agreed to inventory its collection. Remains that can be clearly identified as belonging to an individual or a surviving tribe as well as all burial artifacts will be offered to the Native Americans for reburial. In return the Indians dropped their demand that the Smithsonian surrender all its remains, many of whose origins are unknown.

For the Indians, said Walter Echo-Hawk, senior counsel for the Native American Rights Fund, the agreement marks the "beginning of the end of their spiritual nightmare." In fact, some scholarly institutions have gone further: Stanford University has consented to return an entire collection of skeletal remains of 550 Indians, most of them from the Ohlone tribe, to their descendants. Nonetheless, many curators and anthropologists are worried that a sweeping national policy would empty museums across the land. Scholars argue that preserved skeletons and other human artifacts, particularly those of great antiquity, provide es-

antiquity

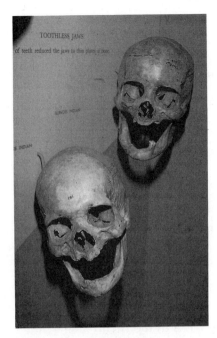

Indian skulls on display at the Smithsonian. Agreeing to defuse an ethical dilemma.

sential information on problems ranging from the organization of tribal societies to the origin of certain diseases, like rheumatoid arthritis.

To that argument, Native Americans answer that 1) most of the unearthed Indian bones lie moldering and unexamined in museum basements; and 2) little if any data gathered from their study are shared with the descendants. According to Suzan

Shown Harjo, executive director of the National Congress of American Indians, the only bit of information the Smithsonian ever imparted to her group was that their ancestors ate corn. "We could have told them that anyway," says Harjo, citing the accuracy of Indian oral tradition.

impart

Returning Indian remains to the proper heirs is not always easy. What contemporary group, asks David Hurst Thomas of New York City's American Museum of Natural History, can speak for a tribe that no longer exists? "If we find things from 10,000 years ago," he says, "it becomes tricky." Another potential problem: misidentified remains of one tribe might be returned to descendants of a group that was historically its mortal enemy. Beyond that, scholars note, tribes varied widely in their treatment of the dead; for some, the spirit left the remains, while for others, the spirit is still with the bones.

Nevertheless, common sense argues for wider acceptance of the Smithsonian's accord, even at the risk of some loss to scholarship. As Harjo notes, the agreement applies "modern standards of ethics to yesterday's abuses." And it may help forestall the future desecration of lands that others hold sacred in memory.

forestall

COMPREHENSION CHECK

Write brief answers to the following questions.

1. Which culture is having a problem?

2. What is the problem?

3. What arguments are made by the two groups?

4. How was the problem resolved?

5. In your opinion, has the problem been solved fairly?

APPLICATION FOUR

Many of the major problems the world faces in the twenty-first century will involve our global environment. The following reading, excerpted from an environmental science textbook, focuses on some of those problems. Before reading the selection, make an outline using the headings in the reading, leaving spaces between the headings. Next, compare the organization of this reading to that of the previous article, "Returning Bones of Contention." What differences do you find?

Wildlife and Plants: Preserving Biological Diversity

BY DANIEL D. CHIRAS

Why save endangered species?

Aesthetics   As Norman Myers has written, "We can marvel at the colors of a butterfly, the grace of a giraffe, the power of an elephant, the delicate structure of a dia- tom. . . . Every time a species goes extinct, we are irreversibly impov- erished." Wildlife and their habitat are in many ways a rich aesthetic resource. The sight of a female

impoverished

trumpeter swan gently nudging her offspring into the water for their first swim, the eerie cry of the common loon at night, the lumbering grizzly bear on a distant grassy meadow, the sputtering of a pond full of ducks, the playful antics of sea otters, the graceful dive of the humpback whale — these enrich our lives in ways no economist could figure. For the weary urbanite home from the office, the sound of migrating geese stirs deep emotions, a satisfying sense that all is well. Destroying the biological world impoverishes all of us.

Ethics Preserving endangered plants and animals is an ethical issue as well. What right, critics ask, do we have to tear apart the richly diverse biological world we live in? Don't other organisms have a right to live, too? Preserving life has become our duty because we have acquired the means to destroy the world. With that ominous power comes responsibility.

ethical

Economics Economically, it makes good sense to protect the rich biological diversity we inherited from our forebears. "From morning coffee to evening nightcap," writes Myers, "we benefit in our daily lifestyles from the fellow species that share our One Earth home. Without knowing it, we utilize hundreds of products each day that owe their origin to wild animals and plants. Indeed our welfare is intimately tied up with the welfare of wildlife. Well may conservationists proclaim that by saving the lives of wild species, we may be saving our own."

conservationist

From the biosphere we reap fish from the sea; medicines and other products from plants; important plant and animal genes needed to improve domestic crops and livestock; a wealth of wildlife for hunters, anglers, and nature lovers; and research animals that provide valuable insights into human physiology and behavior. The economic benefits of these wild resources are enormous. By some estimates, for example, half of all prescription and nonprescription drugs are made with chemicals that came from wild plants. The commercial value of these drugs is around $20 billion per year in the United States and about $40 billion worldwide. The US Department of Agriculture estimates that each year genes bred into commercial crops yield over $1 billion worth of food. Similar gains can be documented for other major agricultural nations. About half of the increased productivity in corn over the last 50 years has resulted from "genetic transfusions" from wild relatives of corn or from corn's early ancestors grown now only in isolated regions.

"Wild species rank among the most valuable raw materials with which society can meet the unknown challenges of the future," writes Myers. Many developments from wild species now loom on the horizon and may offer us further financial gains and healthier lives. For example, the adhesive that barnacles use to adhere to ships may provide us with a new glue to cement fillings into teeth. A chemical derived from the skeletons of shrimps, crabs, and lobsters may help prevent fungal infections. An antiviral drug is now being developed from a Caribbean sponge. It has already proved effective against herpes encephalitis, a previously lethal brain infection that strikes thousands of people each year.

Plants and animals lost before they can be explored for possible benefits will diminish our opportunities to fight disease and increase productivity. A dozen regions located in the tropics and subtropics are the sources of virtually all commercially valuable plants and animals. They provide a reservoir of genetic material essential for the battle to fight disease, drought, and insects. Their loss would be a global tragedy with far-reaching effects on the food supply.

Ecosystem stability Finally, preserving species and their habitat helps ensure global ecosystem stability and, ultimately, our own future. The endangered biosphere provides us with many invaluable services free of charge. It controls pests. It recycles oxygen, carbon, and dozens of important nutrients. It maintains local climate. It helps control groundwater levels and reduces flooding. Without these hidden benefits humans would be an endangered species.

Human civilization thrives as the biological world thrives. In the short term, wildlife advocates argue, a species lost here and there may be of little consequence for overall ecosystem stability, but in the long term the cumulative effect of such losses threatens our own survival.

Opposing views Critics of the animal protection movement argue that too much energy and money is spent on saving endangered species. Researchers and wildlife departments have spent millions of dollars to save the California condor, which still teeters on the brink of extinction. Tens of thousands of dollars will be needed to resurrect the dusky seaside sparrow, which once thrived in the marshlands of east-central Florida. A few critics argue that money would be spent more wisely on prevention. Other critics want to know why there is so much fuss over endangered species that block "human progress."

Surely, a species lost here or there can have no great significance to us. The world will probably never miss the passenger pigeon or the peregrine falcon. And surely no irreparable ecosystem damage would result from the extinction of these and other species. Biologists argue, however, that if we take the attitude that each species by itself is dispensable, bit by bit we will destroy the rich biological world we live in. Somewhere the line has to be drawn: each endangered species is worth saving, because it stops the momentum toward widespread destruction. In growth-oriented societies this momentum may be difficult to slow down, much less to stop. Therefore, each hurdle put in its way becomes an important force in saving the living creatures that make up our web of life. In the words of the naturalist William Beebe, "When the last individual of a race of living things breathes no more, another heaven and earth must pass before such a one can be again."

How can we save endangered species?

Preserving species is not a simple matter; much work can be done on three overlapping levels: technical, legal, and personal.

Technical solutions Integrated species management is a diversified approach that attacks extinc-

tion on many fronts. Some general suggestions are:

1. Reduce habitat destruction by controlling development. Wetland and estuary destruction should be greatly curbed worldwide.

2. Establish preserves wherever needed to protect nesting grounds and other critical habitats.

3. Reduce commercial and trophy hunting when evidence shows that the hunted species is rare, threatened, or endangered and when synthetic products can replace those acquired from these animals and plants.

4. Improve wildlife management by upgrading habitat and protecting "nongame" species.

5. Strictly control the introduction of alien species, especially on islands.

6. Design careful predator and pest control management programs so as not to indiscriminately eliminate nontarget species. Be more selective in using poisons, and eliminate them wherever possible by selecting environmental control agents. . . .

7. Reduce pollution of air, water, and land.

8. Increase public awareness of the value of wildlife and of factors causing extinction.

9. Increase public participation in habitat improvement, wild-life rescue efforts, and wildlife management (for example, by establishing hot lines and re-wards for reporting poachers).

10. Increase private and govern-mental funding of captive breeding programs that raise endangered species for release and for habitat protection here and abroad.

11. Establish domestic breeding programs to generate research animals, rather than relying on imports. Eliminate un-necessary research on wild animals.

12. Toughen penalties and in-crease policing of animal and plant trade and poaching.

13. Promote international cooper-ation to curb the trade of en-dangered species.

14. Increase expenditures for all protective measures, possibly through new taxes or volun-tary income tax programs un-der which citizens donate money to wildlife and protection.

15. Intensify research efforts to learn more about ecosystem stability and keystone species and to identify critical plant and animal habitats. . . .

Legal solutions Integrated spe-cies management requires laws that protect rare, endangered, and threatened organisms and their habitats. Today, however, poverty caused partly by overpopulation and resource shortages hinders progress in habitat protection.

In 1973, in response to the plight of wildlife and plants in the United States and abroad, the US Con-gress passed the Endangered Spe-cies Act. This act (1) requires the US Fish and Wildlife Service to list en-dangered and threatened species in the country, (2) creates federal protection of the habitat of listed species, (3) provides money to pur-chase this habitat, and (4) enables the United States to help other na-tions protect their endangered and threatened species by banning the importation of these species and by giving technical assistance.

Protection begins with the list-ing of an endangered or threatened species. Since 1973, 334 animals and 205 plants have been desig-nated threatened or endangered in the United States. All federally funded or approved projects that might have an impact on endan-gered species must be reviewed by appropriate agencies, which can deny needed permits or ask for modifications that remove the danger. . . .

The Endangered Species Act is one of the toughest and most suc-cessful environmental laws in the United States. "The real success story of the act," says Bob Davison, a National Wildlife Federation bi-ologist, "is that there are species around today that would not have survived if the law had not forced agencies to consider the impacts of what they're doing while allowing development to proceed. . . . To a large extent, the law has succeeded in continually juggling those two competing interests." A battle over protecting old-growth forests and the spotted owl, which was listed as a threatened species in 1989, is raging in Oregon and Washington today. . . .

To protect rhinos, gorillas, and other endangered species, governments throughout the world have joined in an unprecedented legal effort to stop the illegal trade in rare and endangered species. But in many cases inadequate funding makes enforcement a joke. Inspectors can be paid off by illegal traffickers of endangered species. Governmental agents can patrol only a small fraction of the poachers' range and, at least in the United States, the courts have routinely been lenient toward poachers. In 1985, however, a Montana man was sentenced to 15 years in prison for killing and selling protected eagles and grizzlies. Conservationists are hoping that this sentence, the toughest to be handed down in US history, may mark a turning point.

Legal solutions can barely keep up with runaway population growth and burgeoning agricultural development. Nowhere are these trends more acute than in Af-

burgeoning

rica. Without population control and strict laws to protect wildlife habitat, many of Africa's large herds will be wiped out. International wildlife organizations have stepped in to help raise personal awareness and settle the conflicts between humans and wildlife. Population control programs sponsored by a number of organizations can go a long way in stemming the tide of human population that threatens wildlife throughout the world.

Personal solutions Millions of us walk into fast-food restaurants every day and order a hamburger and fries. In Japan, people flock to fast-food restaurants for sushi and stir-fried vegetables, which they eat with disposable wooden chopsticks. Wealthy Californians head for Catalina Island for the weekend in their expensive hardwood yachts. In Central America, chain saws buzz in tropical rain forests; huge trees topple, and monkeys scurry for new homes in the outlying forests. Birds squawk and fly away, crowding into neighboring forests soon to be cut. The trees are hauled off on trucks to nearby mills, cut apart, and finally whittled down to make disposable chopsticks shipped by the millions to fast-food restaurants in Japan. Some of the wood will be fashioned into fine furniture, parquet floors, paneling, and high-quality coffins to bury the dead of the wealthy nations. On the barren forest ground ranchers plant grasses for their cattle, raised in large part to feed the hungry hamburger crowd of North America.

The hamburger and chopstick connection illustrates the part citizens unknowingly play in the extinction of this planet's rich biological diversity. Through excessive consumerism, apathy, and unchecked population growth, we become a part of the problem. But it need not be that way. You can find out which products come from tropical forests and find alternatives. Share the information with your family and friends.

You can take a more active role, too. Members of a Denver group called Volunteers for Outdoor Colorado are working with local wildlife officials to protect habitat and joining other groups to repair badly eroded hiking trails. . . . From Monterey, California, to Alaska volunteers are spending their free time improving salmon streams badly damaged by sediment and debris from heavily forested areas. Similar groups exist in Washington, New Mexico, and Florida.

Join a group in your area. Contact your state fish and wildlife agency and find out what volunteer groups are up to. If there are no active groups in your area, why not start your own? Begin with a simple project. Your wildlife officials will surely know of a few inexpen-

sive habitat improvement projects that you can tackle.

Since all resource extraction and processing affects wildlife, conservation can have an important effect. Shutting off lights when leaving a room, obeying the speed limit, and keeping the thermostat low in the winter will indirectly benefit wildlife. . . . Your actions, combined with the actions of others like you, will cut down on pollution and land disturbance.

You can help educate others about protection of endangered species. You can join groups and spread the word through educational campaigns, lobbying, television ads, posters, books, pamphlets, and the like. Support organizations and politicians who fight against pollution, habitat destruction, commercial and trophy hunting, indiscriminate pest and predator control, and collection of animals and plants for research and home use.

Joining wildlife groups is one of the best ways to learn from dedicated experts with well-developed plans for wildlife protection. . . . Some organizations such as the Nature Conservancy and the Trust for Public Lands purchase habitat for rare and endangered species. Others, such as the National Wildlife Federation, Sierra Club, Audubon Society, and Wilderness Society, concentrate much of their effort in the legislative arena to promote sound environmental policy.

COMPREHENSION CHECK

Complete your outline by listing examples that explain or support the headings. Then write brief answers to the following questions.

1. Although the author presents opposing views, what position does he take on saving endangered species? How do you know this is his position?

2. What "slippery slope" fallacy is discussed in paragraph 9? Is it a valid reason? Explain.

3. Should the decision to save endangered species be based primarily on ethical or economic concerns? Explain your decision.

What Do You Think?

✪ **DISCUSSION QUESTIONS**

Prepare for class discussion by jotting down brief answers to the following questions.

1. Can you think of any incidents where your good intentions at resolving a problem only made matters worse? Describe the incident. Why do you think things turned out so badly?

2. Given that good intentions and even supposedly well thought-out plans may create greater problems than they solve, why should we bother to come up with solutions? Are there times when a "go with the flow" or "let it be" approach to problems is a wiser course to follow?

3. One of the assumptions behind many environmental solutions is that technology can "save" us. Is this a realistic assumption? Why or why not?

4. In what ways are problem solving and debating similar? Dissimilar?

WRITING ASSIGNMENTS

You will need the list of problems that you developed in the Introductory Chapter Activity and the method for problem solving on pages 264–265. The type of writing you are asked to do in Chapter 8 can take a variety of different forms: brief essays, flow charts, or lists. Choose the format that best presents your ideas. With your instructor decide which of the following assignments you will complete.

1. Choose one of your personal problems and apply the problem-solving method to find a solution. Work individually and share your conclusions with the class. Have other students identified similar problems? Have they chosen similar solutions and developed similar plans for implementation?

2. Working in groups of three, select one of the national or global problems you have listed and work toward a solution (omit step 6 of the problem-solving method). Library research will be very useful especially if you do not have a great deal of background knowledge on the topic. You will also want to consider the solutions that others have suggested.

3. Working in groups of three, select one of the school or community problems on your list. Work toward a solution and develop a realistic implementation plan. It may be necessary to interview local or school people and/or consult your local or school newspapers to obtain the necessary background information. Consider actually implementing your solution.

4. Working individually or in small groups, brainstorm your version of life in the year 2060. Imagine that the world's energy, pollution, hazardous waste, food, and transportation problems have been solved. How have their solutions affected people's lives? Describe the daily routine of a young business executive. Or you may want to focus more on how social issues — such as educational opportunity, sexism and racism, homelessness, daycare, illness, and drug abuse — have been solved. Describe the daily routine of a mother and her young daughter or of an elderly couple. Take time to brainstorm your ideas; then go back and focus on those ideas that you wish to develop. Finally, prepare a joint written or oral presentation in which you offer your vision of the future. By all means, be creative!

CHAPTER 9

Reading Research Articles

After reading Chapter 9 you should be able to:

- identify a number of sources where research studies are reported
- understand differences between quantitative and qualitative research
- understand how research is conducted
- better comprehend research articles

CHAPTER OUTLINE AND CHECKLIST

You may use the following checklist in planning your study of understanding research studies. Activities marked with a ⊙ are to be completed in class. Some preclass preparation may be required.

CONTEXT FOR LEARNING

⊙ _____ INTRODUCTORY CHAPTER ACTIVITY

_____ Recognizing and Locating Research

_____ The Link Between Understanding Research and Thinking Critically

_____ How Research Studies Are Reported

_____ GUIDED READING: QUANTITATIVE STUDIES

_____ **"Bystander Intervention in Emergencies: Diffusion of Responsibilities"** by John M. Darley and Bibb Latané

_____ College Research Papers

⊙ _____ DISCUSSION BREAK

APPLICATION: UNDERSTANDING RESEARCH AND WRITING RESEARCH PAPERS

_____ APPLICATION ONE

_____ **"Writing College Research Papers"** by Kevin Gould

_____ COMPREHENSION CHECK

_____ APPLICATION TWO

_____ **"Growing Up Black in White Communities"** by Beverly Daniel Tatum

_____ COMPREHENSION CHECK

_____ What Do You Think?

⊙ _____ DISCUSSION QUESTIONS

_____ WRITING ASSIGNMENTS

Consider the following scenario: Verne is sitting in a large classroom when suddenly he remembers an important piece of information he was supposed to tell Jackie, a friend of his sitting three seats away. Not wanting to disrupt the instructor, Verne quietly takes out a piece of paper, writes his message on it, and then crumples it into a ball. "I wonder," Verne whispers to you, "at what angle should I shoot this in order to deliver my note to Jackie?" You reason that the larger the angle, the farther the ball will travel. In order to keep things simple, you assume that the ball will be traveling at a fixed velocity (speed). Are you correct?

In small groups, discuss how you would go about finding the answer. Write down the steps you would take. If possible, carry out the procedures. Compare your answers/results with those obtained by other groups. Keep this activity in mind as we discuss the steps involved in conducting research.

Recognizing and Locating Research

Formal and informal research

Doing research can be as simple as finding the answers to questions by examining the data right in front of you. It's done all the time. Children do it from the vantage point of their mothers' laps. Dropping spoons, children soon learn one of the basic laws of physics: Dropped objects fall. Basketball players spend hours on the court researching the best techniques for their jump shots. Students sometimes spend the first twelve years of school researching how little work must be done to pass!

In each instance, the person collects data to arrive at some conclusion through a process of informal research. People have "guesses" about the world and attempt to resolve their hunches either by making themselves aware of the surrounding data or by systematically testing it — for example, by setting their odometer every time they try a different route to work. For the most part, this research is conducted as an integral part of their lives, done unobtrusively, sometimes unconsciously, on a need-to-know basis.

However, in other areas, such as medicine, business, and academia, research is conducted very formally. It is supported through corporate sponsorship, charitable contributions, and some of our tax dollars. This is research in which a larger group shares a collective stake: a cure for AIDS, a more efficient engine, a more competitive product, an instructional approach that improves the performance of at-risk youth.

Locating research

Where can all this research be found? Each field of study — education, medicine, criminal justice, engineering, and so on — has a number of journals where research findings are regularly published. What would prevent someone from fabricating a study, writing an article about it, and having it published? Each journal has a board of editors and guest reviewers who evaluate papers submitted for publication. Each paper must be reviewed by or referred by scholars in the field before it can be published. Their work is similar to the peer editing you may have done on a friend's paper. Most of these journals do not make it to your local newsstand or library, but they can be found in academic libraries such as those found on college campuses.

Finding a research article on a specific subject is not difficult because there are companies whose business it is to systematically read through several hundred journal and magazine articles each month and group the articles according to their topics. An index to these articles is published regularly. You may be familiar with *The Readers' Guide to Periodical Literature*, an index that catalogues many popular magazines found at the newsstands, such as *People, Sports Illustrated,* and *Hispanic Business*. In addition to this index, an academic library will contain several more indices, ones that deal primarily with a particular area, such as *Psychological Abstracts, Business Periodicals Index, General Science Index, Art Index, Humanities Index,* and *Education Index*.

The Link Between Understanding Research and Thinking Critically

The results of formal research are often used to support people's opinions. Arguments may be won on the strength of research findings, and plans implemented on the basis of statistical data. For example, in his article "When Jobs and Family Care Clash," which appears in Chapter 6, Cal Thomas refers to numerous research studies to convince readers that mothers with small children should not be employed outside the home. How should we evaluate research findings? Certainly, we can analyze how relevant the findings are to the conclusion being drawn. For example, we might question the assumptions linking the mother-child bond to the conclusion that mothers with small children shouldn't work. We can also ask questions about how those findings were obtained. What methods and instruments were used to obtain the research data? Who was chosen to participate in the study? What questions did the researchers ask their subjects? Knowing the answers to these questions can help us decide whether to accept or reject the research findings.

Becoming familiar with how research is conducted and reported builds a strong basis for analyzing research results. Many students are intimidated by research articles. Perhaps they aren't familiar with the format and terminology used in writing research articles. Perhaps they are overwhelmed by the statistical analyses. Chapter 9 is designed to demystify the reading and understanding of research articles. We believe that if you are comfortable with reading research articles, you will be more willing to think critically about their findings.

You will want to use your reasoning skills as you go through this process. Ask yourself how important given research findings are to modern civilization. Research results may provide new knowledge that increases our understanding of our world and allows us greater choice. Being able to think critically will help us deal with those choices. Of course, new knowledge can bring destruction. Can you think of an example? Many researchers at colleges and universities conduct research because they believe that knowledge is a powerful tool. One of the basic assumptions of Western thought and culture is that through research one can "know the truth." Equally important is the belief that the more information one has, the better. What do you think?

How Research Studies Are Reported

Journal articles provide their readers with a complete explanation of a research study and usually conform to an organizational pattern. We will focus first on quantitative research studies and then look briefly at ethnographic and qualitative research studies.

GUIDED READING *Quantitative studies*

The term *quantitative* means "capable of being measured." Quantitative researchers attempt to "quantify"—to measure and provide numbers for—their findings. Quantitative research studies gather sufficient data on a specific question in order to find an answer that is "highly probable." Researchers examine a sample group from a target population and draw conclusions about that sample. They hope to make statements about the entire group or population being studied. They use statistical procedures to analyze their data and arrive at conclusions.

Quantitative research studies are reported in much the same sequence as they are conducted, and knowing the different components of a research study will be useful in understanding and evaluating the findings of the study. In this section, we present a complete research study separated into its organizational components. Each component is preceded by a description and followed by a few questions to check for comprehension.

Abstract The *abstract* begins the report and is essentially a brief overview of the question being studied, the methodology used to research the question, the results of the study, and possible implications.

Bystander Intervention in Emergencies: Diffusion of Responsibility[1]

BY JOHN M. DARLEY, NEW YORK UNIVERSITY,

AND BIBB LATANÉ, COLUMBIA UNIVERSITY

Journal of Personality and Social Psychology 1968, Vol. 8, No. 4, 377–383.

Ss overheard an epileptic seizure. They believed either that they alone heard the emergency, or that 1 or 4 unseen others were also present. As predicted the presence of other bystanders reduced the individual's feelings of personal responsibility and lowered his speed of reporting ($p < .01$). In groups of size 3, males reported no faster than females, and females reported no slower when the 1 other bystander was a male rather than a female. In general, personality and background measures were not predictive of helping. Bystander inaction in real-life emergencies is often explained by "apathy," "alienation," and "anomie." This experiment suggests that the explanation may lie more in the bystander's response to other observers than in his indifference to the victim.

[1]This research was supported in part by National Science Foundation Grants GS1238 and GS1239. Susan Darley contributed materially to the design of the experiment and ran the subjects, and she and Thomas Moriarty analyzed the data. Richard Nisbett, Susan Millman, Andrew Gordon, and Norma Neiman helped in preparing the tape recordings.

Write brief answers to the following questions.

1. What is the title of the research study? Who are the authors, and with what institutions are they affiliated?

2. What is the bibliographic reference for this study?

3. What does "Ss" mean? (We will discuss the meaning of "$p < .01$" later.)

4. What research question is being investigated?

5. What general finding was reported?

6. What inference is suggested by the researchers?

Rationale   The *rationale* or *statement of the problem* outlines the context for the study. It describes a particular problem, tells what others have found out already, and explains what else needs to be learned (that is, the question that this researcher is investigating). The research question is often stated in terms of a *hypothesis*; it is a statement that reflects the researchers' educated guess regarding the research question.

Several years ago, a young woman was stabbed to death in the middle of a street in a residential section of New York City. Although such murders are not entirely routine, the incident received little public attention until several weeks later when the New York Times disclosed another side to the case: at least 38 witnesses had observed the attack—and none had even attempted to intervene. Although the attacker took more than half an hour to kill Kitty Genovese, not one of the 38 people who watched from the safety of their own apartments came out to assist her. Not one even lifted the telephone to call the police (Rosenthal, 1964).

Preachers, professors, and news commentators sought the reasons for such apparently conscienceless and inhumane lack of intervention. Their conclusions ranged from "moral decay," to "dehumanization produced by the urban environment," to "alienation," "anomie," and "existential despair." An analysis of the situation, however, suggests that factors other than apathy and indifference were involved.

A person witnessing an emergency situation, particularly such a frightening and dangerous one as a stabbing, is in conflict. There are obvious humanitarian norms about helping the victim, but there are also rational and irrational fears about what might happen to a person who does intervene (Milgram & Hollander, 1964). "I didn't want to get involved," is a familiar comment, and behind it lies fears of physical harm, public embarrassment, involvement with police procedures, lost work days and jobs, and other unknown dangers.

In certain circumstances, the norms favoring intervention may be weakened, leading bystanders to resolve the conflict in the direction of nonintervention. One of these circumstances may be the presence of other onlookers. For example, in the case above, each observer, by seeing lights and figures in other apartment house windows, knew that others were also watching. However, there was no way to tell how the other observers were reacting. These two facts provide several reasons why any individual may have delayed or failed to help. The responsibility for helping was diffused among the observers; there was also diffusion of any potential blame for not taking action; and finally, it was possible that somebody, unperceived, had already initiated helping action.

When only one bystander is present in an emergency, if help is to come, it must come from him. Although he may choose to ignore it (out of concern for his personal safety, or desires "not to get involved"), any pressure to intervene focuses uniquely on him. When there are several observers present, however, the pressures to intervene do not focus on any one of the observers; instead the responsibility for intervention is shared among all the onlookers and is not unique to any one. As a result, no one helps.

A second possibility is that potential blame may be diffused. However much we may wish to think that an individual's moral behavior is divorced from considerations of personal punishment or reward, there is both theory and evidence to the contrary (Aronfreed, 1964; Miller & Dollard, 1941; Whiting & Child, 1953). It is perfectly reasonable to assume that, under circumstances of group responsibility for a punishable act, the punishment or blame that accrues to any one individual is often slight or nonexistent.

Finally, if others are known to be present, but their behavior cannot be closely observed, any one bystander can assume that one of the other observers is already taking action to end the emergency. Therefore, his own intervention would be only redundant—perhaps harmfully or confusingly so. Thus, given the presence of other onlookers whose behavior cannot be observed, any given bystander can rationalize his own inaction by convincing himself that "somebody else must be doing something."

These considerations lead to the hypothesis that the more bystanders to an emergency, the less likely, or the more slowly, any one bystander will intervene to provide aid. To test this proposition it would be necessary to create a situation in which a realistic "emergency" could plausibly occur. Each subject should also be blocked from communicating with others to prevent his getting information about their behavior during the emergency. Finally, the experimental situation should allow for the assessment of the speed and frequency of the subjects' reaction to the emergency. The experiment reported below attempted to fulfill these conditions.

Write brief answers to the following questions.

1. What problem does the researcher present?

2. What findings from three other research studies are cited? Who are the researchers?

3. What hypothesis do the researchers intend to prove?

Methodology/Procedure   In the *methodology* section, the researchers note in full detail all the steps taken to conduct the research. They describe the *subjects* (Ss) — that is, the people (or animals) who participated in the study, how they were selected, and precisely what they were asked to do. They also describe the *instruments*, or materials used in the study, such as tests or questionnaires.

In addition, the methodology section includes the *research design*. Because researchers are asking a particular question involving only a few variables, they need to design an experiment that controls the environment as much as possible. They want to make sure that their results are due to the variables that they are looking at and not some other, unaccounted-for phenomenon. For example, in the sample study, the researchers took great care to set up an environment wherein the subject responded to a perceived emergency based on a particular set of circumstances. Obviously, scientists in a laboratory have an easier time controlling their research environment; much as we may try to get them to behave in more manageable ways, human beings do not lend themselves to test-tube experiments!

Having created the research environment they want, researchers now introduce a new variable into that environment and see what happens. The new variable is called the *independent variable*, and the variable that is affected by the independent variable is called the *dependent variable* (because it is dependent on the independent variable). The dependent variable represents the effect or outcome of having introduced the independent variable.

Procedure

Overview   A college student arrived in the laboratory and was ushered into an individual room from which a communication system would enable him to talk to the other participants. It was explained to him that he was to take part in a discussion about personal problems associated with college life and that the discussion would be held over the intercom system, rather than face-to-face, in order to avoid embarrassment by preserving the anonymity of the subjects. During the course of the discussion, one of the other subjects underwent what appeared to be a very serious nervous seizure similar to epilepsy. During the fit it was impossible for the subject to talk to the other discussants or to find out what, if anything, they were doing about the emergency. The dependent variable was the speed with which the subjects reported the emergency to the experimenter. The major independent variable was the number of people the subject thought to be in the discussion group.

Subjects Fifty-nine female and thirteen male students in introductory psychology courses at New York University were contacted to take part in an unspecified experiment as part of a class requirement.

Method Upon arriving for the experiment, the subject found himself in a long corridor with doors opening off it to several small rooms. An experimental assistant met him, took him to one of the rooms, and seated him at a table. After filling out a background information form, the subject was given a pair of headphones with an attached microphone and was told to listen for instructions.

Over the intercom, the experimenter explained that he was interested in learning about the kinds of personal problems faced by normal college students in a high pressure, urban environment. He said that to avoid possible embarrassment about discussing personal problems with strangers several precautions had been taken. First, subjects would remain anonymous, which was why they had been placed in individual rooms rather than face-to-face. (The actual reason for this was to allow tape recorder simulation of the

other subjects and the emergency.) Second, since the discussion might be inhibited by the presence of outside listeners, the experimenter would not listen to the initial discussion, but would get the subject's reactions later, by questionnaire. (The real purpose of this was to remove the obviously responsible experimenter from the scene of the emergency.)

The subjects were told that since the experimenter was not present, it was necessary to impose some organization. Each person would talk in turn, presenting his problems to the group. Next, each person in turn would comment on what the others had said, and finally, there would be a free discussion. A mechanical switching device would regulate this discussion sequence and each subject's microphone would be on for about 2 minutes. While any microphone was on, all other microphones would be off. Only one subject, therefore, could be heard over the network at any given time. The subjects were thus led to realize when they later heard the seizure that only the victim's microphone was on and that there was no way of determining what any of the other witnesses were doing, nor of discussing the event and its possible solution with the others. When these instructions had been given, the discussion began.

In the discussion, the future victim spoke first, saying that he found it difficult to get adjusted to New York City and to his studies.

Very hesitantly, and with obvious embarrassment, he mentioned that he was prone to seizures, particularly when studying hard or taking exams. The other people, including the real subject, took their turns and discussed similar problems (minus, of course, the proneness to seizures). The naive subject talked last in the series, after the last prerecorded voice was played.[2]

When it was again the victim's turn to talk, he made a few relatively calm comments, and then, growing increasingly louder and incoherent, he continued:

> I-er-um-I think I-I need-er-if-if could-er-er-somebody er-er-er-er-er-er-er give me a little-er-give me a little help here because-er-I-er-I'm-er-er-h-h-having a-a-a real problem-er-right now and I-er-if somebody could help me out it would-it would-er-er s-s-sure be-sure be good . . . because-er-there-er-er-a cause I-er-I-uh-I've got a-a one of the-er sei––—er-er-things coming on and-and-and I could really-er-use some help so if somebody would-er-give me a little h-help-uh-er-er-er-er-er c-could somebody-er-er-help-er-uh-uh-uh (choking sounds). . . . I'm gonna die-er-

er-I'm . . . gonna die-er-help-er-er-seizure-er [chokes, then quiet].

The experimenter began timing the speed of the real subject's response at the beginning of the victim's speech. Informed judges listening to the tape have estimated that the victim's increasingly louder and more disconnected ramblings clearly represented a breakdown about 70 seconds after the signal for the victim's second speech. The victim's speech was abruptly cut off 125 seconds after this signal, which could be interpreted by the subject as indicating that the time allotted for that speaker had elapsed and the switching circuits had switched away from him. Times reported in the results are measured from the start of the fit.

Group size variable The major independent variable of the study was the number of other people that the subject believed also heard the fit. By the assistant's comments before the experiment, and also by the number of voices heard to speak in the first round of the group discussion, the subject was led to believe that the discussion group was one of three sizes: either a two-person group (consisting of a person who would later have a fit and the real subject), a three-person group (consisting of the victim, the real subject, and one confederate voice), or a six-person group (consisting of the victim, the real subject, and four confederate

[2]To test whether the order in which the subjects spoke in the first discussion round significantly affected the subjects' speed of report, the order in which the subjects spoke was varied (in the six-person group). This had no significant or noticeable effect on the speed of the subjects' reports.

voices). All the confederates' voices were tape-recorded.

Variations in group composition Varying the kind as well as the number of bystanders present at an emergency should also vary the amount of responsibility felt by any single bystander. To test this, several variations of the three-person group were run. In one three-person condition, the taped bystander voice was that of a female, in another a male, and in the third a male who said that he was a premedical student who occasionally worked in the emergency wards at Bellevue hospital.

In the above conditions, the subjects were female college students. In a final condition males drawn from the same introductory psychology subject pool were tested in a three-person female-bystander condition.

Time to help The major dependent variable was the time elapsed from the start of the victim's fit until the subject left her experimental cubicle. When the subject left her room, she saw the experimental assistant seated at the end of the hall, and invariably went to the assistant. If 6 minutes elapsed without the subject having emerged from her room, the experiment was terminated.

As soon as the subject reported the emergency, or after 6 minutes had elapsed, the experimental assistant disclosed the true nature of the experiment, and dealt with any emotions aroused in the subject. Finally the subject filled out a questionnaire concerning her thoughts and feelings during the emergency, and completed scales of Machiavellianism, anomie, and authoritarianism (Christie, 1964), a social desirability scale (Crowne & Marlowe, 1964), a social responsibility scale (Daniels & Berkowitz, 1964), and reported vital statistics and socioeconomic data.

Write brief answers to the following questions.

1. How is the methodology section labeled in this research study?

2. How is this section further divided? What are the headings?

3. Look carefully at the sections "Group size variable" and "Time to help." What do the researchers describe as the "major independent variable" of the study? The "major dependent variable"?

Results   Once the researchers have informed their readers of all the steps performed in the study, they present an analysis of their *results*. In this section, they must explain the statistical procedures used to analyze their data. This is where a good background in statistics is helpful. If the reader doesn't have that background (and many of us don't), he or she must assume that the peer reviewers selected by the journal editors prior to the article's publication have done their jobs. In any case, it is important to read through the results section and understand as much as possible.

In quantitative studies, research findings are often expressed as probabilities: How likely is it that the findings obtained in the study are due to chance as opposed to the variables being studied? For example, suppose that results from a study indicate that the more education a person receives, the greater the amount of his or her lifetime earnings. Researchers must use statistical tests to determine whether the results they obtained are due to "chance" (a capricious coincidence) or, according to the laws of probability, to a relationship between the variables. When the probability of chance as the cause of the research findings is considered very small (less than 5 or 1 percent), then the findings are called *significant*. Significant (and nonsignificant) findings are given in the results section of the report and are expressed as "statistical procedure x indicates that finding y is significant ($p < .05$) or ($p < .01$)." In the event that the findings are not found to be significant, these are also reported as "not significant findings ($p > .01$) or ($p > .05$)."

Results

Plausibility of manipulation Judging by the subjects' nervousness when they reported the fit to the experimenter, by their surprise when they discovered that the fit was simulated, and by comments they made during the fit (when they thought their microphones were off), one can conclude that almost all of the subjects perceived the fit as real. There were two ex-

ceptions in different experimental conditions, and the data for these subjects were dropped from the analysis.

Effect of group size on helping The number of bystanders that the subject perceived to be present had a major effect on the likelihood with which she would report the emergency (Table 1). Eighty-five percent of the subjects who thought they alone knew of the victim's plight reported the seizure

TABLE 1   Effects of Group Size on Likelihood and Speed of Response

Group size	N	% responding by end of fit	Time in sec.	Speed score
2 (S & victim)	13	85	52	.87
3 (S, victim, & 1 other)	26	62	93	.72
6 (S, victim, & 4 others)	13	31	166	.51

Note. — *p* value of differences; $\chi^2 = 7.91$, $p < .02$; $F = 8.09$, $p < .01$, for speed scores.

before the victim was cut off, only 31% of those who thought four other bystanders were present did so.

Every one of the subjects in the two-person groups, but only 62% of the subjects in the six-person groups, ever reported the emergency. The cumulative distributions of response times for groups of different perceived size (Figure 1) indicate that, by any point in time, more subjects from the two-person groups had responded than from the three-person groups, and more from the three-person groups than from the six-person groups.

Ninety-five percent of all the subjects who ever responded did so within the first half of the time available to them. No subject who had not reported within 3 minutes after the fit ever did so. The shape of these distributions suggests that had the experiment been allowed to run for a considerably longer time, few additional subjects would have responded.

Speed of response   To achieve a more detailed analysis of the re-

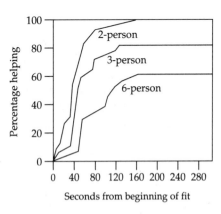

Figure 1   Cumulative distributions of helping responses.

sults, each subject's time score was transformed into a "speed" score by taking the reciprocal of the response time in seconds and multiplying by 100. The effect of this transformation was to deemphasize differences between longer time scores, thus reducing the contribution to the results of the arbitrary 6-minute limit on scores. A high speed score indicates a fast response.

An analysis of variance indicates that the effect of group size is highly significant ($p < .01$). Duncan multiple-range tests indicate that all but the two- and three-person groups differ significantly from one another ($p < .05$).

Victim's likelihood of being helped An individual subject is less likely to respond if he thinks that others are present. But what of the victim? Is the inhibition of the response of each individual strong enough to counteract the fact that with five onlookers there are five times as many people available to help? From the data of this experiment, it is possible mathematically to create hypothetical groups with one, two, or five observers.[3] The calculations indicate that the victim is about equally likely to get help from one bystander as from two. The victim is considerably more likely to have gotten help from one or two observers than from five during the first minute of the fit. For instance, by 45 seconds after the start of the fit, the victim's chances of having been helped by the single bystanders were about 50%, compared to none in the five observer condition. After the first minute, the likelihood of getting help from at least one person is high in all three conditions.

Effect of group composition on helping the victim Several varia-

[3] The formula for the probability that at least one person will help by a given time is $1 - (1 - P)^n$ where n is the number of observers and P is the probability of a single individual (who thinks he is one of n observers) helping by that time.

tions of the three-person group were run. In one pair of variations, the female subject thought the other bystander was either male or female; in another, she thought the other bystander was a premedical student who worked in an emergency ward at Bellevue hospital. As Table 2 shows, the variations in sex and medical competence of the other bystander had no important or detectable effect on speed of response. Subjects responded equally frequently and fast whether the other bystander was female, male, or medically experienced.

Sex of the subject and speed of response Coping with emergencies is often thought to be the duty of males, especially when females are present, but there was no evidence that this was the case in this study. Male subjects responded to the emergency with almost exactly the same speed as did females (Table 2).

Reasons for intervention or nonintervention After the debriefing at the end of the experiment each subject was given a 15-item checklist and asked to check those thoughts which had "crossed your mind when you heard Subject 1 calling for help." Whatever the condition, each subject checked very few thoughts, and there were no significant differences in number or kind of thoughts in the different experimental groups. The only thoughts checked by more than a

TABLE 2   Effects of Group Composition on Likelihood and Speed of Response*

Group composition	N	% responding by end of fit	Time in sec.	Speed score
Female S, male other	13	62	94	74
Female S, female other	13	62	92	71
Female S, male medic other	5	100	60	77
Male S, female other	13	69	110	68

*Three-person group, male victim.

few subjects were "I didn't know what to do" (18 out of 65 subjects), "I thought it must be some sort of fake" (20 out of 65), and "I didn't know exactly what was happening" (26 out of 65).

It is possible that subjects were ashamed to report socially undesirable rationalizations, or, since the subjects checked the list *after* the true nature of the experiment had been explained to them, their memories might have been blurred. It is our impression, however, that most subjects checked few reasons because they had few coherent thoughts during the fit.

We asked all subjects whether the presence or absence of other bystanders had entered their minds during the time that they were hearing the fit. Subjects in the three- and six-person groups reported that they were aware that other people were present, but they felt that this made no difference to their own behavior.

Individual difference correlates of speed of report   The correlations between speed of report and various individual differences on the personality and background measures were obtained by normalizing the distribution of report speeds within each experimental condition and pooling these scores across all conditions ($n = 62 - 65$). Personality measures showed no important or significant correlations with speed of reporting the emergency. In fact, only one of the 16 individual difference measures, the size of the community in which the subject grew up, correlated ($r = -.26$, $p < .05$) with the speed of helping.

Write a brief answer to the following question.

1. What significant and nonsignificant findings are given?

Discussion/Implications   Next comes a *general discussion of the findings* and/or *implications of the study*. Included here is an interpretation of the findings. What exactly do the figures, tables, and charts mean? What implications might be drawn from the findings? Are the results of the study generalizable to a larger population — that is, would the results be the same for other groups? Researchers often include in this section recommendations for future action or research.

Discussion

Subjects, whether or not they intervened, believed the fit to be genuine and serious. "My God, he's having a fit," many subjects said to themselves (and were overheard via their microphones) at the onset of the fit. Others gasped or simply said "Oh." Several of the male subjects swore. One subject said to herself, "It's just my kind of luck, something has to happen to me!" Several subjects spoke aloud of their confusion about what course of action to take, "Oh God, what should I do?"

When those subjects who intervened stepped out of their rooms, they found the experimental assistant down the hall. With some uncertainty, but without panic, they reported the situation. "Hey, I think Number 1 is very sick. He's having a fit or something." After ostensibly checking on the situation, the experimenter returned to report that "everything is under control." The subjects accepted these assurances with obvious relief.

Subjects who failed to report the emergency showed few signs of the apathy and indifference thought to characterize "unresponsive bystanders." When the experimenter entered her room to terminate the situation, the subject often asked if the victim was "all right." "Is he being taken care of?" "He's all right isn't he?" Many of these subjects showed physical signs of nervousness; they often had trembling hands and sweating palms. If anything, they seemed more emotionally aroused than did the subjects who reported the emergency.

Why, then, didn't they respond? It is our impression that nonintervening subjects had not decided *not* to respond. Rather they were still in a state of indecision and conflict concerning whether to respond or not. The emotional behavior of these nonresponding subjects was a sign of their continuing conflict, a conflict that other subjects resolved by responding.

The fit created a conflict situation of the avoidance–avoidance type. On the one hand, subjects worried about the guilt and shame they would feel if they did not help the person in distress. On the other hand, they were concerned not to make fools of themselves by overreacting, not to ruin the ongoing experiment by leaving their intercom, and not to destroy the anonymous nature of the situation which the experimenter had earlier stressed as important. For subjects in the two-person condition, the obvious distress of the victim and his need for help were so important that their conflict was easily resolved. For the subjects who knew there were other bystanders present, the cost of not helping was reduced and the conflict they were in more acute. Caught between the two negative alternatives of letting the victim continue to suffer or the costs of rushing in to help, the nonresponding bystanders vacillated between them rather than choosing not to respond. This distinction may be academic for the victim, since he got no help in either case, but it is an extremely important one for arriving at an understanding of the causes of bystanders' failures to help.

Although the subjects experienced stress and conflict during the experiment, their general reactions to it were highly positive. On a questionnaire administered after the experimenter had discussed the nature and purpose of the experiment, every single subject found the experiment either "interesting" or "very interesting" and was willing to participate in similar experiments in the future. All subjects felt they understood what the experiment was about and indicated that they thought the deceptions were necessary and justified.

All but one felt they were better informed about the nature of psychological research in general.

Male subjects reported the emergency no faster than did females. These results (or lack of them) seem to conflict with the Berkowitz, Klanderman, and Harris (1964) finding that males tend to assume more responsibility and take more initiative than females in giving help to dependent others. Also, females reacted equally fast when the other bystander was another female, a male, or even a person practiced in dealing with medical emergencies. The ineffectiveness of these manipulations of group composition cannot be explained by general insensitivity of the speed measure, since the group-size variable had a marked effect on report speed.

It might be helpful in understanding this lack of difference to distinguish two general classes of intervention in emergency situations: direct and reportorial. Direct intervention (breaking up a fight, extinguishing a fire, swimming out to save a drowner) often requires skill, knowledge, or physical power. It may involve danger. American cultural norms and Berkowitz's results seem to suggest that males are more responsible than females for this kind of direct intervention.

A second way of dealing with an emergency is to report it to someone qualified to handle it, such as the police. For this kind of intervention, there seem to be no norms requiring male action. In the present study, subjects clearly intended to report the emergency rather than take direct action. For such indirect intervention, sex or medical competence does not appear to affect one's qualifications or responsibilities. Anybody, male or female, medically trained or not, can find the experimenter.

In this study, no subject was able to tell how the other subjects reacted to the fit. (Indeed, there were no other subjects actually present.) The effects of group size on speed of helping, therefore, are due simply to the perceived presence of others rather than to the influence of their actions. This means that the experimental situation is unlike emergencies, such as a fire, in which bystanders interact with each other. It is, however, similar to emergencies, such as the Genovese murder, in which spectators knew others were also watching but were prevented by walls between them from communication that might have counteracted the diffusion of responsibility.

The present results create serious difficulties for one class of commonly given explanations for the failure of bystanders to intervene in actual emergencies, those involving apathy or indifference. These explanations generally assert that people who fail to intervene are somehow different in kind from the rest of us, that they are "alienated by industrialization," "dehumanized by urbanization," "depersonalized by living in the cold society," or "psychopaths." These explanations serve a dual function for people who adopt them. First, they explain (if only in a nominal way) the puzzling and frightening problem of why people watch others die. Second, they give individuals reason to deny that they too might fail to help in a similar situation.

The results of this experiment seem to indicate that such personality variables may not be as important as these explanations suggest. Alienation, Machiavellianism, acceptance of social responsibility, need for approval, and authoritarianism are often cited in these explanations. Yet they did not predict the speed or likelihood of help. In sharp contrast, the perceived number of bystanders did. The explanation of bystander "apathy" may lie more in the bystander's response to other observers than in presumed personality deficiencies of "apathetic" individuals. Although this realization may force us to face the guilt-provoking possibility that we too might fail to intervene, it also suggests that individuals are not, of necessity, "noninterveners" because of their personalities. If people understand the situational forces that can make them hesitate to intervene, they may better overcome them.

Write brief answers to the following questions.

1. Were the subjects in the study apathetic toward the student who appeared to have a seizure?

2. What explanation do the authors offer for why some subjects did not respond?

3. Do subjects' personalities affect their rate of responding?

4. Did male subjects report the emergency faster than female subjects? Explain your answer.

5. What theories of bystander behavior do the researchers believe their study calls into question?

References   At the end of the study is a list of *references*. Here, full publication information is given for any articles that were cited within the text of the study. References are listed in alphabetical order and usually follow the format established by either the Modern Language Association (MLA) or the American Psychological Association (APA).

References

Aronfreed, J. The origin of self-criticism. *Psychological Review*, 1964, 71, 193–219.

Berkowitz, L., Klanderman, S., & Harris, R. Effects of experimenter awareness and sex of subject on reactions to dependency relationships. *Sociometry*, 1964, 27, 327–329.

Christie, R. The prevalence of machiavellian orientations. Paper presented at the meeting of the American Psychological Association, Los Angeles, 1964.

Crowne, D., & Marlowe, D. *The approval motive*. New York: Wiley, 1964.

Daniels, L., & Berkowitz, L. Liking and response to dependency relationships. *Human Relations*, 1963, 16, 141–148.

Milgram, S., & Hollander, P. Murder they heard. *Nation*, 1964, 198, 602–604.

Miller, N., & Dollard, J. *Social learning and imitation*. New Haven: Yale University Press, 1941.

Rosenthal, A. M. *Thirty-eight witnesses*. New York: McGraw-Hill, 1964.

Whiting, J. W. M., & Child, I. *Child training and personality*. New Haven: Yale University Press, 1953.

Ethnographic and qualitative studies

Quantitative research is not appropriate for all research studies. If your goal is to demonstrate that variable x influences the outcome in situation y in this particular z fashion, then quantitative research is useful. However, some researchers believe that trying to look at phenomena, events, or situations in terms of this laboratory model just doesn't provide an accurate picture of reality. Ethnographic or qualitative research methods seem more appropriate to them.

Ethnographic Research   Anthropologists have long used ethnographic research methods to study cultural phenomena. In ethnographic research, the researcher observes the subject being studied in its natural setting. For example, the movie *Gorillas in the Mist* is a story about the ethnographic research that Dian Fossey conducted on gorillas in Africa.

Another topic that researchers might choose to investigate using an ethnographic approach would be how children learn in certain environments. The researchers would spend time in that setting, take field notes, and later write a report that interpreted their findings. In ethnographic research, the researchers have a general field of inquiry, but not a well-defined research question or hypothesis, because they believe that such a question limits or biases the observations of the viewer.

Qualitative Research   The term *qualitative* means having to do with "any of the features that make something what it is." The concept of describing is important: When you are trying to explain the characteristics of something, it is necessary to describe it. Qualitative researchers attempt to describe what exists. They may gather their data through in-depth unstructured interviews, or they may combine interviewing with observational case studies. Their research reports on general patterns that can be extrapolated from the pages of information they have gathered from a relatively small sample of participants. The second reading in the Application section of this chapter, "Growing Up Black in White Communities," is part of a qualitative research study. Qualitative research does not use precise research questions, nor does it attempt to control the multitude of variables in a particular situation or derive statistical results that can be generalized to a larger population.

Choosing among different types of research

How can one distinguish between the different types of studies? Imagine that you are a researcher interested in researching the experience of Latino administrators at predominantly white institutions of higher education. You might develop the hypothesis that most Latino administrators do not have positions within the mainstream organizational structure. Researching this topic would involve conducting a quantitative study. After defining "mainstream organizational structure," you would select a sample of your target population and collect your data, perhaps through the use of a questionnaire.

Or you might decide that you wanted to study the "working environment" of Latino administrators at white institutions. You would select a few Latino administrators and perhaps spend several days or months with each one, taking notes on all their activities. Later, you would develop your field notes into a report that described what you had observed. In this case, you would be employing an ethnographic methodology.

Finally, if you decided that you wanted to examine how Latino professionals interpreted their experiences at white institutions, you might select several professionals at different institutions and conduct a series of unstructured, open-question interviews with them. After sifting through the pages of transcript from these interviews, you would write a research report outlining the major themes and patterns your investigation uncovered. This would be a qualitative study.

As you can see in each of the three cases, the general topic is the same, but a very different approach is taken depending on the purpose of the study; this, in turn, has a direct effect on the *kind* of data being collected.

College Research Papers

In many college courses, you will be asked to write what are commonly called "research papers." In this context, the term *research* usually means "library research." You must search for information in books, periodicals, reference works, and research journals in order to find evidence that will support your thesis.

Unless enrolled in research methods courses or in graduate school, students are not usually required to conduct their own research studies — although these can be fun to do! Rather, you will spend your time first compiling information about the views of others and about various research studies that are presented or reported in different articles, and second analyzing or evaluating that information.

Sometimes, you will be given specific questions to research. For example: Is there evidence of widespread police brutality in our cities? What are the consequences of a tight monetary policy? What is the status of the protest movement in Ireland today? More often, however, you will be assigned topics or general areas from which to develop a research question. On the one hand, this allows you to select a topic you are genuinely interested in; on the other hand, it can leave you with no sense of direction.

Another drawback to having a specific research question is the possibility that your library has no relevant information. Thus, we suggest that you spend a couple of hours determining what information on the topic is available and, based on an assessment of what is possible, develop a research question. For example, you may want to investigate the effects of television commercials on boys but discover that all the studies you have access to include both boys and girls. In this case, it may be best to revise your research question to include both boys and girls.

Students are often frustrated when their specific research questions aren't directly addressed in a chapter or an article. But if they were, there would be no need for writing the paper! Students also forget that *finding* information is part of the process of writing the paper. In any event, remember: Always be flexible when writing research papers.

✪ **D,ISCUSSION BREAK**

Prepare for class discussion by writing brief answers to the following questions.

1. List three research findings that have been reported recently in the news. Consult current periodicals, watch the news, or read newspapers to find reports of different research. Results of studies dealing with diet, medicine, and education are topics commonly reported on by the media. What type of research methodology do you think each study used? Do any of the studies refute (disagree with) research findings from a previous study?

2. How is a science lab different from society? What are the advantages and disadvantages of the different kinds of research methodology presented in this chapter?

3. Where do you think research questions "come from"? Can a researcher be free from bias? Is a researcher ever totally objective? Explain your answers.

4. The media are constantly reporting the results of research studies. What is your reaction to these findings? In general, do you believe what they say? Have you ever changed your behavior because of a research study? Explain your answers.

Application: Understanding Research and Writing Research Papers

APPLICATION ONE

The author of this essay, Kevin Gould, is a second-semester senior who suffers from both cerebral palsy and retinitis pigmentosa (a condition of slow deterioration of the retina). Although neither condition is uncommon, finding them in combination in one individual is a rare occurrence.

Despite his handicaps, Gould has enjoyed academic success throughout his undergraduate experience. As you read Gould's essay, make a mental comparison between Gould's and your strategies for doing research and dealing with the frustration of completing research papers.

Writing College Research Papers

BY KEVIN GOULD

concrete

There is a four-stage process that I always go through when I find out that I need to do a research paper. The first thing that I do is panic. What? How am I going to do *this*? Then I go through a brief period where I don't make any concrete or conscious decisions; I just start to weigh the pro's and con's of doing the paper. Is it worth it? I have to make a conscious decision as to whether or not I should attempt the project. For me, it is a major commitment to complete this kind of task because of the time and effort I need to expend. I think about how the paper will interfere with my other courses and my schedule. This brings me to the fourth and final stage of my process. I tell myself, "Stick with it and don't second guess your decision." Basically I have the option to quit, but I don't . . . it isn't a good thing to do.

Some people are really insensitive. They act as if they were totally independent of others, but no one really is. It is just a fact of life that we are all dependent in our own fashion. For example, my handicap makes me dependent upon those who are sighted, but I have had professors who were totally unwilling to help me with my research paper. In these circumstances I just decide to do the paper anyway because of my pride. I'll be damned if someone is going to stop me. My point is that they are no better than I am; we're both human beings.

internalize

I try not to internalize the actions of some professors who are unable or unwilling to address my educational restrictions. It's their problem, but it puts me in a difficult position. Now is when the "fun" starts.

I have to find a reader, which isn't the easiest thing to do, and getting one who is willing to go to the library is next to impossible. If

I am able to find a reader then there are still problems because you have to go by what THEY think is important for the paper. They may read a book to you and you realize that's not what you need. It's a GIANT process. Sometimes my research papers are not really good, and the process that I have to go through is trying. I have to mentally prepare myself to do the best I can.

If I can get some information together then I wind up with cassette tapes where most people will have paper all over the living room floor. The problem is trying to organize the information on the tapes. After I get it together I may still have a major problem; not all professors will accept a research paper on tape. They require a typed text. And so the process continues because I then must find someone to type the paper. Some professors will give me extensions on the due date, but only if I go to their offices, plead, promise to water and weed the lawn and totally convince them I am good for it.

For all this work, I get a B. I've killed myself and that's what I get . . . that's it.

COMPREHENSION CHECK

Write brief answers to the following questions.

1. Briefly, what steps does Gould take to complete a research paper?

2. What is the tone of Gould's essay? Explain your answer.

3. What does Gould mean when he says, "I try not to internalize the actions of some professors who are unable or unwilling to address my educational restrictions"?

4. What assumptions can be made about Gould's standards of academic performance?

Our second reading presents data collected from a qualitative research study. Qualitative studies also provide a context for their research by first discussing the significance of the topic under investigation and by reviewing other relevant research. The methodology section describes how data were obtained, and the study includes a discussion of important findings, usually in the form of general patterns or central themes found in the data.

The following excerpt by Beverly Daniel Tatum includes a description of the methodology used in her study and a profile of one of the students interviewed.

Growing Up Black in White Communities

BY BEVERLY DANIEL TATUM

Telling their stories

African-American college students raised in predominantly White communities were recruited, by letter and through a "snowballing" method of personal referrals, from two elite, coeducational New England colleges to participate in the study. Twenty-four students volunteered to participate in in-depth individual interviews about their family life, school and peer relationships in their communities of origin, their current level of racial awareness, and adjustment to their current predominantly White college environment (see Interview Guide, Appendix A). All of the interviews, which were approximately two hours long, were conducted by the same Black female interviewer.

All of those who volunteered were interviewed; however, six of those were either children from interracial marriages, adopted by White families, or recent immigrants to the United States. While the experiences of these adolescents are also worthy of investigation, this discussion is limited to the remaining eighteen subjects, all of whom had two Black parents, and grew up in the care of at least one of them while residing in the United States.

These participants (six men, twelve women) ranged in age from 18–22, with a median age of 20. Ten were raised in two-parent households, while eight were primarily *rear*

reared in one-parent families. Family size ranged from one to three children. All but one of the thirty-six parents were at least high school graduates, twenty-one were college graduates, and twelve had post-graduate degrees. Family incomes ranged from under $20,000 to over $100,000. The median family income was $55,000. Eleven of the participants have lived in a predominantly White community since they were in pre-school or younger. Four moved to their predominantly White neighborhoods in elementary school, and the remaining three moved in junior high school. However, all have attended predominantly White schools since their elementary years. Probably due primarily to the recruiting patterns of their colleges, most are from suburban areas of East Coast cities, ranging as far South as Washington, D.C., and as far North as Massachusetts. Only three of the participants are from other regions, two from the Midwest and one from the Southwest.

thematically

socialization

The taped interviews were transcribed and analyzed thematically, with particular attention to details regarding parents' attitudes toward racial socialization (race vs. class consciousness), school experiences, and changing self-perceptions regarding racial identity. Gender differences in the nature of the growing-up experiences were also considered. Though there is a great deal of in-

dividual variation in responses to the very open-ended interview questions, there were common threads in the stories they told.

For example, many students reported experiencing feelings of confusion and isolation. Some felt as if they were caught between two worlds, unsure of whether they belonged in their White community (particularly as adolescents), yet unsure of whether they could belong in a Black community. As they struggled to resolve this issue of identity and belonging, they experienced various changes in their view of themselves as Black individuals, as well as changes in their attitudes toward other Blacks and toward Whites. Although the design of the study does not allow for cause and effect conclusions about the relationship between the expression of parental values and children's struggles with racial identity, there is clearly variation in parental socialization as described by their children, and there seems to be a relationship between the race-consciousness of parents and the ease with which students developed a positive identification with other African-Americans.

In order to illustrate both the variation and the commonalities of experience among participants of varying family backgrounds, profiles of five students, three women and two men, are presented here. The names of individuals in each profile have been changed. . . .

commonalities

profile

"The 'burbs are kind of nice"

Karen describes herself ethnically as African-American and economically "well off." An only child, she and her parents lived with her grandmother until Karen was eleven, in the same predominantly Black neighborhood where her parents had grown up. When her parents were financially ready to purchase their own home, they found an affordable house they liked in a nearby, predominantly White community.

Though Karen was initially disappointed to be moving away from a close network of friends and relatives, their new neighbors were friendly. "After I got there, I was fine." Though they were living in a White suburb, Karen's parents maintained close ties with their old friends, most of whom were African-American, some of whom had made similar moves to the suburbs.

vaguely

Karen vaguely remembers her earliest school experiences, but she does remember that there were only two or three Black children in her private elementary school. Her classes were very small, and she had a lot of friends. "When you're younger I don't think that you have as many hang-ups about race or anything as you do when you get older. Because it didn't seem there that anyone was ever really excluded." As she pointed out, "when there's only twelve people in your class, there's only so much excluding you can get away with."

After the sixth grade, she enrolled in a slightly larger private school from which she graduated. Though she knew other Black students who "hated every minute of it," she "enjoyed the smallness of it. I enjoyed being able to go to teachers and just being able to sit down and talk about whatever . . . it was pretty homey like." Being active in sports also helped her feel included, and she was often invited to parties by her White teammates when some of the other Black students were not. There was little dating going on among her group of friends ("guys and girls just used to hang out"), so the fact that she wasn't dating didn't bother her. "It was just the way the cookie crumbles."

Karen began to recognize some racism in high school, and was confused by it.

". . . we were talking about something and someone was like, 'Oh, but you're not really Black anyway.' I was like, 'What?!' . . . when they get really comfortable with you, it just like comes out . . . obviously they think that everyone who's Black is either carrying a gun or talking in some sort of slang . . . when it was time to apply to schools, people were like, 'Oh, you don't have to worry; you're a minority. Everyone needs minorities.' You're like, 'Wait. I've been in school with you for the past seven years. I've been going to class like you have. I don't think I've been sitting in my room every day going, "Oh when it's time to apply to college, it's not going to matter anyway. I'll go whether I can read or can't read, whether I can add or can't add."' I was very pissed off . . . I told them how pissed off I was at them."

Unsure of whether these comments were malicious in intent or simply a reflection of ignorance, she found it "hard to decipher sometimes where that person stood." Her parents were helpful in talking to her about these situations as they arose, and she felt satisfied with the preparation they had provided.

Her parents "strongly suggested" that she consider attending a Black college, but Karen rejected the idea primarily because of her school and peer culture. Her school was "this kind of pre-college building ground where you get sent to the most prestigious universities in America, whatever malarkey they teach you."

Though she sees her predominantly White experiences as helpful in making the adjustment to college, she wonders if "it should have been a different choice . . . it's not horrible, I suppose. It's just tough." A pre-med student, Karen believes some of her male professors (particularly in science) have a lot of problems dealing with "female students, with Black students, with any minority group students

on the whole." The social environment has also been disappointing. "A lot of the campus events are really centered around drinking beer and having these parties. After a while it's quite boring."

By contrast, the people she knows attending Black colleges "seem to be really enjoying their experience." She herself spent the previous summer in a program for pre-med minority students, and it was "fun going to class," not being the only one. Her social life was great, too. "I just never had gone out and had so much fun in a long, long time." She is now seriously considering applying to a Black medical school.

Though Karen describes herself as "fine with everyone in the Black community," her circle of friends is not exclusively African-American. She acknowledges that there are certain White students "you want to stay away from," but others she has become friendly with through her sports involvement. She has observed other Black students from White communities struggling with their identity, and objects to the "Blacker than thou" attitude some of them have. "It seems to me that a lot of people are all of a sudden defining what Blackness is. Like who's really Black, who's not . . . I don't know, it just doesn't go over well with me." Her own view is that they should be more understanding of the variety of backgrounds Black students come from and how that might influence the social choices they make.

In reflecting on her own identity development, Karen said,

"I think a lot of it, the changes that I went through have been after I came here . . . in all of the other schooling I've had it really didn't ever come up as a huge thing. I mean at home I don't think I was ever lacking. I mean my parents have all these books for me, like books by Black authors, poetry, jazz music, I mean I had it all at home. But I think it was different in school that you really didn't start to learn how much you were being excluded historically and things like that in school until you get here and you get a chance to do other things, like you get a chance to take Black studies courses . . . I've done a fair amount of work in African-American literature, especially women's literature. And so that's something I never, ever had a chance to do in high school . . . hundreds of people, myself included, that graduated from high school who had no idea of all the great things that any other cultural group has done. A lot of that may be the problem why people can say things that they say . . . do things that they do, just because they don't understand any more either. It's just perpetuated by this lack of knowl-

perpetuate

edge. But I think that a lot of the changes I've gone through have happened here just by getting a different sort of education and having the ability to choose for myself what I want to take, what I want to learn about . . . But on the whole I don't think I act any different than I did necessarily. I think it's just now I know more."

Though Karen believes her parents would prefer for her to choose a Black partner, she does not see interracial relationships as a problem. "Of more importance to me is the person's personality . . . whether I enjoy them and like having fun with them." Where would she like to live in the future? "Maybe I'll want to live in the 'burbs somewhere. The 'burbs are kind of nice, growing up in the 'burbs wasn't bad."

In many ways Karen seems to be truly bicultural, moving back and forth between Black and White communities with relative ease. Though she has had some difficult experiences in college, she does not seem demoralized by them in the way that Janice was. Karen's family's ongoing involvement with a network of African-American friends and family members, their apparent willingness to discuss racial issues, and the reinforcement of African-American culture at home through music and literature certainly suggests a level of race-consciousness. This aspect of Kar-

bicultural

demoralize

resilience

en's family life seems to have contributed to her resilience.

Though she certainly identified with her White peers in high school, even then she seemed secure enough in her own African-American identity to confront their racism when it was necessary. The opportunity to learn more about her heritage in college has been important for the further develop-

heritage

ment of that identity. It seems regrettable that there were no opportunities for such learning in high school. It also seems unfortunate that her guidance counselor did not understand enough about her developmental needs as a Black adolescent to at least suggest that she also consider an historically Black college.

COMPREHENSION CHECK

Write brief answers to the following questions.

1. Who participated in Tatum's study? How did Tatum find these subjects?

2. How did Tatum collect her data? What methodology did she use?

3. How were the data analyzed?

4. What was one of the "common threads" she found in the stories?

5. Briefly, what were Karen's experiences?

6. How does Tatum analyze Karen's experiences?

What Do You Think?

❖ **DISCUSSION QUESTIONS**

Prepare for class discussion by writing down brief answers to the following questions.

1. In "Writing College Research Papers," Gould describes some of his professors as "insensitive." Do you agree?

2. What process should you follow to complete research papers?

3. Students complain that it is almost impossible to write a research paper without feeling as though they were plagiarizing the ideas of others. They wonder what is original in their papers. How can students avoid plagiarizing and be original?

4. Compare the two research studies presented in this chapter. What similarities and differences do you find? Did you find one study more believable than the other? Explain your answers.

5. Both studies relate to human experiences and behaviors. What personal experiences have you had that support or refute their findings?

WRITING ASSIGNMENTS

Select one of the following topics and in a few paragraphs develop a thoughtful written response.

1. Why is it important to spend time analyzing the impact of new technical knowledge on society? Be sure to include examples to explain your ideas.

2. Write a response to the following statement: "Some critics believe research is inherently political, because it is supported by either

nations or organizations to maintain their powerful positions. They also believe that the questions researchers ask are subjective and are an outgrowth of their views and of the society in which they live."

3. In many textbooks, references used by the authors are listed at the end of each chapter. Many of these references are research articles. Select a research article listed in the reference section of one of your textbooks and find the original study in the appropriate journal. After reading the article, write a brief summary of the study.

4. One of our major goals in Chapter 9 was to demystify the reading of research articles. Have we succeeded? Explain your answer.

CHAPTER 10

Evaluating Evidence

After reading Chapter 10 you should be able to:

- ask questions about factual evidence

- distinguish between the concepts of validity and reliability

- ask questions about research data, statistics, and reports of research found in newspaper and magazine articles

- understand how research is used in college textbooks

You may use the following checklist in planning your study of evaluating research studies. Activities marked with a ✪ are to be completed in class. Some preclass preparation may be required.

CONTEXT FOR LEARNING

✪ _____   INTRODUCTORY CHAPTER ACTIVITY

_____   **"Women Find Men Frustrating"** from United Press International

_____   Evaluating Quantitative Research

_____   Evaluating Qualitative Research

_____   Reports of Research Versus Research Reports

APPLICATION: ANALYZING RESEARCH

_____   APPLICATION ONE

_____   **"Shere Hite: Embattled as Usual"** by Elizabeth Mehren

_____   COMPREHENSION CHECK

_____   APPLICATION TWO

_____   **"The Numbers Game"** by Jerry Adler

_____   COMPREHENSION CHECK

_____   APPLICATION THREE

_____   **"Woman's Work Is Never Done"** by Jim Miller

_____   COMPREHENSION CHECK

_____   APPLICATION FOUR

_____   **"Altruism"** by D. G. Meyers

_____   COMPREHENSION CHECK

_____   What Do You Think?

✪ _____   DISCUSSION QUESTIONS

_____   WRITING ASSIGNMENTS

⊙ **INTRODUCTORY CHAPTER ACTIVITY**

Keep the following questions in mind as you read the newspaper article below: Do you believe the research findings? Why or why not? If you could ask the researcher any questions, what would you ask? Share your questions with other members of the group. Keep a record of your questions; we will come back to them.

Women Find Men Frustrating

FROM UNITED PRESS INTERNATIONAL

New York — A new Shere Hite report on female sexuality — seven years in the making — shows 88 percent of the 4,500 women surveyed by the researcher indicated they feel frustrated in their relationships with men.

The report was based on Hite's sampling via "confidential essay questionnaires" of "women from all over the United States."

Her report will be published Oct. 26 in "Women and Love," the third book in the Hite series.

The survey showed that 88 percent of the 4,500 married and single women indicated they were frustrated in their relationships with men, and 83 percent have their closest emotional relationship with a woman.

Some 82 percent of married women indicated they feel lonely in their relationships, and 98 percent of single women said they love the freedom of calling their life their own, and find love affairs with men full of anxiety and ambiguous and arrogant behavior by men.

Other signs of dissatisfaction were:

- 70 percent of women married five years or more are having sex outside their marriages; 82 percent are "not in love" with their husbands but care for them.

- 71 percent of married women have left their relationships emotionally and now lead essentially double lives, finding the only way to survive in their marriages is to focus most of their emotional energy elsewhere.

- Only 13 percent of women married more than two years say they are in love with their husbands.

Hite's two earlier books focused on female and male sexuality. All her books were based on anonymous survey questionnaires, a method criticized by some researchers.

Evaluating Quantitative Research

The easiest way to evaluate a research study is to ask questions about four components: the subjects who participated, the instruments used, the research design (how the research study was conducted), and the statistics presented and their applicability to other situations or populations. In this section, we take up a discussion of each of these four areas.

Criteria for a representative sample

Recall that in a quantitative study, data are collected from a small sample, and then the findings are generalized to a larger population. Suppose we were interested in college students and their food likes and dislikes, and decided to do a research study that investigated students' opinions of the food served at their school cafeterias. Since it would be impossible to canvass every student on every campus in the United States, we would need to select a *sample group* for our study that was *representative* of the *target population* we were considering.

What is a representative sample? In order for a sample to be representative of the total population, it must meet the criteria of size, breadth, and randomness.

Size   The first criterion, *size* of a sample, depends on the total target population. Consider the advertisement that claims, "Four out of five doctors recommend that you use Brand X if stranded on a desert island." The audience is left in the dark as to how many doctors were questioned, but clearly, if the sample population included only five doctors, the sample is too small! Choosing the proper sample size is a complex process, and there are several types of sampling procedures possible depending on the specific set of circumstances. However, in general, the greater the number of participants, the greater the likelihood that the sample reflects the total population. For example, given two research studies done on the food served at your college, one that surveyed 25 students and one that surveyed 250, all other things being equal, we would have more confidence in the results of the study that interviewed 250 students.

Breadth   The second criterion for our subject population is *breadth*. If our goal is to make statements about the eating preferences of all college students in the United States, then we must include students who incorporate all the characteristics of the total population. This would mean paying attention to factors such as gender, ethnic background, geographic location, and school size. For example, we shouldn't gather data only from the Northwest or only from large schools.

Randomness   The third criterion is *randomness*. Once we have determined the appropriate number of subjects and have considered the characteristics of our population, we must be sure that students are randomly selected to participate — that is, that everyone has an equal chance to be in the study. For example, if we decided to collect our data at the cafeteria from 11:00 to 12:00 during the week, how random would our sample be? Not all students would have the same opportunity to participate; students who had classes from 11:00 to 12:00 would automatically be excluded from the study. In addition, we would also be excluding those people who skipped lunch. To ensure randomness, we should collect data over several days and at different meal times.

Evaluating research instruments

How should we evaluate our research instruments? In this case we might use a questionnaire. Our instrument must be both valid and reliable.

Validity   An instrument is said to be good when the results obtained from using that instrument are *valid* — that is, when the results measure what we intend to measure. In Chapter 6, we used the term *validity* to refer to the truthfulness of the premises (reasons) given in an argument. When we want to evaluate a research instrument, we also look for validity, but here we are referring to the truthfulness of the results of that instrument.

For example, if we say we are surveying students for their opinions on college food, then results of our survey must do just that—survey opinions on college food, not attitudes toward the college meal plan. In this case, the task seems rather straightforward; however, in more complex research tasks, one may dispute the validity of the instruments being used. For example, if someone said he wanted to test your creativity quotient, you might want to know how he defined creativity and how he was going to measure it. In order for an instrument to be valid, it must measure what it claims to. If you didn't agree with how creativity was measured, you would find the test invalid.

Our food preference survey must also be constructed fairly. Consider question 5 from our hypothetical questionnaire:

> Question 5: My college serves delicious fried chicken.
> (circle one)
>
> agree very strongly   agree strongly   agree   disagree

How many opportunities does a student have to make a positive choice? Three. How many opportunities does a student have to make a negative choice? Only one. This is an example of an unfairly constructed question. It is advisable to have an equal number of positive and negative choices for your responses.

Reliability   The results of an instrument must also be *reliable*, that is, consistent. For instance, if a creativity test says that you are a remarkably creative person today, then it should say the same thing tomorrow. The research instrument should give consistent results from one time to another, barring any significant changes in the circumstances. In the case of our study, if the survey shows on Monday that 76 percent of college students find college meals "fine cuisine," then 76 percent of college students should feel the same way on Thursday, barring any interference from extraneous (outside) variables such as a new chef or spoiled food.

Evaluating the research design

How researchers conduct a study is important. In our cafeteria study, for example, we must be careful to control for any extraneous variables — variables that unintentionally could influence the results we get. We have already considered some elements of the research design in selecting our sample and in choosing the times and place where we will gather our data. Since we want students' individual responses, we will need to make sure that students have privacy while completing the questionnaire. Seven students sitting at one table might be inclined to share answers or even exert peer pressure on one another's responses. Our goal is to consider the many variables that might interfere with our results and try to control for them. The more successful we are at controlling all the variables, including the ones we are *not* examining, the better our research design.

Evaluating statistical data

Once the data are collected and the statistical analysis has been completed, the researcher must report those findings. We have already pointed out that unless you have a strong background in statistics, you will have to assume that the researchers applied the correct statistical procedures. However, by understanding a few statistical concepts, you can make some judgments about the statistical findings as they are being reported, and thus decide whether you should accept the research findings. A basic understanding of these concepts increases the number of critical thinking skills you can apply to your analysis. We will consider four concepts: averages, percentages, magnitudes, and generalizing findings.

Averages   You may remember from previous math classes three types of averages: mean, median, and mode. Assume that the following test scores are the ones you earned last semester in chemistry. Your instructor says that she will average your marks and that you can decide which average you would like her to use — mean, median, or mode. Which average would give you the highest mark?

Test Scores
63 95 95 84 78 87 72 56 40

1. To compute the mean, add up all test scores and divide by the number of test scores. Your answer is _____ .

2. To compute the median, arrange all the scores in rank order (that is, highest to lowest, or lowest to highest):

    _____ _____ _____ _____ _____ _____ _____ _____ _____

    Now find the score that is halfway between the highest and lowest scores. Your answer is _____ .

3. To compute the mode, find the score that appears most frequently. Your answer is _____ .

Given your answers, which average will you tell your instructor to use?

When studies report averages, you want to know how that average was computed. As the test scores example illustrates, it makes a difference!

Percentages   Percentages by themselves don't tell us very much. At a recent conference, a presenter announced with great enthusiasm, "Last year we increased the number of Native Americans at our institution by 300 percent." But before everyone had finished applauding, he added, "We now have three Native American students enrolled full-time in our undergraduate classes." Three students! 300 percent! Without the context for a percent, you can easily jump to the wrong conclusions.

Consider this example. "Less than .001 percent of the patients taking 'Wonder Drug Elixir' suffered near-fatal reactions." This sounds like a relatively small percentage, but if the number of patients taking the drug was 1,000,000, then .001 percent would equal 1,000 — no small number when you are talking about human lives.

In order to interpret percentages correctly, you must be sure you know the base figure you are starting with. Without the absolute numbers, it is very easy to be misled.

Magnitudes   The magnitude or size of the number given can be as confusing as percentages. In this case, the confusion works in reverse. Presented with a relatively large or small number, out of context, you can easily misread the significance. For example, the closest star next to our sun is heading in our direction at the rate of 50,000 miles per hour, but given its distance from us it will take over 57,000 years to arrive. Alternately, this star is only 4.1 light years away. This sounds like a relatively small number unless you know that 1 light year equals approximately 6 trillion miles.

Generalizing findings   Researchers must be careful when they draw conclusions about their data. For example, if they have been looking at a sample population of first-year college students, then they cannot generalize their findings to all college students. If 82 percent of married women indicated they feel lonely in their relationships and 98 percent of single women said they love the freedom of calling their life their own, the researchers cannot then claim that the institution of marriage is defunct.

Evaluating Qualitative Research

Qualitative research tends to be more open-ended and does not try to prove or disprove a specific hypothesis. It also does not try to find statistically "significant" or "not significant" results. The researcher's goal is to accurately portray patterns, behaviors, and significant events in the data. In evaluating qualitative research, it is important to focus on the methods used to arrive at these findings.

One way to evaluate qualitative research is to investigate the safeguards the researcher used to minimize researcher bias. What steps were taken to increase objectivity? Was there an outside reader to check the researcher's findings, to check on the researcher's bias? In addition, did the researcher make clear the assumptions and theoretical framework under which the study was conducted? Finally, were the study's limitations clearly set forth? The number of subjects (called participants) in qualitative studies is usually too few to make general statements (generalizations) about the group, and researchers thus must take care not to generalize their findings.

Reports of Research Versus Research Reports

How often do you believe the research findings reported in newspapers and magazines? Most of us will read many more reports of research than we will read research reports themselves. Newspapers, magazines, and television programs report the results of new studies regularly. Many of them focus on the results and provide us with little information with which to evaluate the instruments, research design, and subjects. However, there is usually enough given for us to ask questions. With a basic understanding of the research process, we are now in a position to evaluate the research evidence presented. And if we are the ones reporting the research, we can prepare answers for possible questions.

By far the best defense against being wrongly informed is to be well informed. This can only come from being exposed to a wide variety of informational sources. You should not rely on only one television station, one newspaper, or one magazine for your information. The more avenues of information you have available, the greater your chances of developing a rich context for the information presented. Furthermore, be careful not to read or listen to only those with whom you agree. When you expose yourself to views that contradict your own, you have the opportunity to expand or strengthen your own thinking.

Application: Analyzing Research

APPLICATION ONE

Return now to the questions you posed regarding the review of Hite's study in the Introductory Chapter Activity. Reread the review, as well as the section on evaluating quantitative research. Can you think of some other questions you would now like to ask? For example, did your questions consider representativeness? Validity and reliability? Research design? (What extraneous variables might have influenced her findings? Who would be most likely to sit down and answer an essay questionnaire?) Did you consider the generalizability of her findings? Compare your answers with those of your classmates.

Now read the following excerpt from an article presenting some of the critical comments on Hite's research made by other social science researchers. Do you agree with their comments?

Shere Hite: Embattled as Usual

BY ELIZABETH MEHREN

self-proclaimed

New York—The controversy over self-proclaimed cultural historian Shere Hite, best-selling author of "The Hite Reports" on female and male sexuality, took curious new twists last week as renewed questions surfaced about her methodology as well as her personal conduct. . . .

Eleanor Singer, president of the American Association for Public Opinion Research, said from her office at Columbia University that Hite's "kind of research, if it is thought of as survey research, is damaging to all of survey research. No public-opinion researcher would claim this as a piece of public-opinion research."

equivalent

Robert Groves, an associate professor of sociology at the University of Michigan and senior study director of that institution's Survey Research Center, blasted Hite's methodology as "the equivalent of medical malpractice in our field."

In a telephone interview from his office in Ann Arbor, Groves called the newest Hite report "such a public display of incompetence that all others who are involved [in survey research] in a serious way are associated by default."

Groves faulted Hite's sample as self-selecting, and called the 4,500 responses she received from 100,000 questionnaires mailed out "an incredibly low" response rate.

Lewis [director of a *Los Angeles Times* poll] said he was surprised not only by Hite's results but also by her "very crude" techniques of research. "I have never seen findings like that in 20 years of polling." Lewis said.

crude

In her continued defense of her methodology, Hite said while only a "very few social scientists are methodologists," most of her critics admit they have not read her book or her introductory essay on methodology. She termed that "shocking, really. I really don't see why we are arguing over statistics."

Write brief answers to the following questions.

1. In general, what view do survey specialists and social science researchers have of Hite's methodology?

2. On what specific factors is this opinion based?

3. How does Hite respond to criticism of her work?

4. Is her response valid?

APPLICATION TWO

Mark Twain once remarked, "There are lies, damn lies and statistics." "The Numbers Game" discusses the difficulties of reporting reliable statistics and "the vast potential of statistics for misleading the public by intention." Many of the isolated figures used to support popular social and political debates are misleading, confusing, or inaccurate. Adler contends, "Great issues of public policy are being debated by people who have no idea what they're talking about." First read the information bracketed in boxes, then read the article to find specific examples of misleading statistics.

The Numbers Game

BY JERRY ADLER

Ideas: Statistics can be scary, not just in what they say but because they're misused, confusing and wrong. Why are we told so many of these true lies?

How many battered wives are too many?

That's an easy one; in an ideal world, even one is too many. But we live in a glaringly imperfect world, in which battered wives are only one exhibit in a panorama of human misery clamoring for our attention. So

panorama

when O. J. Simpson's history of wife-beating came to light after his arrest, women's advocacy groups were quick to point out that what was really shocking was how often this happens among ordinary families. Undoubtedly many Americans were shocked to read in *Time* magazine that *4 million* American women are assaulted by a "domestic partner" each year. It must have been especially shocking to those who read in *Newsweek* that the number of women beaten by "husbands, ex-husbands and boyfriends" was *2 million* a year.

This is terrible. Not because of the implication that either *Time* or *Newsweek* is wrong by a factor of 2, but because the divergence reflects society's actual state of ignorance on such an important and theoretically verifiable statistic. Nor is this a problem unique to the question of how many men beat their wives. Great issues of public policy are being debated by people who have no idea what they're talking about. Estimates of homelessness range from 223,000 to 7 million. A United States senator announced in debate that 50,000 American children were abducted by strangers each year — a figure so striking that it took five years to dislodge from public consciousness, although it exceeded the real number by approximately 45,000. After a year of hand-wringing over a Roper poll that seemed to indicate that nearly a quarter of Americans believed the Nazi Holocaust might never have happened, the poll

divergence

> ## 22% of Americans say the Holocaust may not have happened.
>
> This 1992 Roper poll phrased its question with a confusing double negative. Reworded, a 1994 survey found that only 1% doubted the extermination.

was shown to be flawed because many people didn't understand the question. In a new poll with better questions the naumber of Americans who agreed that it was "possible . . . the Nazi extermination of the Jews never happened" went down to 1 percent. But the mere fact that professional researchers could make such a mistake by inadvertence suggests the vast potential of statistics for misleading the public by intention.

inadvertence

Both *Time* and *Newsweek* acted in good faith on credible sources. In fact, the figures on domestic violence they published are not so far apart as others they might have chosen. *Newsweek*'s data came from a 1985 survey by an acknowledged authority in the field, University of Rhode Island sociologist Richard J. Gelles. *Time*'s was based on a 1992 article in the *Journal of the American Medical Association,* which cited a "landmark" study in 1975. But neither study's figure is consistent with a study by the U.S. Department of Justice that counted a total of 2.5 million

credible

crimes against women annually — including robberies, rapes and assaults by strangers. (The study was based on interviews, not on police crime reports, which undercount rape and domestic violence.) And none of these comes close to the assertion in a packet of statistics from the National Clearinghouse for the Defense of Battered Women that "an estimated 800,000 women are battered each year" *just in Pennsylvania* — a state with approximately 5 percent of the U.S. population.

Of course, battered women are hard to count. They may be ashamed, retribution   or afraid of retribution, or they may not even recognize that they have been abused. *Murdered* women, on the other hand, are an unambiguous category. The FBI's Uniform Crime Report says that about 1,400 women a year are killed by husbands or boyfriends, accounting for roughly a third of all female homicide victims. But the Center for Women's Policy Studies, citing a 1981 study, claims that "each year, 4,000 women are killed by husbands or partners who have abused them." The *total* number of female homicide victims was only 4,936 in 1992, by FBI figures. A "fact sheet" from the American Medical Association played the trump card of modern statistics, asserting that family violence "kills as many women in five years as the total number of Americans who lost their lives in the Vietnam War." Unfortunately, that would imply nearly

10,000 homicides of women a year — more than twice as many as the FBI has found.

Sheer size

America is a big country, and it hides a lot of problems in its sheer size and diversity. Perhaps that is why, as Christina Hoff Sommers points out in "Who Stole Feminism" (320 pages. Simon & Schuster. $23), several best-selling authors have claimed that 150,000 women die annually from anorexia (misinterpreting a study that found 150,000 *cases* a year, almost none of them fatal). That's *three* times the number of Americans killed in Vietnam!

This gives rise to the suspicion that many of the statistics Americans receive come from sources less interested in precisely measuring a given problem than in showing that it's even worse than anyone thought. "People who want to influence public policy have a real strong feeling that the end justifies the means," says Cynthia Crossen, a *Wall Street Journal* reporter and author of the recently published "Tainted Truth: The Manipulation of Fact in America" (272 pages. Simon & Schuster. $23). "If they can save *even one* woman from being battered, they don't see the harm." Advocacy groups tend to consider questions about their statistics as tan-   tantamount tamount to an attack on their goals. When a reporter questioned some of the data supplied by the National Coalition Against Domestic Violence,

> ### 50,000 children are abducted by strangers each year.
>
> Sen. Paul Simon cited this figure in Congress in 1983, and it was widely used for years. But a 1988 Justice Department study found fewer than 5,000 stranger abductions that year.

coordinator Rita Smith became defensive: "Boy, there certainly is a *backlash* in this country," she said. "People don't want to believe women are in danger."

But surely one can deplore domestic violence and seek to end it even if it isn't worse than Vietnam. Increasingly, though, political and social debate in America takes the form of an attack on the other side's statistics, a singularly *sterile* and unenlightening exercise. This seems to have led not toward more reliable statistics but toward more exaggerated ones. Thus in the debate over a gay-rights ordinance in Colorado, one side asserted that homosexuals were responsible for a hair-raising 50 percent of sexual attacks on children, while the other claimed to study the same question and put the figure at a suspiciously minuscule .7 percent. But *advocacy* groups, precisely because they present themselves as disinterested defenders of the public interest, ought to be held to a higher standard. Instead, says American University so-

ciologist James Lynch, they sometimes "willfully distort numbers to benefit their cause."

At risk?

Crossen's book considers the question of hungry children. There is no cause more worthy, which is why the 1991 "Survey of Childhood Hunger in the United States" by the Food Research and Action Center received a respectful hearing. One of the study's "key findings" was that 11.5 million American children under the age of 12 were either hungry or "at risk" of hunger—an astonishing one child out of four. The "at risk" category is often a fruitful one for social-action groups seeking to magnify a problem. In this study of low-income families, children were said to be at risk if their parents answered yes to any one of eight questions. One was this: in the last 12 months, "Did you ever rely on a limited number of foods to feed your children because you were running out of money to buy food for a meal?" Not being able to afford what you might otherwise buy (even once in a year) is a pretty tautological definition of poverty.

To be fair, though, hungry kids—like a lot of things we seek information on—aren't that easy to count. The quest for increasingly subtle and intimate data on American society has begun to run into the law of diminishing returns. Even the most basic statistic of all, the United States Census, is increasingly disputed.

More complicated questions fall into an epistemological abyss; despairing of counting illegal aliens directly, New York City once tried to estimate the figure by working backward from water usage. Luckily it failed, otherwise the statistic would be floating around in databases to confuse journalists yet unborn. But even our best statistics on some important questions are based on a long chain of "assumptions," the scientific term for "faith." The figure for the homeless population used by the Clinton administration dates from a 1987 study by Martha Burt of the Urban Institute. Burt surveyed 381 shelters and soup kitchens in 20 large cities — a fraction of the total. Researchers questioned a random sample of clients and then applied a variety of statistical manipulations to the data: adding in children (who were not counted directly) and assuming that the rate of homelessness in small cities was one third that in large ones. Finally Burt assumed that she missed anywhere from one fifth to one third of the homeless, which gave a possible range of 400,000 to 600,000 — from which the administration, for its own reasons, plucked the top figure. Meanwhile, the late Mitch Snyder, the charismatic homeless advocate, made one simple assumption — that 1 percent of the population was homeless — and arrived at a figure of 2.5 million, which was duly quoted alongside Burt's.

charismatic

Credible source

Are journalists to blame for some of the confusion, then? Researchers at magazines such as *Newsweek* are not habitually careless with numbers. But by and large they consider their job done when they find a number that can be attributed to a credible source. Gelles thinks they need a higher standard. "This is really simple," he says. "You've got numbers that are made up and numbers that come from scientific data. Reporters don't ask, 'How do you know it?' They're on deadline. They just want the figures so they can go back to their word processors."

Yes, it would be better if journalists were more skeptical of statistics. But they're not the ones who have turned public-policy debate in America into a tug of war over data. What's important to know about spouse abuse is that it's wrong, whether it kills 1,400 women a year or some other number. Data on sexual molestation — even if it were accurate — ought to have no bearing on anyone's civil rights. Someday we'll remember that facts are only the shadow cast by truth.

With T. Trent Gegax in New York and Mary Hager in Washington

Write brief answers to the following questions.

1. List some of the misleading statistics cited in the article. What statistical inaccuracies can be traced to poor or misleading research design?

2. What are some of the difficulties in gathering information on such groups as homeless people or battered women?

3. What obligation do reporters have to make sure the statistics they use are accurate?

APPLICATION THREE

The following article, also from *Newsweek* magazine, discusses the findings of a recent study on two-career families. Preview the article by reading the headings, the information framed in the box, and the caption under the picture.

Woman's Work Is Never Done

BY JIM MILLER

A stinging new study of two-career families

After eight hours on the job as a social worker, a trip to the grocery store and a stop at the day-care center to pick up her son, Joey, Nancy Holt staggers through the front door of her California home. Waiting is a heap of unopened mail, a half-eaten piece of cinnamon toast on the hall table, and a flashing red light on the phone machine. In the words of Arlie Hochs-child, a professor of sociology at Berkeley, Nancy's first shift may be over—but her "second shift" at home is just beginning.

When both parents work, who buys the groceries, cooks the meals, scrubs the floors, irons the clothes? Who changes the diapers, rocks the baby, sews the Halloween costumes, reads the bedtime story? The answer

As if one job weren't enough: *Who cooks? Cleans? Reads bedtime stories?*

will come as no surprise to most working mothers. As Hochschild shows in *The Second Shift* (309 pages. Viking. $18.95), her stinging new study of "working parents and the revolution at home," it is usually mothers — with only a little, if any, help from their husbands — who are taking charge. Women like Nancy Holt perform the majority of household tasks, doing most of the parenting, trying in effect to perform two full-time jobs in one 24-hour day. Through a variety of case studies, Hochschild brings the *dilemma* of the working mother to life as never before, illustrating in vivid detail the different ways different couples are trying to cope. The result is a book with some of the detail and texture of a good novel.

dilemma

Hochschild starts with several raw — and startling — statistics. On average, according to her *computations*, American women in the past

computations

two decades have "worked roughly fifteen hours longer each week than men." Over a year, that adds up to "an *extra month of twenty-four-hour days*."

In order to find out just what these figures actually mean in human terms, Hochschild and a research associate, Anne Machung, conducted in-depth interviews with 50 working couples in the Bay Area between 1980 and 1988; in addition, Hochschild observed several of these families more closely as they went about their daily routines. Noting the *nuances* of their interactions, she developed a sense of the dynamics at work in their relationships.

nuance

Take the case of Nancy and Evan Holt. On a typical workday, Evan, a furniture salesman, and Nancy both leave home at 8 a.m. and return roughly 10 hours later; this "first shift" they share equally. Nancy, an *ardent* feminist, has tried desperately

ardent

Who's Minding the Home?

In her survey of Bay Area working couples, Arlie Hochschild asked 100 husbands and wives to describe their approach to housework and child care. Some findings:

Women care more:
Describing a typical day, 97% of the wives mentioned their house — but only 54% of the husbands did.
97% of the women mentioned their children; only 69% of the men did.

Women do more:
Wives report doing 75% of the housework.
Only 18% of the husbands share housework equally.

Men are shirkers:
61% of the men do little or no housework.

Money matters:
Only those wives who earned more than their husbands did less than half the household tasks.

to convince Evan of the justice of sharing the "second shift" equally as well. For a time, Evan did help out with meals. But following a classic strategy of passive resistance, he somehow always "forgot the grocery list, burned the rice, didn't know where the broiler pan was." So now Nancy and Evan go their separate ways in the evening.

After arriving home, Nancy prepares dinner, plays with their son, Joey, cleans up after dinner, does the laundry, gives Joey a bath and puts him to bed. Meanwhile, Evan opens the mail, eats dinner, retreats to his hobby shop, enjoys a beer — and, as part of his negotiated "share" of the housework, looks after the family dog.

Hochschild's acid comment: "Other men, I found, had second-shift fetishes, too. When I asked one man what he did to share the work of the home, he answered, 'I make all the pies we eat.' . . . Another man grilled fish. Another baked bread. In their pies, their fish, and their bread, such men converted a single act into a substitute for a multitude of chores in the second shift — a token. Evan took care of the dog."

fetish

Traditional prerogatives

Parts of this book will doubtless make some male readers cringe. But Hochschild is no knee-jerk ideologue. Many of her findings are quite unexpected. In general, for example, working-class husbands who wished their wives could stay at home actually did slightly more around the house than ostensibly more liberal middle-class professionals who supported the idea of their wives working but resisted doing any housework themselves. Similarly, several women resisted sharing the child care, jealously guarding traditional prerogatives.

ideologue

prerogative

In her last chapter, Hochschild surveys some possible solutions to the dilemmas she describes. She speaks wistfully of liberated husbands and of countries like Sweden, where the state subsidizes a wide range of services to help working parents, from day-care centers to 12 months of paid maternity and paternity leave. Here, Congress has belatedly begun to address the need for day care. But for now, most of the nation's growing army of working parents will have to fend for themselves—enlightened, one hopes, by the insights and arguments in this timely book.

COMPREHENSION CHECK

Write brief answers to the following questions.

1. What kind of research is being conducted in this study — quantitative or qualitative?

2. How did the researchers collect their data?

3. What are the major findings of the research?

4. Do you accept the findings? Are they consistent with your experience? Should we be concerned about these findings? Why? Do we need to develop "some possible solutions to the dilemmas"? If so, what would you suggest?

5. Given the researcher's goals, was the research design appropriate? Explain.

APPLICATION FOUR

Recall the research study on bystander intervention we read in Chapter 9. What happens to research once it has been published in some scholarly journal? Many of the findings are synthesized, summarized, and reported in newspapers, popular magazines, and textbooks. Studies that catch the public's interest can result in interviews for the researchers by network celebrities. One graduate student conducting research on the different kinds of graffiti found in men's and women's public bathrooms even received inquiries about his research from the international press!

With regard to the Darley and Latané study from Chapter 9, we tracked down a passage on altruism in a psychology textbook that discussed their research. Preview the passage by reading the headings and studying the two figures. As you read the selection, compare the style and content of the text with the original research study.

Altruism

BY D. G. MEYERS

Altruism—an unselfish regard for the welfare of others—became a major concern of social psychologists after Kitty Genovese, walking from a train station parking lot to her nearby Queens, New York, apartment at 3:20 A.M. on March 13, 1964, was murdered by a knife-wielding stalker. "Oh, my God, he stabbed me!" she screamed into the early-morning stillness. "Please help me!" Windows opened and lights went on as thirty-eight of her neighbors heard her screams. One couple even pulled chairs up to the window and turned out the light to see better. Her attacker fled and then returned to stab her eight more times and sexually molest her. Not until he departed for good did anyone so much as call the police. It was then 3:50 A.M. . . .

Bystander intervention

commentator
lament
apathy

Reflecting on the Genovese murder, most commentators lamented the bystanders' "apathy" and "indifference." Rather than blaming

them, social psychologists John Darley and Bibb Latané (1968b) attributed their inaction to an important situational factor—the presence of others. Given the right circumstances, they suspected, most of us might behave like the witnesses to the Genovese murder.

After staging emergencies under various conditions, Darley and Latané assembled their findings into a decision scheme: We will help if and only if the situation enables us first to *notice* the incident, then to *interpret* it as an emergency, and finally to *assume responsibility* for helping (Figure 20-3). At each step the presence of other bystanders can turn people away from the path that leads to helping. In laboratory experiments and in street situations such as the car break-ins, people in groups of strangers are more likely than solitary individuals to keep their eyes on what they are doing or where they are going and thus not to notice an unusual situation. Some who did notice the

scheme

bystander

solitary

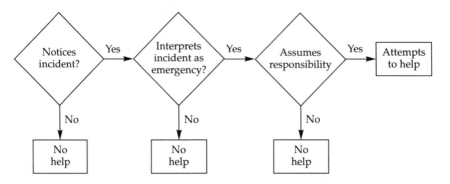

Figure 20-3   The decision-making process for bystander intervention. (From Darley & Latané, 1968b.)

blasé

unambiguous

car break-ins — and also observed the blasé reactions of the other passersby — perceived the burglar as a locked-out car owner.

But sometimes, as with the Genovese murder, the emergency is unambiguous and people still fail to help. The witnesses looking out through their windows noticed the incident, correctly interpreted the emergency, *and* failed to assume responsibility. To find out why, Darley and Latané (1968a) simulated a physical emergency in their laboratory. University students participated in a discussion over an intercom. Each student was in a separate cubicle, and only the person whose microphone was switched on could be heard. One of the students was an accomplice of the experimenters. When his turn came, he was heard calling for help and making sounds as though he were being overcome by an epileptic seizure.

How do you think the other students reacted? As Figure 20-4 indicates, those who believed that they were the only one who could hear the victim — and therefore thought they bore total responsibility for helping — usually went to his aid. Those who thought others could also hear were more likely to react as did Kitty Genovese's neighbors. And the more the responsibility for helping was shared, the less likely it was that any single listener would help.

bore
(to bear)

In hundreds of additional experiments psychologists have studied the factors that influence bystanders' willingness to relay an emergency phone call, to aid a stranded motorist, to donate blood, to pick up dropped books, to contribute money, and to give time to someone. For example, Latané, James Dabbs (1975), and 145 collaborators took 1497 elevator rides in three American cities and "accidentally"

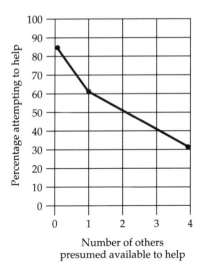

Figure 20-4 When people thought they alone heard an epileptic seizure victim calling for help, they usually helped. But when they thought four others were hearing it, too, fewer than a third responded. (From Darley & Latané, 1968a.)

dropped coins or pencils in front of 4813 fellow passengers. The women coin-droppers were more likely to receive help than the men—a gender difference often reported by other researchers (Eagly & Crowley, 1986). But the major finding of all this research was the *bystander effect*—that any particular bystander is less likely to give aid if other bystanders are present. Thus, when one other person was on the elevator, those who dropped

the coins were helped 40 percent of the time. When there were six passengers, help came less than 20 percent of the time.

From their observations of behavior in tens of thousands of such "emergencies," altruism researchers have discerned some patterns. The odds of our helping someone are best when:

discern

We have just observed someone else being helpful.

We are not in a hurry.

The victim appears to need and deserve help.

The victim is in some way similar to ourselves.

We are in a small town or rural area.

We are feeling guilty.

We are focused on others and not preoccupied.

We are in a good mood.

This last result, that happy people are helpful people, is one of the most consistent findings in all psychology. No matter how people are put in a good mood—whether by having been made to feel successful and intelligent, by thinking happy thoughts, by finding money, or even by receiving a posthypnotic suggestion—they become more generous, more eager to help (Carlson & others, 1988).

COMPREHENSION CHECK

Write brief answers to the following questions.

1. What is altruism?

2. What kinds of events prompted social psychologists to study bystanders' behavior?

3. What is Darley and Latané's decision-making scheme for intervention? On what do they base their theory? (Cite the relevant research.)

4. What other factors may influence people's decision to help? What evidence is given to support these factors?

5. Compare the Darley and Latané research study you read in Chapter 9 with this textbook version of the study using the following criteria: purpose, tone and style, amount of detail and information about the study, organizational structure, and your ability to evaluate the evidence presented. Which selection did you enjoy the most? Why? Was one selection easier to understand? Explain your answer.

What Do You Think?

✪ DISCUSSION QUESTIONS

Prepare for class discussion by jotting down brief answers to the following questions.

1. Do people accept research findings too easily? Explain your answer. How can we guard against accepting results so readily?

2. What research findings can you think of that have later been refuted?

3. If you had the opportunity to conduct a research study, what area(s) would you investigate? For example, you might wish to investigate the relationship between students' class attendance and their final course grades. You might investigate people's reaction to news seen on television versus heard on the radio. Or you might examine the effects of telephone "call waiting" on the length of phone conversations.

4. Given your area of interest (question 3), what kind of research would best answer your research question? How would you ensure the objectivity of your study? Be as specific as possible.

WRITING ASSIGNMENTS

Select one of the following topics and in a few paragraphs develop a thoughtful written response.

1. Select a chapter from one of your college textbooks that cites several research studies. Using the reference section of the chapter, locate the original study in the appropriate journal. Evaluate the research study. Be sure to include a discussion of the areas you considered. (Students who completed Writing Assignment 3 in Chapter 9 may use the same research study.)

2. Find a popular magazine article, a newspaper story, or an editorial in which the author cites research findings to support his or her writing. Can you evaluate these findings? Explain. Now locate the original study in the appropriate journal. Write a brief evaluation of this study.

CREDITS

(Numbers in parentheses indicate pages on which material appears in this book.)

Chapter 1

Martin Jones, "Peer Pressure and Academics." Used with permission of Martin Jones. **(16—18)**

Diane Ravitch, "Test Scores Don't Lie: Back to Basics," *The New Republic*, March 6, 1989. Used with permission of *The New Republic*. **(19—23)**

Daniel Lewis, "Breaking Habits," reprinted by permission of the author. **(24—25)**

L. Steinberg, "Environmental Influences on Achievement," *Adolescence*, 1989, pp. 377–379. Used with permission of McGraw-Hill, Inc. **(26—29)**

Chapter 2

"Rocky," an excerpt from R. C. Anderson, R. E. Reynolds, D. L. Schellert, and G. T. Goetz, "Frameworks for Comprehending Discourse," *American Educational Research Journal* 14, 1977, pp. 367–381. **(40—41)**

Vicki Anderson, "Literally Handicapped." Used with permission of Vicki Anderson. **(55—57)**

B. T. Watkins, "Berkeley Mathematician Strives 'to Help People Get Moving,'" *The Chronicle of Higher Education*, June 14, 1989. © 1989, *The Chronicle of Higher Education*. Excerpted and used with permission of *The Chronicle of Higher Education*, Washington, D.C. **(58—60)**

Frank H. Shih, "Asian-American Students: The Myth of a Model Minority," *Journal of College Science Teaching*, March/April 1988, pp. 356–359. © 1988 by the National Science Teachers Association. Used with permission of the National Science Teachers Association, 1742 Connecticut Avenue, N.W., Washington, D.C. **(61—67)**

Photo of two students. © 1992 Pamela Gentile, San Francisco, California. **(64)**

Photo of Frank H. Shih. Courtesy of Frank H. Shih, Stony Brook, New York. **(67)**

R. J. Wilson, "The New Americans," from R. J. Wilson, J. Gilbert, S. Nissenbaum, K. O. Kupperman, and D. Scott, *The Pursuit of Liberty*, Vol. 2, 2nd ed., pp. 633–

Chapter 3

Chapter 4

Amy Bayer, "Are Lotteries A Ripoff?" Reprinted by permission from *Consumers' Research* magazine, Washington, D.C. **(218–223)**

Chapter 7

Carole Bowe, Cindy Osgood, and Kimberhly Hopkins, "Student Dialogues." Dialogues used with permission of Carole Bowe, Cindy Osgood, and Kimberhly Hopkins. **(241–243)**

Nike advertisement. Reprinted with permission of NIKE, Inc. **(244)**

Elisabeth Ford, "Arguing Family Style." Used with permission of Elisabeth Ford. **(245–247)**

Stephen Jay Gould, "The War on (Some) Drugs," *Harper's*, April 1990. Used with permission of Stephen Jay Gould, Cambridge, Massachusetts. **(248–250)**

Chapter 8

G. Tyler Miller, Jr., "Is Food Relief Helpful or Harmful?" from *Environmental Science* 4/E © 1993 by Wadsworth, Inc. Used by permission. **(262–263)**

Carol Wilson, "Setting Limits: The Key to Working, Studying and Parenting." Used with permission of Carol Wilson. **(269–270)**

Michael Blumenthal, "Human, All Too Human," *The New York Times*, July 23, 1989. © 1989 The New York Times Company. Used with permission of The New York Times Company. **(271–273)**

John Elson, "Returning Bones of Contention," *Time*, September 25, 1989. © 1989 The Time Inc. Magazine Company. Used with permission of Time Inc. **(274–275)**

Photo of North American Indian skulls. Brad Markel/Gamma Liaison, Inc., New York City, New York. **(275)**

Daniel D. Chiras, "Wildlife and Plants: Preserving Biological Diversity," *Environmental Science*, 3rd ed. (Redwood City, California: Benjamin/Cummings Publishing Company, 1991), pp. 181, 183, 185–187. Used with permission of Benjamin/Cummings Publishing Company. **(276–282)**

Chapter 9

John M. Darley and Bibb Latané, "Bystander Intervention in Emergencies: Diffusion of Responsibility," *Journal of Personality and Social Psychology* 8 no. 4, (1968). © 1968 by the American Psychological Association. Used with permission of the American Psychological Association, Arlington, Virginia, and Bibb Latané, Florida Atlantic University, Boca Raton, Florida. **(293–306)**

Kevin Gould, "Writing College Research Papers." Used with permission of Kevin Gould. **(312–313)**

Beverly Daniel Tatum, "Growing Up Black in White Communities," in F. Miller, ed., *Adolescence, Schooling and Social Policy*. Reprinted by permission of the author. **(314–319)**

Chapter 10

United Press International, "Hite: Women Find Men Frustrating," *Hampshire Gazette*, 1987. Used with permission of United Press International, Washington, D.C. **(325)**

Elizabeth Mehren, "Shere Hite: Embattled as Usual," *The Boston Globe*, November 16, 1987. Copyright 1987 Los Angeles Times Syndicate. Used with permission of the Los Angeles Times Syndicate. **(333)**

Jerry Adler, "The Numbers Game," from *Newsweek*, July 25, 1994. © 1994 Newsweek, Inc. All rights reserved. Reprinted by permission. **(334–338)**

Jim Miller, "Woman's Work Is Never Done," *Newsweek*, July 31, 1989. © 1989 Newsweek, Inc. All rights reserved. Used with permission of Newsweek, Inc. **(339–342)**

Photo of mother and child. Robert Maass/Sipa Press, New York City, New York. **(340)**

D. G. Meyers, "Altruism," *Psychology*, 3rd ed. (New York: Worth Publishers, 1992), pp. 584–587. Used with permission of Worth Publishers, Inc. **(343–345)**

Additional Notes

Page 40: The sentence "The notes were sour because the seams split," was used by John G. Barnitz and Argiro L. Morgan in their study "Aspects of Schemata and Syntax in Fifth Grade Children's Inferential Reading Comprehension of Causal Relations," an article published in *Reading Psychology: An International Quarterly*, vol. 4 (Dec. 1983), pp. 337–348.

Page 87: "Columbus" entry from *The Standard American Encyclopedia*, vol. 4, ed.-in-chief Walter Miller (Chicago: Standard American Corporation, 1937).

Page 151: "Argument" entry from *Webster's New World Dictionary*, 2nd concise ed., general ed. David B. Guralnik (New York: Simon & Schuster, 1982), p. 38.

Page 191: Passage from David A. Conway and Ronald Munson, *The Elements of Reasoning* (Belmont, Calif.: Wadsworth Publishing, 1990), p. 39.

Page 192: Passage from T. J. Deloughry (1989), "An Anthropologist's Unusual New Subject: The American College Student." *The Chronicle of Higher Education* (June 7), p. A31.

From "A Game of Life" by Lavinia Edmunds
(final paragraphs from article appearing on pp. 184—185)

In practice, local transplant decisions can be made independent of the UNOS guidelines, which do not cover medically urgent situations. But within that system, in what order would these patients be given hearts that become available in this region? According to UNOS rules, those patients in intensive care or requiring cardiac or pulmonary assistance are given Status 1; those at home are assigned Status 2. Within Status 1, surgeons are to make decisions based on medical urgency. The second consideration is the patient's distance from the transplant center (the heart's viability can diminish with delay). The final consideration: how long the patient has been on the waiting list.

Thus Cindy Johnson would receive the first available heart. In the jargon of those who work in organ procurement, she is stat, considered likely to die within 12 hours. Following Johnson would be Chatsworth, the only other Status 1 patient on the list, despite his diminishing chance of survival. Then would come college student Smith, the Status 2 patient who has been waiting the longest. Ranking fourth is Billy Forbush, equal in urgency to Smith but with less time on the waiting list. And he will get a heart only if someone will pay for the operation; some hospitals are allotted one or two such "charity" cases a year. Fifth is Rodriquez, whose foreign background does not come into play here unless the transplant center has done more than 10 percent of its transplants on foreign nationals (a restriction adopted after foreign nationals were shown to take a large share of American kidneys). Because Long lives farther from the transplant center than the other Status 2 patients, she is last on the list.

SUBJECT INDEX

SKILLS INDEX